Rackets: Volume III

Decriminalized Prostitution:
The Common Sense Solution

Brian Saady

© 2017 by Brian Saady. All rights reserved.

Prerogative Publishing

Although every precaution has been taken to verify the accuracy of the information contained herein, the author and publisher assume no responsibility for any errors or omissions. No liability is assumed for damages that may result from the use of information contained within.

Book cover design by Daniel Ryves

Images for the cover art were derived from bigstockphoto.com

Printed in the U.S.A.

First Edition / April 2017

ISBN: 978-0-9987245-7-7

www.briansaady.com

Contents

Introduction..1

1. History of Prostitution...7
2. Decriminalization of Prostitution..........................43
3. Nevada Brothels..73
4. International Perspective.....................................88
5. Human Trafficking..108
6. Feminism..142
7. Prostitution Scandals...153

Names and Organizations..184

References and notes..186

ACKNOWLEDGEMENTS

"That was so well-written, Brian. It was…it was…as though I had written it *myself*."
"Uncle Freddy"

Those words came from a friend of mine (my former boss) several years ago when reviewing some of my work. We've had a few good laughs about that comment since then. Nevertheless, he loved my writing and he gave me several editorial duties at work. I had dreamed of becoming an author for several years, but I hadn't taken any steps toward accomplishing that vision. However, those work assignments sparked something inside of me that prompted me to pursue my dream.

I'd like to thank all of my friends and family members who supported me along the way. In particular, I'd like to thank my friends, Brian Sharff and Dan Luby. You both provided me with the praise and constructive criticism that was necessary to complete an endeavor like this. Also, this project would never have materialized without the technical assistance from my friend, Cory Waters.

I'd also like to thank my wife, Zanilia. Your help was invaluable. Your critical analysis challenged me to push beyond my mental boundaries. You'll never know how highly I value your opinions. You not only assisted me with numerous tasks, but you also inspired me in so many other ways.

Lastly, I'd like to thank my mom, Marguerite Saady. None of this would have been possible without you. I could have never accomplished my dreams without your help. I can't stress enough the significance of your support. You've been my biggest supporter from the beginning to the end. I know that you spent countless hours refining these books in the pursuit of perfection. In fact, this book series would never have been published without your hard work, insight, eye for detail, corrections, revisions, among numerous other efforts.

Thank you.

INTRODUCTION

The 19th-century Russian author Fyodor Dostoyevsky once wrote that a society can be judged by the conditions within its prisons. In that same vein, you can determine the strength of a society by how it treats those living on the outskirts of society, the most vulnerable and stigmatized citizens. Prostitutes are nearly at the bottom of the American social hierarchy, just above pedophiles, rapists, and violent criminals. Prostitutes are vilified in such a way that suggests they are somehow victimizing other people. In fact, that stigma has enabled some of the most sinister serial killers and rapists to target prostitutes because their victims have been deemed by our culture as unworthy of the most basic human rights.

Throughout history, many nations have changed their prostitution laws back and forth according to the ebb and flow of social movements as this is a very symbolic and polarizing issue. In the end, these changes have had little to do with implementing the most cost-effective and practical policies. Instead, the motivation behind prostitution laws has been more related to enhancing political careers.

There were four major social movements that coincided during the early 20th century and created a perfect storm resulting in the prostitution laws that are still in place today. It may be surprising to learn that nearly every state in the U.S. lacked prostitution laws until WWI. Before then, prostitution laws had been enforced at the local level and most every major city had a red-light district where this activity was decriminalized. In fact, in 1894 one infamous New York Police Captain, Alexander "Clubber" Williams, defiantly testified to a corruption committee that he permitted rampant prostitution in his precinct because it was "fashionable."

The views within this book advocate the decriminalization of indoor prostitution. The terms "decriminalized" and "legalized" are synonymous for most people. However, there are differences. Decriminalization occurs when prostitution laws are overturned, but it doesn't encourage prostitution nor open the door for broad commercialization. The police simply don't pursue prostitution arrests as long as it takes place indoors among consenting adults. Decriminalization will improve the human rights conditions for those most marginalized in society and save the taxpayers tremendous resources. Conversely, there are positive aspects to legalized prostitution, but that model tends to grant significant power to brothel owners, not the prostitutes, which can lead to further exploitation.

It's undeniably idealistic to expect that prostitution can be abolished through the criminal justice system. Despite brutal efforts in some cases, no society throughout history has accomplished that goal. On the other hand, decriminalization reduces the harms associated with this vice. Various American cities had informal regulation systems for prostitution during the 19th century. Those were successful social experiments, but they're generally unknown to the masses due to a lack of interest by most historians.

Now, prostitution is so strongly stigmatized that many people are afraid to publicly support legalized or decriminalized prostitution. Conduct an informal poll with your friends or colleagues and you will see that many of them will denounce legalized prostitution in a group setting. However, some of those same people will support it if they're asked privately. They're afraid to admit their true beliefs because there is a false connotation that only a "whore" or a "whoremonger" would support such a policy. That's a shame because decriminalization will reduce the harms associated with this activity by making it easier for outreach workers to give prostitutes the help needed to exit the industry. Banning prostitution does nothing to address the social and economic problems that push many people into prostitution; those laws only make the conditions worse. In fact, one of the better-kept secrets in American politics has to do with the success rate that various cities have had with diversion and harm reduction programs for prostitution. Unfortunately, not enough of these programs exist in America.

Oddly enough, decriminalizing indoor prostitution would appease conventional mores because it would reduce the volume and visibility of street prostitution by funneling much of that activity indoors. For some, it's a natural assumption that liberalizing prostitution laws will lead to increased diseases and less public safety, but that isn't the case. The U.S. has arguably the most rigorous anti-prostitution laws among the 35 most economically developed nations, yet it has the 2nd highest rate of HIV among those countries. In fact, most of those nations, 27 out of 35, don't waste their resources enforcing prostitution laws because it is either decriminalized or legalized.

You will read about various countries with better policies regarding prostitution. However, one of the most enlightening prostitution systems exists within the U.S. It is Nevada's legalized and regulated system which is far superior to any other state in America. Nevada brothels have virtually eliminated most of the violent crime related to black market prostitution, along with the transmission of STDs. Then again, we don't live in a utopian society and Nevada's legalized brothel system has its flaws, but the positives far outweigh the negatives. However, the backstory of how Nevada legalized prostitution is absolutely fascinating and it provides another striking example of the corrupt nature of politics.

In recent years, the media has flooded the American public with prostitution propaganda and created a moral panic. There is a historical precedent; the same thing happened roughly 100 years ago and it was part of why states began implementing prostitution laws. Now, nearly every report in the media about prostitution conflates the issue with terms like "sex slaves" and "sex trafficking." Human trafficking has become a highly politicized issue and the main culprits behind the controversy are the anti-trafficking organizations. Obviously, human trafficking is one of the most horrific crimes imaginable and it's a genuine problem. But there are organizations that exaggerate the extent of the problem. These activists are hell-bent in their ideology and they often are swayed by financial conflicts of interest because the federal government pays lucrative contracts to these groups. Nonetheless, many of the self-described "rescue" organizations don't have enough money to sufficiently help trafficking victims because their resources were spent making public relations and "awareness raising" campaigns. In some cases, these organizations expect trafficking victims to make public appearances and fulfill media obligations. In essence, these victims are being used as props. It's despicable.

In addition, the U.S. government has an official "zero tolerance" policy on human trafficking, but the details in this book will thoroughly demonstrate that our government's promise has merely been a facade. For example, there are some very politically connected multinational corporations that have been associated with human trafficking, yet the U.S. government has demonstrated little to no motivation to punish those companies. In fact, those corporations continue to receive very generous contracts from the federal government.

There is also an increasingly popular notion that prostitution and human trafficking can be reduced with something known as the "Swedish model." The Swedish government decided to arrest only the men who pay for prostitution, not the women who sell sex. Their government has taken an ideological stance which considers all prostitution as an act of coercion and violence against women. These officials have successfully exported their agenda internationally and the people behind this propaganda effort largely consist of a group of radical feminists with shocking worldviews.

These radical feminists have conducted an influential public relations campaign with this issue to curb debate. Hence, many international media outlets glowingly cite the press releases of the Swedish government without further examination. However, the devil is in the details and you will read several facts proving that the Swedish model fails to achieve its mission. It doesn't protect women and subjects them to much worse work-related conditions than they faced before the Swedish model was implemented.

The Swedish model has gained a lot of support because of its symbolic nature. However, prosecuting the men who pay for sex does nothing to address the various social and economic issues that cause prostitution, such as lack of public housing, marketable job skills, substance abuse treatment, etc. Nonetheless, the Swedish model is the favored model for most radical feminists. Many people even assume that the radicals speak for most self-described feminists, but that couldn't be more wrong. You will read the perspective from several segments within the feminist movement regarding their views on prostitution and several of these groups support decriminalization.

Our tax dollars commit extensive resources into combating prostitution, resulting in roughly 100,000 prostitution arrests every year, even though the line where prostitution is defined is quite blurry. This country is inundated with pornography and a $2.5 billion strip club industry in which it is perfectly legal for a bare-naked stripper to writhe at full friction in the lap of a paying customer. Likewise, semi-celebrities have leaked their sex tapes to extend their 15 minutes of fame and it's often a successful ploy. Also, it's perfectly legal for a woman to date or marry a man for his money. There are even several perfectly legal "sugar daddy" websites dedicated to this particular purpose. In fact, the reality TV show "Who Wants to Marry a Multi-Millionaire?" had 22 million viewers and a show with the same premise "Joe Millionaire" had 40 million viewers. However, statistics show that the majority of those viewers support laws banning prostitution. Somehow they didn't notice even a hint of irony.

Our government has maintained its prostitution laws, like drug and gambling laws, despite rampant examples of hypocrisy. These laws are not likely to be overturned mostly due to "family values" conservatives who warn against the tyrannous nature of big government. They publicly lament the "nanny state" while cherry-picking various freedoms of yours to suppress. Meanwhile, many of the self-proclaimed "pristine" elected officials have been involved in their own prostitution scandals. For the purpose of brevity, one chapter focuses heavily on this subject. Albeit, there are so many of these scandals that an entire book could be dedicated to this subject. As a matter of fact, the label of "prostitute" would be quite flattering for some of these politicians. Their corrupt actions routinely affect other people negatively, but prostitution is an act between two consenting adults.

Likewise, several people jokingly refer to politicians as the "real whores" because they do the bidding of powerful corporate interests. In an interesting twist, many of these political sex scandals intertwine with some major corruption scandals. For instance, one of the leading Congressional war hawks accepted millions of dollars in bribes, including escort services, from military contractors. Similarly, one of the foremost federal bureaucrats responsible for implementing an "anti-prostitution" pledge was guilty of this same crime. In fact, his policies crushed efforts by non-profit organizations worldwide that were solely focused on reducing HIV rates. In a separate example, a routine media investigation into conflicts of interest resulted in a political prostitution scandal. In the process, that scandal exposed that several government officials have routinely violated our nation's laws against covert propaganda. You will read about these and several other prostitution scandals that reveal the underbelly of how our democratic system actually functions.

1

"You can make prostitution illegal in Louisiana, but you can't make it unpopular."

To call prostitution "the world's oldest profession" isn't technically accurate, but prostitution has been documented in some of the earliest civilizations. Prostitution has largely been ignored by historians, thereby making it difficult to trace the exact origins, but the earliest known records date back to 2400 BC in Sumer. In fact, the Sumerians used a term, "kar.kid," to describe a prostitute who was working on behalf of the church.[1] Oddly enough, prostitution is considered one of the oldest taboos, but historical records demonstrate that many of the earliest societies practiced "temple prostitution," in which the women's work was believed to honor the gods and the proceeds benefited the church or the state. In one instance, in 1800 BC, the Babylonian Code of Hammurabi granted specific rights to sacred prostitutes with six of its codes. Some of those codes granted more rights to sacred prostitutes than all other women. She could receive property from her father, in addition to income from her brother's work on the land.[2] On the other hand, temple prostitution was compulsory work for every Babylonian woman. They were forced to serve time as prostitutes, some more than others depending on their social class, because it was very lucrative for the church.[3]

The Greek lawmaker Solon created state-sponsored brothels around 500 BC with the proceeds dedicated to building a temple in honor of Aphrodite (the Greek goddess of love, beauty, and sexuality).[4] The prostitutes in those brothels were slaves of the state, known as deichtrides, who stood on display in the doorways and at the windows. They were severely ostracized and banned from entering the streets before nightfall so as not to disturb the public.[5]

There was a social hierarchy among prostitutes in ancient Greece just as there is in modern society; the middle class prostitutes were known as auletrides. They were free women, but only because they bought their freedom. They often sang, danced, and performed music in public and thus were generally well accepted. It was also possible for an auletride to move up the hierarchy to join the highest class of prostitute--as a hetaera.[6]

The elites of Greek society frequented with high class prostitutes or hetaerae. "Courtesan" would later become the term for this kind of prostitute who catered to the upper echelon within various cultures. These women differed in that they weren't desired solely for their looks, but also for their intellect and social skills. They needed to be highly educated in order to converse with the highest level of Greek society, including politicians.[7] Notably, a mistress of Alexander the Great, a hetaera named Thais of Athens, is believed to have convinced him to burn down Persepolis.[8]

Prostitution was also quite prevalent during the Roman Empire. In fact, the word prostitute comes from the Latin meaning "to set forth in public" or "exposed for sale."[9] They also used another term, "meretrix," which in Latin meant "she who earns."[10] Unfortunately, this was basically the only option for poor free women to earn a living and most Roman prostitutes were slaves of Syrian or Egyptian descent. Roman prostitutes were essentially outcasts of society with few legal rights, but there was one week in April that acknowledged their existence. The Floralia festival was an annual celebration to honor the goddess of fertility, Flora. All kinds of lewd debauchery ensued in the Roman Colosseum, including spectacles with prostitutes who "fought" in mock gladiator battles.[11]

In modern times, the following words would be political suicide, but the Roman emperor Marcus Porcius Cato promoted prostitution during a speech in 60 BC. He stated, "Anyone who thinks young men ought to be forbidden affairs with prostitutes is certainly very ignorant of the freedom of our time, and indeed not in harmony with the customs of our ancestors. Name any epoch when this was not normal. When was such behavior ever censured or forbidden? These things have always been allowed. Prostitution is a legally sanctioned privilege."[12]

The economy was declining in 40 AD when Gaius Caligula became the first Roman emperor to tax prostitution. The tax wasn't like our modern income tax system based on actual wages. Instead,

Caligula taxed prostitution like modern day pimps, demanding a flat fee no matter the circumstances. The tax was due whether the woman worked or not. And that tax remained in place until 498 AD. Caligula even added a brothel to the palace and forced the wives and daughters of some leading officials to work there as well. Historians tend to disagree as to what motivated such a decision. Some believe that he wanted to humble the aristocracy in a public gesture, but the most plausible explanation is the obvious one; he was an egomaniacal tyrant guided by lust who enjoyed abusing his power.[13]

The Romans regulated and taxed the industry with their own government officials, aediles. The aediles registered prostitutes in a public index and inspected the brothels in an attempt to maintain public order.[14] Indeed, they required brothels to be closed from sunrise to three p.m. In the process, aediles were given a lot of latitude to enforce their regulations, but they weren't entitled to complete immunity from abusing their power. To demonstrate, a prostitute named Manila won a case in court against an aedile, Auslis Hostilus Manicinus, after he had invaded her home. This man came to her home in his "party clothes," which was a festive garland on his head that signaled his clear intentions, while she was with a customer. In response, she shooed him and his unwelcome advance away by throwing stones at him.[15]

Throughout history, many nations have shifted back and forth on plans of action to handle this issue of prostitution. Again, prostitution was either tolerated or directly enabled through temples or state-sponsored brothels in early societies. However, that changed dramatically in the 6th century AD when prostitution was formally banned by the Visigoths' King (modern day Spain). These women were punished with 300 strikes from a stick and deported from the city. If they were caught re-entering the city, they again received 300 strikes and were forced into community service.[16]

Some other historic rulers attempted to ban prostitution as well, yet none were able to effectively root out the demand for this vice despite the use of brutal, corporal punishment. Notably, the Roman Emperor Frederick Barbarossa banned his soldiers from traveling with prostitutes in 1158 AD. This wasn't a matter that he took lightly as any woman who violated the law had her nose cut off; the soldiers had a finger cut off or an eye poked out.[17] Despite such harsh penalties, this illegal activity continued to occur rampantly. In a similar fashion, nearly a full century later (1254 AD), the French King Louis IX decreed that prostitutes would be exiled and stripped of all of their money and possessions, including their clothing. Once again, this policy wasn't very effective so Louis IX officially decided to have all of the brothels in his country torn down in 1269.[18]

On the other hand, several European countries sanctioned this vice with designated red-light districts. Two of the most prominent were in Paris and Venice. In fact, the Great Council of Venice in 1358 considered prostitution to be "absolutely indispensable to the world."[19] Furthermore, the red-light districts in Florence and Venice featured police protection for public safety and were supported by the government because their leaders believed that it reduced homosexuality.[20]

Many decades passed before prostitution was universally condemned by the church. It had been viewed as a necessary outlet for male sexual urges and would thus maintain decency throughout society. Saint Thomas Aquinas said, "Prostitution in the cities is like the toilets of the palaces. Take them away and the palaces will be destroyed by the stench and putrefaction."[21] His beliefs were similar to Saint Augustine, who centuries earlier stated that if you ban prostitution then "you will pollute all things with lust; set them among honest matrons, and you will dishonor all things with disgrace and turpitude."[22] In fact, the Catholic Church's policies during the 10th century were labeled a "pornocracy" by some historians due to the fact that several clergymen owned brothels.[23] This type of culture remained in place for centuries until the Protestant Reformation; Martin Luther and John Calvin fundamentally opposed prostitution and premarital sex.

The wheels had been set in motion for the newfound conservative principles of the Protestant Reformation. European sentiment regarding prostitution reversed course drastically in the late 15th century. The catalyst behind such a turnaround was the epidemic of syphilis, initially known as "large pox." This disease was first discovered in Naples, Italy in 1495 and it eventually ravaged Europe.²⁴ Syphilis is a horribly degenerative disease if left untreated. Unfortunately, the first effective treatment wasn't discovered until centuries later. Thus, most state-sponsored brothels were officially shut down in the 16th century as part of the Protestant Reformation. Furthermore, prostitutes faced fierce hostility during this period. For instance, groups of young men in Italy, known as "monastic brotherhoods," gang raped women who walked the streets alone at night. These assaults were even condoned as long as the men yelled "whore" beforehand.²⁵

The demand for prostitution thrived in Colonial America despite the corporal punishments enacted for this crime. For example, the first prostitution arrest took place in Boston in 1673. A madam named Alice Thomas was punished with forced labor and whipped in the streets for allowing women and men the "opportunity to commit carnal wickedness."²⁶ Even though this was a country partially founded by Puritans, it is estimated that one in twenty-five women were prostitutes during the Revolutionary period.[A]²⁷ As a matter of fact, the workers who built the White House had a makeshift brothel nearby at their service. The brothel also offered drinking and gambling, but it was shut down after some of the workers left early from their shifts to go to the brothel.²⁸

Prostitution laws were selectively enforced at the local level via disorderly conduct laws such as vagrancy or lewdness. However, much to the surprise of most modern Americans, this

---

[A] New Orleans wasn't American territory until 1803, but it's interesting to note that many of its early founders were prostitutes. New Orleans was a French colony and was founded in 1721. The French king decided to empty a prison and 88 prisoners, most of whom were prostitutes, were sent to New Orleans to found the city.

Oddly enough, Benjamin Franklin's swinger lifestyle may have indirectly aided the American Revolution. In the late 1750s, Benjamin Franklin was an ambassador to Great Britain and some historians believe that Franklin was acting as a spy when he ingratiated himself with the British elite by frequenting places such as the Hellfire Club. This club held secret members-only parties dedicated to drinking, orgies with prostitutes, and sacrilegious ceremonies. Some historians also believe that Franklin was later able to gain secret information during British negotiations with the colonies as a direct result from some relationships that he formed within the Hellfire Club.

vice has been quasi-decriminalized and/or tolerated for the majority of our nation's history. With that said, some of the first habitual offender laws were created in Massachusetts and they were generally aimed at prostitutes. A woman who committed a third prostitution offense netted a five-year sentence. In fact, some Massachusetts reformers requested drastic "police state" changes, including a police register for all hotel visitors and boarding houses.[29]

During the 1800s, police throughout the country generally allowed brothels to operate openly. Nevertheless, brothels were occasionally destroyed by masses of rioters. With that said, "brothel riots" weren't the result of conservative reformers who took the law into their own hands. No, prostitution is certainly a polarizing issue and thus brothels were a convenient target of the misdirected anger of working-class vigilante groups. These uproars were generally sparked by events completely unrelated to prostitution, such as food riots.[30] One such brothel riot was in reaction to the castration and murder of a soldier.[31]

Prostitution is now typically viewed as an urban problem, but it was pervasive and generally accepted during the expansion of the American western states where 1 in 10 women were prostitutes.[32] Thousands of men trekked westward in search of riches, but there were also a high number of prostitutes following them. In fact, the term "hell on wheels" originated from the women who traveled behind the Union Pacific railroad workers in wagons.[33] Likewise, the term "gold digger" derives from this era in relation to the women who flocked West to cater to the miners during the Gold Rush.[34]

Obviously, the primary factor behind the tremendous demand for prostitution was a very disproportionate male to female ratio. To be specific, in 1860 there were only 30 women in the silver mining town of Virginia City, NV with a population of 2,236.[35] There was so little female companionship in the West that it was accepted custom for heterosexual men to have all-male dances on Friday and Saturday nights. Half of the men would pin a white piece of cloth or handkerchief to their left arms to signify that they were playing the roles of women. Later they'd switch cloths and switch gender roles for dancing. Some men would even put on skirts.[36]

The disparity in the male to female population was much the same in San Francisco at the beginning of the gold rush. "Whenever a woman appeared on the street, business was practically suspended," wrote Herbert Asbury in *The Barbary Coast: An Informal History of the San Francisco Underworld*. "She was followed through the town by an adoring crowd, while self-appointed committees marched ahead to clear the way and protect her from the too boisterous salutations of the emotional miners."[37]

Business owners obviously knew that prostitution was an effective recruiting tool for luring workers out west, therefore they supported laissez-faire policies. Likewise, there has long been an association with tolerance and support of prostitution from the U.S. military. During early western expansion, numerous women traveled with the soldiers. Many of them were prostitutes who also provided additional services such as laundry and cooking. Consequently, many "laundresses" had common-law marriages with military men. In fact, laundresses received one ration a day, a place to live, and medical assistance.[38] However, due to budget cuts, Congress officially banned this practice in 1878.[39]

Wherever there were military forts, there were usually brothels nearby, known as hog ranches. These brothels weren't officially sanctioned by the military, but they weren't condemned either. Military officials usually didn't interfere with their business because it was futile to crack down on the sex trade. Consider the example from one of the first hog ranches established in 1849 in Laramie, Wyoming. The Army purchased the property so that they could shut it down, but that decision was basically nullified as the women simply set up shop six miles away in a ranch named Openly Lewd. Another brothel in the area, Three-Mile Hog Ranch, still exists today as a historic site.[40]

As the Civil War ensued, prostitution was rampant among the troops on both sides. Camps were set up for the wives of soldiers, but many prostitutes pretended to be the wives of soldiers. In fact, the term "hooker" became popularized during this period in Washington, D.C. The Union General, Joseph Hooker, directed that brothels be isolated in a section of Lafayette Square, known as "Hooker Row."[41] However, that term existed before the Civil War and, according to one theory, the word "hooker" originated in Corlear's Hook of New York City, then a waterfront with an infamous red-light district.[42]

Naturally, venereal diseases were transmitted at high rates during the Civil War even though many prostitutes had access to condoms. Unfortunately, these "sheepskins" or "French letters" weren't very effective. That sparked a recurring theme throughout American history in which prostitution policies were re-evaluated during times of war. Due to the high rates of venereal disease, Union Provost Marshal Lt. George Spaulding ordered that all of the "public women" were to be ousted from Nashville.[43] For this reason, a steamboat captain, John Newcomb, was forced by the army two days later, despite his protests, to bring the area's diseased prostitutes to Louisville, KY on his ship. However, when Newcomb arrived in Louisville with about 500 to 600 women, he was told by local officials that those women wouldn't be allowed to enter their city. He was then ordered to bring them to Cincinnati, but he had the same problem upon arrival. Newcomb tried various other cities along the Ohio River with no luck and after a month of exhausting all of his options Newcomb brought the women back to Nashville, TN. The local press delighted in detailing this fiasco and nicknamed Newcomb's ship "The Floating Whorehouse."[44]

Rather than accepting defeat, Union Provost Marshal Lt. George Spaulding came up with a different plan to reduce the harm of diseases from prostitution. He devised a licensing system after the women were returned to Nashville. All of the area's prostitutes were ordered to submit to weekly medical exams and those who passed their tests were then given licenses that required a $0.50 weekly fee. On the other hand, the women who refused to submit to such tests were sent to a workhouse for 30 days. Those who didn't pass their medical tests were sent to a specially organized hospital. Altogether, this system effectively reduced venereal disease and a similar licensing system was set up in Memphis, TN in 1864.[45]

Outside of the battlefields, prostitution was widespread and ingrained in popular culture to such an extent that six of the fourteen Broadway theatres shared the same city blocks with a brothel during the Civil War.[46] Meanwhile, the sexual double standard was glaringly apparent. Prostitutes were considered vile sinners, but men's roles were often absolved. *If* someone was arrested for prostitution, it was generally the woman who faced the harshest penalties while the man who paid for sex was usually unscathed by law enforcement. This was considered a "gentleman's privilege" for middle and upper class white males who were the least likely to be arrested. And, if they were arrested, authorities were known to sometimes scribble out names in reports and dispose of mugshots for prominent members in the community. An excerpt from an article in the *Boulder County Herald* in 1882 about a prostitution arrest exemplified this dynamic, "Marshall Bounds and assistant Titus went to said house and arrested X and Y."[47]

The most upscale establishments for prostitution, known as parlor houses, had an air of exclusivity for the patrons and often required a letter of reference.[48] You would think that prostitution alone would be enough for most of the patrons, but many of these businesses purposely projected a sophisticated atmosphere. Parlor houses were often expensively decorated with fine art and offered premium amenities, along with card games and billiards. One of the most well-known establishments of this kind was the Everleigh Club in Chicago. It had a reflective glass floor and three string orchestras.[49]

Rarely were parlor houses shut down by the police because the madams generally stayed within the good graces of the law by paying bribes to local law enforcement. Likewise, madams typically ingratiated themselves within the community by making charitable donations to local schools, hospitals, and churches. In addition, they paid substantially higher rents than other businesses.[50]

Of course, every prostitute didn't work in an upscale parlor house. Many saloons doubled as covert brothels and the women often stayed in the backrooms known as wine rooms, family rooms, or ladies parlors.[51] Hence, the draw of prostitution enabled saloons to charge sky high alcohol prices. Brothels could easily charge a whole dollar for a beer in the 1870s; that same drink would sell for five cents in a regular tavern.[52] Consequently, the booming profits from prostitution-related alcohol and the potential income persuaded women to become "dance hall girls." They sang, danced, and cavorted with men in taverns while earning commissions from the drinks that their customers purchased. They weren't required to have sex with the men, but many dance hall girls doubled as prostitutes in adjoining rooms.[53] Also, many urban theatres used the draw of prostitution to lure more customers by giving free entrance to these women as long as they stayed in the third tier.[54]

Prostitution was a $3 million annual industry in the U.S. by the mid-19th century, more than many fully legal business sectors.[55] Meanwhile, the moral crusaders of the time generally ignored the fact that few opportunities existed for a woman to earn a livable wage. The debate was dominated by religious ideology with the primary conclusion being that prostitution was solely caused by a lack of virtue. Rev. James Curry of New York once proclaimed, "If a girl or woman wishes to go wrong she will do so no matter if she is working for $3, $30, or $300 a week."[56]

Unfortunately, there weren't any credible prostitution studies until 1858 when William Sanger published a first of its kind in America, *The History of Prostitution: Its Extent, Causes and Effects Throughout the World*. What in modern times is patently obvious, wasn't necessarily the case back then. William Sanger, along with future researchers, documented that economic conditions generally pushed women into prostitution. Most professions wouldn't hire women at that time and, if so, there was rampant sexual harassment and wage discrimination. One study by a Berkeley Chief of Police found that most of the prostitutes he interviewed had previously worked for degrading, low paying employers, generally as a domestic or factory worker.[57] Domestic servants were not only paid poorly and treated like trash, but they didn't even have the benefit of autonomy outside the workplace. Their employers often tried "to change the way they dressed, courted, and carried on their social lives."[58] One woman explained, "I'd rather do this than be kicked around like a dog in a kitchen by some woman who calls herself a lady."[59]

William Sanger's research also identified some of the widely ignored social factors that led women into prostitution. Many women were running away from failed and abusive marriages or families. Also, a woman was viewed no different from a prostitute if she had engaged in premarital sex. Society, in general, assumed that she couldn't regain her honor, therefore choosing to make more money as a prostitute was an understandable decision.[60] Sanger's research also focused on ways to improve public health and safety, a line of thinking lost on most of the American public at the time. Conversely, many European countries attempted to regulate the industry, including medical checkups, but there weren't the necessary medical advances to treat venereal diseases at that time.[B][61]

The anti-prostitution movement didn't become a national movement in America until the turn of the 20th century with the Progressive Era. Nearly every major city had unofficial vice districts operating with the full knowledge of the local police. In particular, the first American red-light district was located in Dodge City, KS. That city was a major stop for the railroad and a red light was left outside the brothels to locate the train crews in case of an emergency. As red-light districts became more common in America, some cities insisted that a red shade or curtains be placed in the windows of brothels during the day as a warning to passersby.[62]

Some large and midsized cities even established formal public health regulations, such as medical testing, and that became a galvanizing force for reformers who united nationally to try and stop this trend. Thus, when various local governments attempted

---

[B] The Contagious Disease Acts were passed in England during the 1860s in response to having had one of the highest rates of disease in the world. Prostitutes who refused medical exams faced prison time. These examination laws were contested strongly by feminist reformers, such as Josephine Butler, who referred to them as "surgical rape" because they were indiscriminately probed with metal objects. By the 1880s, these kinds of efforts by Christian and women's groups pushed lawmakers to stop regulating and testing prostitutes in England. In fact, these inspections were a moot point because there was little scientific progress at that time to stop the spread of diseases. Also, gonorrhea surfaced during this period of time. The disease's nickname, "the Clap," derived from a large prostitution district in Paris named Clapier.

to officially sanction prostitution, it became a call to arms for the Progressives. These protests were a reflexive reaction to the taboo subject of regulated prostitution. However, that doesn't mean that there weren't merits to these experiments with regulation.

St. Louis was the first American city to formally legalize and regulate prostitution in 1870. This may be surprising, but the city's police were early supporters of "the social evil ordinance." St. Louis established a very thorough, yet overly authoritarian set of regulations. Every prostitute and brothel owner was forced to pay monthly licensing fees. Also, all prostitutes had to pass medical inspections from the city's board of health. However, those women were quarantined in what was known as the "social evil hospital" if they failed their medical exams. In fact, there were guards in the building and the women weren't allowed to leave until cleared by the medical staff. Regardless, some of them managed to escape this "One Flew Over the Cuckoo's Nest" type of setup.[63]

There were, however, positive takeaways from this social experiment. The social evil ordinance didn't allow for street prostitution and it funneled much of that activity indoors. For instance, the Chief of Police, James McDonough, stated in his annual report of 1872 that the number of street prostitutes "have been almost entirely discontinued" and child prostitution "has been greatly diminished, if not wholly removed."[64] These results should have spurred further debate as to how to modify their regulatory system to include common-sense, middle-ground compromises to ensure the women's fundamental rights. However, this experiment was too politically charged for its time. Thus, the city terminated this regulatory system in 1874 primarily due to the lobbying efforts of religious and feminist leaders, including the wife of the St. Louis Police Commissioner.[65]

Other cities such as Philadelphia, Cincinnati, and Chicago attempted to create a comparable system of regulation, but they were defeated by similarly organized lobbies who feared that regulations would "legitimize" prostitution.[66] The state of New York even passed a similar bill in 1871, but it received a pocket veto by the Governor. Nonetheless, New York state legislators continued with similar proposals a few more times, but every one of those bills was defeated.[C67]

Iowa is hardly a bastion of liberal-minded social experiments, but Henry Vollmer, the newly elected 25-year-old mayor of Davenport, publicly announced a bold new policy for the city in 1893. Prostitutes had to register with the police and pass health exams. Also, the madams were "arrested" monthly like clockwork. That forced them to appear in court to pay civil fines that essentially served as licensing fees. To sum up, this system was effective in maintaining public order and well received in the community. In fact, Sharon E. Wood, author of *The Freedom of the Streets: Work, Citizenship, and Sexuality in a Gilded Age City*, wrote, "Regulation had become so lucrative and so well established that even a reform Republican (mayor) could not easily displace it."[68] Indeed, this system stayed in place, even after Vollmer left office to join the U.S. House of Representatives, until 1909 when Iowa passed a state law banning prostitution.

Joel Best, author of *Controlling Vice: Regulating Brothel Prostitution in St. Paul, 1865-1883*, documented a similar system. He concluded that the regulatory system in St. Paul, MN effectively maintained public order in their city. The regulation system wasn't an exemption from the rule of law for brothel owners, rather it provided them protection from violent customers. Also, brothel owners had an incentive to keep the sex trade behind closed doors and within the good graces of the community because the police still had the right to arrest them if necessary. Hence, most of the high-ranking city officials supported this system, including the mayor, and the police chief, along with the majority of the police force. Albeit, one particular judge was offended by this system for moral reasons. He decided to exercise his power and increased the brothel owners' monthly fines. In reaction, Mayor William Lee offered a rebuttal, "For six thousand years the attempt had been made to eradicate (prostitution) but the attempt was useless."[69] Nevertheless, the police simply responded by arresting these madams less often to even out the costs of their "licensing fees."

[C] Susan B. Anthony was one of the organizers who helped stop regulation from passing in New York.

The peak of commercialized sex coincided with the beginning of the Progressive Era. To review, the Progressives of today are highly liberal, but they were the leading social conservatives of that era who pioneered the prohibition of alcohol. Therefore, San Francisco's mayor became a symbolic target of the Progressives when the city established a regulatory system similar to the one in St. Louis. From 1913 to 1915, prostitutes in San Francisco were examined every four days at a city facility, the Municipal Clinic for the Prevention of Venereal Disease. If they passed their tests, they received certificates and were exempt from legal trouble. On the other hand, San Francisco didn't impose extreme quarantine measures as St. Louis did. Prostitutes in San Francisco were banned from working in the sex trade if they had diseases, but they were provided with free health care. As a result, this was generally well supported locally, but opposition lobbyists coordinated across the nation to shut down the program. In the end, San Francisco's mayor decided to close the city's testing clinic due to political pressure because a large group threatened to boycott the Panama-Pacific International Exposition (a world's fair) held in San Francisco.[70]

The Progressives were led by religious leaders such as Charles Parkhurst, a Protestant Minister who urged for more "protest" from the Protestants.[71] The Progressive Era united various anti-vice crusaders such as the Anti-Cigarette League, the American Purity Alliance, and the Anti-Saloon League.[72] These groups were already united with many other issues such as labor rights, women's rights, minimum wage laws, etc. Thus, in 1900, a reform group known as the "New York Committee of Fifteen" conducted undercover investigations and released their first report with the title "The Social Evil." A similar group with ties to the New York Anti-Saloon League, known as the "Committee of Fourteen," did a comparable investigation of prostitution three years later. Forty-three different cities followed suit with similar commissions from 1910 to 1917 and flooded their communities with advocacy research in hopes of banning prostitution.[73]

Reverend Parkhurst gained national recognition for his efforts to root out New York City's open corruption with vice activity. In 1893 he successfully lobbied for criminal charges of neglect of duty to be levied against a notoriously corrupt police captain, Bill Devery, who refused to shut down his precinct's brothels. As mentioned in *Dealing from the Bottom of the Deck*, Bill Devery (a part owner of the New York Yankees) was a Tammany Hall crony who "taxed" all of the city's illegal gambling businesses. He implemented a similar payoff system with all of the area's brothels. And Devery was relatively open about these arrangements. In particular, one of his patrolmen was accused of accepting bribes, but how he handled the situation was noteworthy. He told the officer, "If there's any graftin' to be done, I'll do it. Leave it to me."[74] Despite the litany of evidence, Devery was acquitted in the end. However, Parkhurst gained a partial victory, albeit temporarily, when one of history's most notable Progressives, Teddy Roosevelt, served as the superintendent of the New York City Police Department in 1895. Roosevelt was a staunch rival of Devery and the blatant nature of Gotham City's vice rackets declined noticeably while he was at the helm.

The New York State Senate was then conducting a corruption investigation, through the Lexow Committee, and it was like shooting fish in a barrel. Many high-level officials were quite candid about ignoring vice crimes in exchange for bribes. Police Captain Alexander "Clubber" Williams was questioned by the committee in regard to the 83 brothels that brazenly operated in his precinct. He replied, "Well, they were fashionable."[75] In fact, Williams is credited with nicknaming New York City's most notorious red-light district, "the Tenderloin," which was located in his precinct.[76]

Vice crimes generally went unpunished in most large cities, just like New York City. In fact, this dynamic peaked during the first two decades of the 20th century and accordingly this period was labeled the "Golden Age of the Brothel in America" by some historians.[77] A few cities, such as New Orleans, Shreveport, Houston, and El Paso, had specific legislation that determined the exact location of those areas; otherwise, the police decided which city blocks would host this gray market activity. Also, judges tended to reinforce those rules by being more punitive if a prostitution arrest occurred outside the red-light district.[78]

New Orleans had probably the most well-known and flamboyant red-light district, Storyville. This area was named after a city councilman, Alderman Sidney Story, who made the proposal. The Storyville red-light district went into effect on New Year's Day of 1898 and pertained to a specific 16 square block area (adjacent to the French Quarter) that had been home to primarily black residents. Every known prostitute in the city was forced to relocate to the area or face an eviction notice.[79]

Storyville hosted 2,200 registered prostitutes at its peak.[80] Other than registering with the city, prostitution wasn't regulated in any way. In theory, Storyville's early supporters hoped that their social experiment would unfold successfully like many other cities by sequestering the vice into a small area for the police to monitor and maintain public order. New Orleans already had a serious overall crime problem, but the police were more concerned with how this area had developed a notoriety for interracial sex. Many tourists traveled to the area for this reason from around the nation and internationally.[81] In response, the city passed some Jim Crow ordinances to thwart this racial comingling, including a ban on alcohol sales within businesses if both black and white people were on the premises. The city council followed up with a more direct attack by forcing all of the black prostitutes to relocate to a separate district in the uptown area. However, a group of Storyville madams sued the city on grounds of discrimination and the court sided with the madams.[82]

Some top New Orleans jazz greats, such as Louis Armstrong, started their music careers in Storyville brothels.[D][83] The Storyville area even offered a pretense of legitimacy as it catered to the adjacent business district with guidebooks, known as blue books, which listed the local brothels and rated their services. However, not everyone approved of this formalized red-light district and a local resident, George L'Hote, sued the city over the ordinance. His case made it all the way to the Louisiana State Supreme Court, but the court ruled against him because the ordinance didn't actually legalize prostitution; it was banned in all areas outside Storyville.[84]

[D] James Brown also began his music career in a brothel, but that was in Georgia.

Most local governments had a laissez-faire approach to prostitution and that motivated several social justice reformers to band together during the Progressive Era. Iowa became the first state to pass injunction and abatement laws in 1909. Again, state prostitution laws didn't exist up until that point in history! Every state eventually followed suit by passing those same laws. They allowed police to shut down brothels as "public nuisances" if there were complaints from concerned citizens and the judge agreed with their opinions.[85] Consequently, many cities began shutting down their red-light districts, but some notable cities such San Francisco, New Orleans, and San Antonio didn't enforce the new laws.[86]

There were four leading factors that prompted every state to create their own prostitution laws, the first being the Progressive movement. The second factor was the highly sensational "white slave" panic. This political movement began in earnest in response to a series of articles printed in the Pall Mall Gazette in the 1880s. A British journalist, William T. Stead, arranged an undercover sting operation to "purchase" and "arrange to sell" a 13-year girl for that story. Naturally, Stead's column gained massive exposure and directly resulted in some positive changes throughout Europe, such as establishing laws to punish statutory rape and sex trafficking.[87]

William T. Stead's work was based on actual events and raised numerous ethical and moral questions. In fact, he was nominated for a Nobel Peace Prize. However, these issues didn't capture the hearts and minds of Americans until decades later. Also, the response snowballed into an overblown media spectacle that pumped up newspaper sales and advanced political agendas for various opportunists.

The term "white slavery" became commonplace in American newspapers in the early 20th century, but the moral outrage on the part of many readers was misplaced. Simply put, few Americans were concerned with this issue when the victims were minorities. Roughly sixty years earlier, beginning in the 1850s with the California gold rush, startling numbers of young Chinese women were sold by their families into sex slavery. These women were, in some cases, literally shipped in crates labeled as cargo to San

Francisco.[88] Chinese gangs known as "tongs" controlled the traffic of these women and forced them into a brutal form of indentured servitude that few were able to escape.[89] In a particularly disheartening twist, one woman, Ah Toy, was able to buy her freedom, but she ultimately became one of the most notorious sex traffickers in the area.[90]

This trafficking of young Chinese women lasted for decades and the extent of the problem was much worse than that of the future "white slave trade." At its peak, there were roughly 1,500 to 2,000 Chinese women forced into sex slavery in San Francisco, but there wasn't extensive public uproar because of rampant anti-Chinese sentiment.[91] Oddly enough, our nation's first drug laws were directly related to anti-Chinese sentiment because the newspapers proclaimed that Asian men were forcing *white women* into sex slavery with opium. Consequently, that propaganda had a double whammy effect of sorts as it led to both drug and prostitution laws.

The white slave scare was unofficially launched in the U.S. by a journalist George Kibbe Turner. His 1907 article, "City of Chicago," asserted that numerous women in the city were being trafficked by "Russian Jews." Turner's report rapidly gained national attention even though he offered no actual evidence.[92] Similar to our earliest drug laws, unflinching racism and bigotry were prevalent in the buildup to our nation's first state prostitution laws. As an illustration, Turner claimed in a separate article that Jewish pimps seduced young white women with false promises of marriage. He also claimed that Italians used force because "(f)ear is more efficacious with this class than any other, because of the notorious tendency of the low-class Italian to violence and murder."[93]

These kinds of articles were nothing more than yellow journalism. This media panic chose to ignore the clear social and economic conditions that drove numerous women into prostitution. Instead, this narrative offered a simpler explanation that prostitution was rampant due to "mongrel" races being behind this problem. In line with the drug war and the prohibition of alcohol, a wide range of groups (the Immigrant Protective League, the KKK, and the Woman's Christian Temperance Union, among others) advanced their white slave agenda with films, books, magazines, and pamphlets.[94] The general theme involved young, innocent white girls who were seduced, drugged, and ultimately forced into prostitution. Those stories often struck a particularly sensitive nerve by mentioning that these white sex slaves were forced to service black men.

White slavery alarmists spread that message aggressively. In particular, there were posters displayed publicly throughout various cities warning, "Danger! Mothers beware! Sixty thousand innocent girls wanted to take place of sixty thousand white slaves who will die this year in the United States."[95] Nearly all of the white slave tales preyed upon racial stereotypes and presented the peddlers as anything but White Anglo-Saxon Protestants (WASPs). According to the alarmists, the prostitution industry was *solely* a result of illicit sex traffickers who were Eastern Europeans, Jews, Germans, French, Greek, etc. One Chicago religious reformer, Jean Turner-Zimmerman, published *Chicago's Black Traffic in White Girls*. Her book described the peddling as "carried on and exploited by a foaming pack of foreign hellhounds" who were "the moral and civil degenerates of the French, Italian, Syrian, Russian, Jewish, or Chinese races." Conversely, that same author asserted that "an American or Englishman conducting such a business is almost entirely unknown."[96]

That type of narrative has clear parallels to the earliest drug laws when cocaine was posed as a substance that led to black men raping white women; whereas, the same drug was considered something akin to caffeine for white professionals on the go. Consider another example from a different white slave author and activist Ernest Bell. He wrote, "Shall we defend our American civilization, or lower our flag to the most despicable foreigners -- French, Irish, Italian, Jews, or Mongolians?" Meanwhile, he also mentioned that he knew of no trafficking "by English, Scotch, German or Scandinavian men."[97]

Luckily, not everyone was fooled by this genre. Brand Whitlock, former Toledo mayor during this era, offered measured analysis by suitably describing the white slave hysteria as "one of those strange moral movements which now and then seize upon the public mind" as "a sort of pornography to satisfy the American sense of news."[98] The Progressives maximized their propaganda efforts by eliciting fear and by ironically preying upon the public's most base desires. "The moral panic surrounding white slave traffic allowed a certain class to discuss prostitution in the most serious tone while being titillated by the sexual detail. This was porn for puritans," wrote James R. Peterson, author of *The Century of Sex*.[99] To demonstrate, one magazine article was titled "Beautiful White Girls Sold into Ruin" with the caption "Illustrated with a large number of startling pictures."[100]

George Kibbe Turner was able to publish these kinds of lurid tales for a long time with practically no actual fact-checking. However, that changed when he wrote another white slave article that directly implicated Tammany Hall, the New York City Democratic political organization. It was no secret that this group was incredibly corrupt; Tammany Hall directly "taxed" the city's vice rackets, but there was no evidence that they were forcing anyone into prostitution.[E][101] Nonetheless, George Kibbe Turner's article caused a stir nationally and the spotlight forced the city into damage control mode. As a face-saving gesture, they launched an investigation by a commission and grand jury led by John D. Rockefeller Jr.

Rockefeller's name clearly added some credibility to their investigation, but many have concluded that he was chosen by Tammany Hall because his privileged lifestyle didn't coincide with the city's underworld. Therefore, he would be less likely to expose any corruption.[102] In fact, Rockefeller was reluctant at first to commit to such an assignment because he wasn't an expert on the subject, but he ultimately went full bore with the project. Moreover, the commission was originally scheduled to last for thirty days, but Rockefeller donated $250,000 of his money and he worked an extra six months on the assignment. In the end, George Kibbe Turner was forced to indirectly admit, while under oath, that his work was entirely a fabrication. During his testimony, he

---

[E] Maybe no one knew of this corruption better than William Travers Jerome, a former Judge and District Attorney. The police often tipped off the criminals before any raids. Therefore, Jerome decided to issue the warrants and lead raids on these businesses himself. In 1901 alone, he had taken part in 114 raids for gambling and prostitution.

reneged on his claims that syndicates were trafficking young women. Ultimately, the Rockefeller Commission found no evidence of any kind that a syndicate existed. Basically, the only "trafficking" was voluntary.[103]

Despite the clear conclusions of the Rockefeller Commission, the general public was convinced that there was an epidemic of white slavery. They were less interested in a stodgy government commission and more compelled by the graphic reports from a few high-profile cases in the newspapers. One such convicted human trafficker, a man named Harry Levinson, received so much press that a different New York businessman with the same name needed to get a legal name change.

On the other hand, a mixed-race madam named Belle Moore was also labeled by the press as a "white slave trafficker," but the details from her trial demonstrated that reporters were frequently guilty of cherry-picking salacious details to fulfill their narrative. They didn't tell the whole story in the proper context and that was typical of these white slave cases. Belle Moore wasn't involved with underage prostitutes nor did she use any force, fraud, or coercion.

An undercover police officer posed as an Alaskan brothel owner looking to set up a new business in Seattle. He said to Belle Moore, "I don't want colored girls. I want white girls, girls weighing less than one hundred pounds, not more than one hundred ten at most, must be naturally good looking, well-built and be able to get twenty or twenty-five dollars in any whorehouse."[104] The investigators told the press that Moore had arranged the purchase of two young girls. One was described as "so little and so childish that she wept when they took her from one house to another because she had to leave her Teddy bear behind." However, it was all a ruse. The two "girls" turned out to be experienced prostitutes who were 23 and 25 years old. Also, the women weren't forced to do anything. One of them testified, "All I remember is he asked us to go to Seattle, made arrangements for us to go to Seattle, and I said, 'Yes, I would go.'" It was clear to the judge that Belle Moore wasn't guilty of white slavery according to the intent of the law. "White slavery, as popularly understood, is that condition to which young and innocent girls are debased when sold into captivity for immoral purposes," he stated. "The evidence did not show you to be guilty of such a sale." Nonetheless, she was convicted of compulsory prostitution of women and was sentenced to five years.[105]

Belle Moore's case marked a tipping point when *The New York Times* became one of the few newspapers to tone down the rhetoric of white slavery. By 1914, *The New York Times* had denounced the myth of white slavery stating "sensational magazine articles had created a belief in the existence of a great interstate 'white slave' trust. No such trust exists, nor is there any organized white slave industry anywhere."[106] Similarly, various investigations during this period were conducted in St. Paul, Seattle, Minneapolis, Syracuse, Illinois, Wisconsin, and Massachusetts and they found there to be very little forced prostitution. Likewise, one study in San Francisco with 320 prostitutes didn't find a single one of them forced into prostitution.[107]

With all that said, there has existed coercion, exploitation, and human trafficking within the prostitution industry to some extent throughout history, but it was vastly exaggerated to sell newspapers and advance an agenda during the white slave panic. The white slavery narrative also proved to be fruitful for some ambitious prosecutors. A pair of Illinois attorneys were the leaders of this agenda, Clifford Roe (the Assistant State's Attorney) and Edwin Sims (the U.S. District Attorney in Chicago). These men were adamant in their claims. Roe professed that "about one half (of prostitutes) are recruited through the white slave markets."[108] Furthermore, Edwin Sims even insisted that white slave syndicates were so inhuman that they made the "Congo slave traders of the old days appear like Good Samaritans."[109]

This pair seized upon the headlines generated from a case involving a woman named Mona Marshall, who alleged that she had been drugged, raped, and forced into prostitution by a pimp. There were elements of her story that were genuinely factual and terribly disturbing, but other parts seemed far-fetched. That included a tale in which the police reportedly received a note that she dropped from the window of the brothel stating, "I am a white slave." In addition, Marshall's recounting of events included several contradictions with dates and key details. Nonetheless, *The Chicago Tribune* and William Randolph Hearst's *Chicago American* ran wild with the Mona Marshall story and it quickly gained a national audience. This was another contradictory aspect to Hearst's legacy. His newspapers sales benefitted from white slave newspaper reports, yet he profited handsomely as a major landowner in one of New York City's popular red-light districts.[110]

Clifford Roe gained recognition nationwide as the prosecutor of that case and he leveraged his newfound fame to become a revered activist. He subsequently published *Panders and Their White Slaves* and *The Girl Who Disappeared,* which was later fact checked by a notable sociologist Walter Reckless. He found that Roe used heavily altered statements from prostitutes to advance his agenda.[111] In addition, Reckless studied Chicago's "white slave" court cases extensively and found that less than 5% of them actually involved women held against their will.[112] In fairness, although Roe's methods were deceptive, one positive result manifested from his work. It was success in lobbying for much-needed sex trafficking laws to be passed in Illinois. Over a short period of time, twenty-nine different states passed similar laws.[113]

The hysteria from the press undoubtedly influenced Illinois Congressman, James Mann, who introduced the first federal bill to outlaw "white slavery." In fact, Sims and Roe helped draft the bill.[114] This bill passed easily, although the pretenses were astounding. Research for the bill was conducted by the Dillingham Commission that was far from scholarly, nor impartial, and expressed racist opinions.[115] James Mann even asserted that "(t)he white slave traffic while not so extensive, is much more horrible than any black slave traffic ever was in the history of the world."[116] Yes, many politicians spoke of "white slavery" in this manner and it seemed to be a misguided attempt to wipe the slate clean from the wrongs of the past. Nonetheless, the White Slave Traffic Act of 1910, or as it was known "the Mann Act," was signed by President Taft. Taft allocated $50,000 to a then fairly new branch of government to pursue Mann Act violations, the Bureau of Investigation (the precursor to the FBI).[117]

Obviously, no one would deny the need for federal legislation against sex trafficking, but the white slavery aspect clouded the fact that Congressman Mann's bill granted the federal government overly broad and invasive powers in determining morality. In some Mann Act cases, the FBI even jailed the people they were supposed to be protecting -- the sex trafficking victims, in order to guarantee their arrival for testimony in court.[118] The language of the bill specifically banned transporting females across state lines for the "purpose of prostitution, or debauchery, or any other immoral purpose." Hence, the term "immoral purposes" can be interpreted broadly and many people were convicted of a federal crime who were merely unmarried adults engaging in consensual sex that was completely unrelated to prostitution.

By April of 1914, there were 530 Mann Act convictions. However, only 75 of them were for actual cases of sex trafficking involving force, violence, coercion, etc. And almost as many convictions, 51, were for non-commercial sex between consenting adults. Therefore, the vast majority of these convictions involved women who *voluntarily* entered into the sex industry as prostitutes, strippers, nude models, etc.[119]

A landmark U.S. Supreme Court ruling in 1917, Caminetti v United States, upheld the federal government's right to police non-commercial sex between consenting adults. That Mann Act case involved a pair of married men from Sacramento, Drew Caminetti and Maury Diggs, who took their young mistresses on a trip to Reno, NV. Upon arrival, those men were arrested because their wives had informed the police about their journey. This case gained a ton of media exposure because Caminetti's father was then President Woodrow Wilson's Commissioner of Immigration.[120]

With the precedent established by Caminetti v United States, there were over 50,000 Mann Act investigations in the 16 years following that ruling.[121] The volume of Mann Act cases began to decline in the 1930s because juries had become less willing to convict someone for consensual sex unrelated to prostitution. However, as late as 1959, a federal judge still determined that a Mann Act conviction was apt simply for having the *intent* to violate the law, as long as the man had crossed the state line. He stated, "Proof that he accomplished his illicit purpose is not necessary to conviction."[122]

The terms of the law have been amended multiple times since its passage. The Mann Act still exists, but it has increasingly become viewed as an antiquated and farcical law. After all, Jackie Gleason's character, Sheriff Buford T. Justice, planned to charge Burt Reynolds under the Mann Act for taking Sally Field on a cross-country joy ride in the film *Smokey and the Bandit*.

Not everyone welcomed the FBI when it was established because there were valid concerns that this federal agency could abuse its power and those fears were realized with the Mann Act.[123] Mann Act investigations opened the door to unnecessary snooping by government officials. This law justified prying into the personal lives of influential public figures whom they wanted to subvert. Case in point, the first black heavyweight boxing champion, Jack Johnson, was one of the first men to be convicted under the Mann Act. He had a swagger and a lifestyle that slapped Jim Crow in the face. Johnson openly dated white women and often had a harem of white prostitutes parading around his training camp. On top of that, he had a signature style in which he taunted his opponents in the ring, all of whom were white. In fact, one of his victories even caused a race riot.[124]

Johnson's first Mann Act arrest involved one of his girlfriends, Lucille Cameron, who was a prostitute before she met him. The prosecutors were stymied as she testified that she was in no way coerced by Johnson, and, in the end, Johnson was acquitted in that case. As a matter of fact, he married Cameron soon afterward.[125]

Undeterred, the FBI kept Johnson in the crosshairs of their witch-hunt and found a jilted ex-lover to testify against him, Belle Schreiber. The FBI had leverage over Schreiber because she had worked as a prostitute at the most elite parlor house in Chicago, the Everleigh Club. Black patrons were banned from the club and Johnson was ushered out fairly quickly after his entrance, but not before he managed to convince a group of women, including Schreiber, to leave with him. As a result, Schreiber and the others were fired from the Everleigh Club.[126] This group traveled around the country of their own free will with Johnson. However, Johnson and Schreiber eventually went their separate ways. Nonetheless, Schreiber contacted him after their breakup asking for money to set up her own brothel because every madam had declined her services due to her connection with Johnson. In turn, Johnson obliged her request and sent her thousands of dollars.[127]

Yes, Johnson facilitated this young woman's venture in the sex trade, but his Mann Act case clearly didn't relate to "white slavery," according to the intent of the law. To sum up, an all-white jury ruled that he was guilty even though all of his transgressions with Schreiber occurred entirely *before* the Mann Act had been passed. In fact, the judge even admitted afterward that he was determined "to send a message" to all other black men.[128] Likewise, the Assistant U.S. District Attorney Harry A. Parkin agreed, "(T)his negro, in the eyes of many, has been persecuted. Perhaps as an individual he was. But it was his misfortune to be the foremost example of the evil in permitting the intermarriage of whites and blacks."[129]

Charlie Chaplin's left-wing political views also made him a target of the former FBI director, J. Edgar Hoover. As a result, the bureau manufactured a Mann Act charge against him in 1944. FBI investigators went forward with their case after discovering that Chaplin had purchased tickets for his mistress and her mother to travel from Los Angeles to New York. In the end, Chaplin was acquitted, but his image was ruined and he moved to Europe.[130]

These kinds of cases are just the tip of the iceberg as J. Edgar Hoover exploited the Mann Act's broad reach to dig into the sex lives of his political opponents. Hoover's reign brought sexual blackmail to epic proportions. Furthermore, these elected officials were aware of Hoover's meddling and the implied threat of exposure helped him extend his influence over Capitol Hill for decades.

The peak of the white slave panic was a fairly short-lived phenomenon (early 20th century), but a powerful one and the effects were long lasting. And that brings us to the third contributing factor that led to the first state prostitution laws. There was a belief that prostitutes were too "feebleminded" to make their own decisions. That fell in line with the eugenics propaganda that was gaining traction at the time. Eugenics was a genre of "research" posed as scientific proof to legitimize the beliefs of bigots and racists. Eugenicists advocated the sterilization of "inferior races," amongst other cruelties.

Eugenics has since been completely debunked by the scientific community, but many powerful American politicians were firm believers, including Teddy Roosevelt, Woodrow Wilson, and FDR. In fact, Teddy Roosevelt once privately wrote a supportive letter to a leading eugenicist stating that "society has no business to permit degenerates to reproduce their kind."[131]

In an odd way, eugenic beliefs began to influence the legitimate scientific research of the social hygiene movement, which consisted mostly of physicians who wanted to minimize venereal diseases. They weren't morally opposed to prostitution, rather they were concerned about disease. However, John D. Rockefeller Jr. co-opted and manipulated social hygiene research. In fact, he formed the Bureau of Social Hygiene in 1911, which he directed himself and corresponded with over 100 reformers in the movement.[132]

To reiterate, eugenics "research" was wildly popular with America's economic elite in the early 20th century. Names like Carnegie and Rockefeller now have a connotation of credibility and prestige, but a full century ago the Carnegie Institution and the Rockefeller Foundation provided hundreds of thousands of dollars to fund various eugenic research projects. As a matter of fact, John D. Rockefeller's grand jury experience with Tammany Hall became a springboard for expanding the Rockefeller Foundation's support for eugenic research. The Rockefeller Foundation funded groups such as the Kaiser Wilhelm Institute of Anthropology, Human Heredity, and Eugenics in Berlin, which prominently displayed Nazi flags on their premises. The implied credibility from studies by these types of groups eased eugenic beliefs into prostitution legislation. That includes work by the Danish biologist and geneticist Tage Kemp's *A Study of the Causes of Prostitution, Especially Concerning Heredity Factors*.[133]

In a way, John D. Rockefeller pioneered the advocacy research that's pumped out by so many modern think tanks. He provided generous fellowships to some of the most well-known scholars of that era, including Abraham Flexner. As a result, Flexner traveled to Europe to study prostitution and published

"Prostitution in Europe," which criticized legalization and regulation. On that note, historian Nicholas R. Scott aptly noted Rockefeller's attempt to conflate his eugenics agenda into legitimate research. Scott wrote, "Indeed the book's description of the causes of prostitution were the very same elements that eugenicists claimed to have found among the feebleminded."[134]

Eugenics also fit well within the widespread bigotry of the American public who were resistant to the country's increasing ethnic diversity. Accordingly, the first forced sterilization law for criminals was passed in Indiana in 1907.[135] In fact, future President Woodrow Wilson created the Board of Examiners of Feebleminded Epileptics and Other Defectives four years later, while serving as the Governor of New Jersey.[136] As you may have guessed, prostitutes were their first group tested for possible "feeblemindedness."[137]

Naturally, the subject matter of forced sterilization elicits memories of Nazi Germany, but it should be noted that much of the Nazis' eugenic influences came from the U.S. In fact, some of the methods from California's sterilization system were later used as a model by Nazi Germany.[F138] Moreover, California held the precursor to "three strikes" drug laws, in which the conviction for any crime on three separate occasions was punishable by sterilization.[139]

Thankfully, the U.S. government never imposed eugenics measures at a level on par with the Nazis, but, believe it or not, forced sterilization laws were actually upheld by the U.S. Supreme Court with Buck v Bell in 1927. By 1931, twenty-seven states had those laws on the books![140] In fact, these weren't particularly controversial policies. A survey in *Fortune Magazine* found that 66% of Americans agreed with compulsory sterilization in 1937.[141]

To sum up, roughly 6,000 people were forcibly sterilized before Buck v Bell. Approximately another 30,000 people were sterilized or castrated after that case. Not surprisingly, a large percentage of them were prostitutes who weren't actually "mental defects."[142] But psychologists like Henry Goddard were the judge,

---

[F] California hasn't passed any law to compensate the victims that are still living.

jury, and executioner when determining the criteria for feeblemindedness. Even the most fickle factors were applied as Goddard believed in "the unmistakable look of the feebleminded" and "just a glance sufficed" at making that determination.[143]

The influence of the Progressive movement, white slavery, and eugenics indeed prompted state legislators to make prostitution laws, but it was America's entry into WWI that officially ended the open toleration of prostitution. The U.S. military decided to rigidly enforce new federal anti-prostitution bans near military bases. As a result, from July 1917 to Sept 1918, over 100 cities ended their red-light districts because of the federal bans, including Storyville.[G][144]

After the Storyville shutdown, the Mayor of New Orleans Martin Behrman famously declared, "You can make prostitution illegal in Louisiana, but you can't make it unpopular."[145] He was certainly on the mark and the demand for prostitution has been an eternal force. Hence, the military launched various propaganda campaigns emphasizing fears of contracting disease. Those messages added to public service announcements that were in rotation before the war. These bulletins were highly convincing and actually had many Americans genuinely afraid to use public bathrooms and water fountains due to fears of contracting venereal diseases.[146] The military coined slogans such as "a German bullet is cleaner than a whore." Soldiers were also warned that prostitutes "could do more harm than any German fleet of airplanes."[147] Likewise, military pamphlets even stated that prostitutes were sent from Germany to infect American forces.[148]

These kinds of messages were part of a new program called the Commission on Training Camp Activities (CTCA). This program, which was created two weeks after the U.S. entered WWI, focused on imparting wholesome values for the troops as part of their training. Raymond Fosdick, the future President of the Rockefeller Association, led the CTCA. Before that time there was no uniform policy and each general handled the prostitution issue in his own way.[149] However, with Fosdick at the helm, the

---

[G] As a negotiating ploy, a Houston red-light district was shut down during WWI after the Army threatened to close a nearby Army base.

Rockefeller Foundation donated $100,000 to the CTCA and they implemented the Rockefeller brand of social hygiene.[150]

WWI marked a period in which the U.S. government combatted prostitution in an unprecedented manner. In particular, Congress passed the Chamberlain-Kahn Act in 1918 and it established "pure zones" by banning prostitution around the 5-mile perimeter of military bases. Those "pure zones" were patrolled by officers who were authorized to capture any woman if she didn't have a letter of introduction or an approved escort. This wasn't a proud moment in American history. Any woman within the pure zones could be labeled a "suspected prostitute" based solely upon an officer's fleeting suspicion. Consequently, thousands of women were held without formal charges and their rights to habeas corpus were vacated. In the end, about 45% of those cases were dismissed without a record of arrest, but the women first had to pass a medical exam before being released.[151]

Ultimately, the War Department punished 15,520 infected women. Yet, none of the male soldiers who paid for sex were arrested. The women were either jailed, quarantined in barbed wired work camps or with the "feebleminded," or sent to reform schools.[152] Ironically, in some cases, the buildings of these reformatories and detention homes had formerly been brothels that were abandoned after the red-light districts were shut down.[153]

Prior to 1917, only Indiana state law defined and prohibited prostitution. However, the Chamberlain-Kahn Act had a chilling effect and ten states added prostitution-specific laws in 1918. Consequently, all but a few states had added those laws by 1920. Reminiscent of the Mann Act, these new state laws overstepped personal freedom boundaries and issued the government overbearing, unconstitutional power. Indiana, along with some other states, specifically banned commercialized sex, but the language also included promiscuity or "indiscriminate sexual intercourse without hire."[154] Likewise, an Alabama ruling in 1920 came to a similar conclusion that a prostitute was a "loose woman or strumpet," which obviously was open to wide interpretation.[155]

There were additional alcohol-related laws created with the intention of indirectly curbing prostitution, including bans on mixed-gender drinking in saloons. Also, women were required to have an escort in order to enter a bar.[156] Furthermore, the people who were behind the white slave panic ultimately set in motion results that were the exact opposite of their intentions. The mafia expanded into the prostitution industry because the timing of new statewide prostitution laws coincided with the prohibition of alcohol, thereby banding both vices together underground. The conditions in brothels certainly weren't ideal for the women before prohibition, but at least it was a female operated industry with individual madams controlling their businesses. In contrast, the new state laws greatly benefited the pimps and organized criminals. Exploitation, extortion, and human trafficking associated with prostitution increased due to these new laws.

The new prostitution laws were quite profitable for "bookies," or what someone would today call a pimp. The term bookie is now associated with gambling, but then it referred to someone who booked appointments for prostitutes.[157] Those bookies were often connected to the mafia and thus gangsters such as Al Capone and Bugsy Siegel made a fortune from prostitution. For instance, it's estimated that by 1935 Lucky Luciano's henchmen controlled 200 brothels in New York with 1,200 prostitutes, generating about $10 million a year. What's more, he was indicted on 62 counts of forced prostitution a year later, which resulted in a fifty-year sentence.[158]

There is another bitter coincidence involving these first state prostitution laws. The laws were passed at a time when the supply and demand forces behind prostitution began to decline on their own. Women gained many new rights and access to higher paying jobs during the Progressive Era. Undoubtedly economic indicators for women have steadily improved ever since. Likewise, several of the social factors that prodded many women into prostitution began changing during the Progressive Era as well. Women often chose to work as prostitutes due to the stigma attached to premarital sex, but that dishonor drastically faded during the 1920s. After all, the rate of premarital sex was twice as high for women born after 1900 than before. Oddly enough, that was in part enabled by increased sales of automobiles, which were often referred to as "prostitution on wheels."[159]

As birth control became more effective and available, it enabled more casual premarital sex and that obviously reduced the demand for prostitution dramatically. Hence, the famous sex researcher, Alfred Kinsey, found that the percentage of men who had sex with prostitutes decreased by up to 67% over the course of 1926 to 1948.[H160] To put in perspective how extensive prostitution had been, twenty percent of men born between 1933 and 1942 had their first sexual encounter with a prostitute.[161] That number dropped to 7% by the 1950s and by the 1990s it was 1.5%.[162]

Every state since WWI, excluding Nevada and Hawaii, decided against regulating prostitution. Most people are aware of Nevada's legal brothels, but few know about Hawaii's venture with regulating prostitution. From 1930 to 1944, there was an unofficial regulation system for prostitution that was coordinated by the military and police. This supervised red-light district system was developed after a U.S. Army General, Briant H. Wells, called for regulating prostitution near the bases.[163]

Without a doubt, this system was kept quiet because it violated the May Act, a federal law passed in 1941 that banned prostitution near military bases. However, these officials proceeded with this experiment because Hawaii was only a U.S. territory at that time, not a state.[164] Here's how it worked. Street prostitution was banned and the women were required to live and work in houses in the red-light district. Prostitutes had to a pay a $1 licensing fee to the Honolulu Police Department to work as "entertainers." They were fingerprinted and photographed at the police station. That's where they received printed instructions. There were a variety of rules such as a ban on traveling to other Hawaiian islands, owning property or a vehicle, marrying a soldier, using the telephone without the madam's permission, among other severe restrictions. These women had to consent to medical exams every week and

---

[H] The Showtime series "Masters of Sex" portrays the other leading sex scientists of that era William H. Masters and Virginia Johnson. Masters originally conducted his research without a partner. He realized the need for a female research colleague while interviewing a prostitute. The woman explained that she regularly faked orgasms with her customers, but Masters literally couldn't conceive of what she was talking about. He soon afterward took the prostitute's advice and added a female research partner.

this was all sanctioned by the military. As a matter of fact, the Provost Marshall, Frank Steer, once blocked the women from collectively raising their rates.[165]

After the Pearl Harbor attack, many of the brothels were converted into makeshift hospitals. Consequently, the prostitutes left the brothels and moved to new locations, but within a year the police wanted to reinforce the old restrictions. However, with their newfound freedom in hand, this group of prostitutes picketed in front of the local police headquarters. They also organized a labor strike for 22 days in June of 1942 and it forced the police to compromise on their restrictions. However, these kinds of public protests brought this decriminalized system to light and this brief experiment was shut down due to an order by the Governor of Hawaii.[166]

The military's regulations were overly intrusive, like the experiment in St. Louis, but venereal disease rates were "phenomenally low" where prostitution was regulated. Ted Chernin, a newspaper contributor who worked as a radio engineer at Pearl Harbor, later documented the regulated system.[167] He uncovered a report by the Honolulu Police Commissioner, Victor S.K. Houston, who "recognized that while (prostitution) cannot be prevented, it can be regulated and controlled." His report mentioned that Dr. William F. Snow of New York City inspected the houses on behalf of the War Department and commented that he had never seen such a "common sense setup" with such "low rates of venereal disease."[168]

Certain cultural norms tend to become ingrained over time, and thus, there was very little momentum for changing prostitution laws until the 1970s. Obviously, there was a generational paradigm shift during the 60s and 70s that embraced the counterculture and liberalism. After all, *The Happy Hooker* eventually sold over 15 million copies beginning in the 1970s. In fact, a poll in California (Field Poll) in 1971 found that 50% of the respondents supported the legalization of prostitution as opposed to 42% against it![169] In an odd way, it was another example of the reoccurring theme in which the politics of prostitution are reexamined during times of war. This time around, the U.S. military imposed very laissez-faire restrictions regarding prostitution during the Vietnam War.

Also, in an unprecedented manner, various prostitutes formed their own political organizations, thus spawning the catchphrase "Hooker's Lib."[170] The most renowned of these activist groups, COYOTE (Call Off Your Old Tired Ethics), was founded by a former prostitute, Margo St. James. Notably, one very prominent advocate member of COYOTE, Carol Leigh, created the term "sex worker" in the 1970s. Her intention was to reduce the stigma attached to prostitution and assert the legitimacy of her profession in the process. As a result, "sex worker" is now considered the politically correct term in many circles.[171]

Margo St. James has been an incredibly effective lobbyist. She had a knack for maximizing her media appearances and coined some quirky slogans such as "A blowjob is better than no job" or "The real victim of victimless crime is the taxpayer."[172] In addition, COYOTE challenged many state and local prostitution laws. For example, the Rhode Island Division of COYOTE filed a civil class action lawsuit in 1976 in the U.S. Federal District Court of Rhode Island. COYOTE v Roberts was on behalf of all prostitutes and challenged the constitutionality of the state's prostitution laws.

Margo St. James' testimony in 1979 demonstrated that the state's prostitution laws were worded so broadly that all sex between unmarried couples was technically illegal.[173] She also proved that prostitution laws were enforced in a discriminatory manner by race and gender. By citing arrest statistics, Margo St. James illustrated that minority women, rather than their clients, were arrested at significantly higher rates. Thus, the publicity surrounding COYOTE v Roberts motivated the Rhode Island Assembly to amend the state's prostitution laws from a felony, punishable by up to five years in prison, to a misdemeanor. In the process, the assembly accidentally created a loophole that decriminalized indoor prostitution. Consequently, the judge dismissed COYOTE v Roberts because the state had already addressed many of the issues from the case.[174]

Most Rhode Island residents were unaware of the technicality in which indoor prostitution was decriminalized for many years. Then, in 2003, the local newspapers published a story about a judge who dismissed prostitution charges against some massage parlor workers.[175] Their lawyer successfully argued that they were not guilty of a crime because they operated indoors. Thus, a group of conservative feminist and religious leaders were outraged by the court's decision and aggressively canvassed for the state to change its laws.[176] That outcry eventually prompted state legislators to draft proposals to re-criminalize indoor prostitution in 2005, but it didn't happen. However, they persisted for a few years and the Rhode Island legislature eventually reversed the loophole in 2009.[177]

Obviously, politicians face a lot of pressure to appear tough on prostitution, but Rhode Island Rep. Rod Driver remained resolute in his opposition to the bill. "The proponents of the bill keep talking about the victims -- the victims being the women that are in this profession," replied Driver. "So we're going to help the women by putting them in prison, and I have a real problem with that."[178]

Two professors, Scott Cunningham from Baylor University and Manisha Shah from the University of California, later published a research paper, "Decriminalizing Prostitution: Surprising Implications for Sexual Violence and Public Health." It detailed Rhode Island's brief and accidental experiment with decriminalization. There are inherent flaws with these types of social science case studies because these aren't actual scientific studies. Nevertheless, the results made a strong case for decriminalization. For instance, rape and gonorrhea statistics dramatically improved during the period of decriminalization.[179] Therefore, you might be wondering, "Will any more of these types of social experiments ever come to fruition?"

A former San Francisco prostitute, Maxine Doogan, set up her own sex workers' rights organization, Erotic Service Providers Legal, Education, and Research Project (ESPLERP), in hopes of challenging prostitution laws. She initially raised $30,000 on the crowdfunding website GoFundMe.com before her page was shut down.[180] Nonetheless, Doogan, along with two other sex workers and a man who wants the right to be one of their clients, hired a Cincinnati-based law firm, Santen & Hughes. That man has a genuinely emotional argument as he suffers from a condition known as hypospadias which causes "microphallus." This aging man has had to deal with this birth defect due to a side effect from a prescription drug that his mother took during pregnancy. He told his heartbreaking story to *Reason Magazine*. He has *never* been able to maintain a normal romantic relationship due to his medical condition. Thus, prostitution has been the only manner in which he could gain female companionship. As a result, it has enabled him to "feel like a member of humanity."[181]

Just like Margo St. James, this group is fighting their battle in federal court with a lawsuit against the San Francisco District Attorney. Their case challenges that prostitution laws violate their constitutional rights to freedom of speech, association, and privacy.[182] One of this group's attorneys, Jerald L. Mosley (former Assistant Attorney General of California), cites past court cases as precedent. Sodomy laws, for instance, were mentioned by Mosley. Those laws were ruled to be unconstitutional because those laws violated homosexuals' rights to sexual privacy.[183] This group of activists certainly has a strong case, but no one can predict what will be the eventual outcome. Regardless, this case will likely continue to be appealed and eventually be, at a minimum, reviewed by the U.S. Supreme Court. Hopefully, there will finally be a positive outcome with this issue.

2

"(The penitentiary) never addressed my issues that led me to prostitution."
Yvette Brooks-Godley

Most industrialized countries have a form of decriminalized or legalized prostitution. Some nations have experimented with a variety of progressive measures, many of which are detailed in Chapter 4. However, most of those policies aren't politically viable in the U.S at this time. With that in mind, the ideal system would be for indoor prostitution to be decriminalized, as opposed to legalized, because that outcome could fit within American culture. No commercial business can openly profit from prostitution when it's decriminalized, thereby eliminating the possibility of an ultra-commercialized, mega-brothel industry that exists in some other countries. Decriminalization differs from legalization by removing those laws from the books, rather than establishing a government regulated licensing system. The police don't make prostitution arrests as long as that activity takes place indoors among consenting adults.

Let's address some common misperceptions. First and foremost, decriminalization isn't intended to encourage prostitution; instead, the goal is to reduce the harm involved with its black market. Decriminalized prostitution obviously wouldn't permit force, fraud, coercion, human trafficking, exploiting minors, etc. In fact, such a system would reduce those problems because the police would then be able to focus more resources toward those issues. But, many people experience a gut reaction regarding decriminalization. They believe it will lead to more prostitution. However, that is not the case. Most women refuse to join the oldest profession due to the nature of the work -- not the laws.

There are legitimate public safety concerns connected with street prostitution and that's why those laws, along with zoning and private property laws, would still be in place. However, by decriminalizing indoor prostitution, it will reduce street prostitution by funneling much of that activity out of the streets. Consequently, that's a net positive for public safety as indoor prostitution is universally associated with less violence, less coercion, more condom usage, etc.

Of all the economically advanced nations in the world, the United States is the least secular. Therefore, any issue involving sex stifles intellectually honest debate. Some activists, particularly those in the academic community, delve into questions in which the answers are so obvious that a scientific study isn't needed. For one thing, some scholars have examined men's motivations for paying for sex. By the same token, a certain segment of feminism asserts that men who pay for sex are primarily motivated to reinforce a patriarchal society and exert power over women. Those kinds of views ignore the basic human observation that men generally view casual sex differently than women. As an illustration, consider how the pornography industry markets specifically to men, meanwhile a similarly sized industry of romance novels clearly caters to women.

Nonetheless, one apt social experiment, "Gender Differences in Receptivity to Sexual Offers," demonstrated this dynamic with research conducted on the campus of Florida State University. In both studies, college-aged men and women with roughly average levels of attractiveness approached complete strangers of the opposite sex. They only told the strangers that they found them attractive and immediately asked to go to bed with them. Not a single woman agreed to that impromptu proposition in either study, but 75% of men in the first study and 69% in the second study accepted the invitation![1]

With all that said, the terms anti-prostitution and decriminalization aren't necessarily mutually exclusive. Everyone who supports criminal penalties for prostitution isn't necessarily a prude, nor is every person who supports eliminating those laws a lecherous individual. Decriminalization is simply a practical strategy. Criminal penalties will never reduce the social and economic forces that cause someone to choose to become a prostitute. In fact, the criminal justice system's revolving door of repeated arrests, fines, and jail time only makes it more difficult for a person to exit the sex trade. Think about it. Can you name a company that is willing to hire someone who has been arrested for prostitution? There are an estimated 1 million prostitutes in the U.S. and their misdemeanor arrests remain on their records for seven years.[2] In fact, repeat offenders in some states can be charged with felonies and are added to the sex offender registry, both of which remain on their records permanently.

We should take into account what people, who have actually transitioned through that system, have to say. Yvette Brooks-Godley is a brave woman who has been entirely forthcoming about her past and explained that prison resulted in the exact opposite of its rehabilitation goals. "(The penitentiary) never addressed my issues that led me to prostitution," she declares. She had been in and out of jail for prostitution charges on countless occasions, yet her time there helped her become more adept in this underground industry. Through the connections she gained behind bars, she learned the prime locations of where to work and when the vice stings would occur.[3]

Prostitution is generally viewed as an insignificant issue, but enforcing those laws is a heavier drain on public resources than most imagine. On average, twenty-one man-hours are needed for a pair of officers to make a prostitution arrest.[4] There are obviously more serious crimes for them to pursue and, worst of all, these arrests often punish a host of repeat offenders. One newspaper reported about a woman from Springfield, OH who had been arrested 45 times over a five-year period, mostly on prostitution or drug charges. In the end, that one woman's arrests cumulatively cost the city over $100,000.[5] That estimate falls in line with a study during the 1980s which attached a $2,000 total cost for each prostitution arrest to the taxpayer.[6]

Nonetheless, there aren't many available studies into the burdensome costs of enforcing these crimes because so few politicians have been courageous enough to challenge the status quo. However, the city of San Francisco once organized a non-partisan group comprised of local activists, attorneys, police, and members of the mayor's office to research this issue. Ultimately, the San Francisco Task Force on Prostitution determined the total budgetary costs (including law enforcement, jails, courts, etc.) of policing prostitution in their city was over $7.6 million for the year of 1994.[7] Obviously, those costs have increased substantially since then.

As detailed in *The Drug War: A Trillion Dollar Con Game*, the "prison industrial complex" profits from an increased prison population. Money and special interests often explain the motivations behind several of the flaws in the criminal justice system. With that in mind, politicians usually care more about public perception than effective governing. Thus, prostitution stings give the impression of a government that is "tough on crime." Prostitution arrests are low hanging fruit for the law enforcement community because it is highly visible and it doesn't take a brilliant detective to rack up convictions for this crime.

At a time when support for the drug war has drastically declined, several media outlets are now investigating and exposing the profit-based policing and corruption associated with asset forfeiture laws. The proof is in the pudding and some police departments have even written specific guidelines that discourage their officers from seizing cars that are too old or have liens.[8] It's quite clear that police departments overly prioritize drug cases because they can boost their budgets through asset forfeiture. In the process, they neglect more impactful investigations.

Prostitution cases are now a growing portion of the asset forfeiture smorgasbord. Forty-one states currently allow the police to make asset forfeitures in relation to prostitution crimes. Thus, police departments in an increasing number of cities are confiscating the cars of "johns" arrested for prostitution.[9] To be brief, that's a very strong penalty for what is considered by most as a public nuisance misdemeanor. In fact, some courts have overturned those cases because the financial penalties exceed the maximum allowable punishment for those crimes.[10]

To review, as part of a criminal prosecution, the police can confiscate certain assets (cash, jewelry, cars, homes, etc.) if those items were used to commit a crime or were the proceeds of criminal activity. That is known as criminal asset forfeiture and a conviction is necessary for the government to seize that property. Suffice it to say, criminal asset forfeiture is a particularly slippery slope in relation to prostitution charges because those cases typically have a lower burden of proof due to the stigma of the crime. However, the police have a more powerful tool at their disposal--civil asset forfeiture, which was explained in more detail in *Rackets Vol I: The Drug War: A Trillion Dollar Con Game*. Civil asset forfeiture is even more prone to abuse because the police can seize your property without making an arrest. Civil asset forfeiture denies you the right to due process and your assets can be seized based upon mere *suspicion*. Let's examine one such encounter.

The Morality Unit of the Wayne County Sheriff's Office (Detroit, MI) seized a local man's SUV, but the notes from the undercover officer's report should have exonerated him. Neither sex nor any transaction was ever mentioned in their brief interaction. The man in question drove up to the undercover officer who was standing on a street corner. She greeted him, "Hey, baby, what's up?" He replied, "Not much, just driving around." The officer then asked him, "Whatcha looking for?" Before driving away, he responded, "Nevermind, I'm OK, thanks anyways."[11]

That man drove away, without being arrested, because the police clearly didn't have evidence to charge him with a crime. However, those same officers saw him an hour later and decided to enter his license plate number into their system. Thereafter, they found that he had been arrested for soliciting a prostitute four years earlier. That's when they pulled him over and seized his car via civil asset forfeiture.[12] Was that man driving around looking for a prostitute on that day? Maybe so, but the burden of proof should be on the government. After all, that is the same local government that was later humiliated with national headlines due to some Detroit police officers who used money from the drug forfeiture fund to pay for prostitutes, marijuana, tanning booth sessions, and so on.[13]

In general, law enforcement officials often suggest that the proceeds from prostitution-related seizures will help the victims of sex trafficking. However, the exact distribution is rarely written into law. Therefore, nearly every dollar, if not all of the money, goes to the police. For example, the state of Washington proposed one such bill in 2015, but only 10% of the proceeds from asset forfeiture were specifically earmarked to help the victims.[14]

Meanwhile, as Americans are increasingly showing less support for the drug war, the media has renewed its interest in the crime of sex trafficking. This has a certain air of the "white slavery" panic of the last century. As a result, a startling number of people now conflate the entire prostitution industry with human trafficking. This wasn't always the case and prostitution had been a low priority for the Department of Justice with a ranking of 174 out of 204 different criminal offenses, according to an internal survey in 1985.[15] Now, there is an increasing police response to prostitution, in large part due to this recent media coverage. That is reminiscent of what unfolded with the drug war and, likewise, police departments have become more aggressive and statistic-oriented with their anti-prostitution efforts because it can result in multi-million dollar federal grants for human trafficking.

Like drug cases, prostitution arrests can lead to "collars for dollars." In other words, police officers don't receive a commission from making an arrest, but they can earn overtime pay for working after their shifts have ended by filling out paperwork and waiting to book an arrestee. Therefore, police have a financial incentive to make frivolous arrests towards the end of their shifts and prostitutes serve as easy targets.

Numerous cities throughout the country have issues with their police budgets and this type of abuse is one of the causes. Case in point, from January to October of 1994, $63 million was approved for the NYPD's overtime pay and half of the arrests in that period involved prostitution.[16] Likewise, a report by the *Miami Herald* found 128 misdemeanor prostitution cases in which six or more local police officers were listed as witnesses even though only one was needed. That scenario unnecessarily adds to the budget because each witness receives a subpoena and overtime pay.[17]

Prostitution investigations often involve joint task forces from multiple agencies with city, county, and state officials. Many of these investigations are also coordinated with various federal authorities such as the FBI, ATF, and the Department of Homeland Security. Yes, your tax dollars pay for undercover police officers and federal agents to sit in massage parlors and seedy strip clubs, for months at a time, ordering drinks and lap dances. Ultimately, the only constructive outcome from these kinds of wasteful investigations is proving that Chris Rock was wrong when he said, "No matter what a stripper tells you. There's no sex in the Champagne Room."[A]

Police officials routinely insist that these kinds of sting operations improve upon "public safety." To demonstrate, a strip club in rural Coweta, OK (30 miles from Tulsa) was busted in 2013 on prostitution charges after a four-month undercover investigation. Multiple agencies from across the state participated in this case because they feared that the owners would recognize the local cops. "So all these different agencies from different parts of the state worked well together to keep the citizens safe," said Pedro Zardeneta, agent of the Oklahoma Alcoholic Beverage Laws Enforcement Commission.[18]

In some rare cases, vice officers and criminal informants are *literally* paid with taxpayer money to have sex with prostitutes. In particular, one man was angered while visiting a massage parlor in Lehigh Valley, PA after the woman offered him some "VIP" services. This man was certainly upset, but it wasn't for moralistic reasons. He took issue with the fact that he didn't have enough money to pay for the "happy ending." Afterward, he informed the local police about the illegal conduct inside this establishment and they decided to pay him as a confidential informant to go back there while wearing a wire. On four separate occasions, Pennsylvania state officers stationed themselves outside listening to a live recording of him in the massage parlor. The officers were supposed to barge in immediately and make an arrest once both parties agreed to the illegal transaction. But the officers stayed put and laughed among themselves as they listened for the entire duration of this man's sexual trysts on all four occasions.[19]

Likewise, the Nashville, TN police conducted a much larger undercover prostitution sting operation that spanned over three years and cost the taxpayers $120,000. For clarification, that figure doesn't include the actual law enforcement costs. Instead, those funds were paid to several undercover informants to have sex with the prostitutes. They typically received $300 for up to three

---

[A] That line was from Chris Rock's parody of Baz Luhrmann's number one hit, "Everybody's Free (To Wear Sunscreen)," which offered sage life advice to the graduating class of 1999.

prostitution 'buys,' and an extra $100 each additional time. These eager informants brought about hundreds of arrests, but the embarrassment from one particular case forced the department to stop using informants. It turned out that one of the informants paid for a threesome with a husband and wife couple and, apparently, that's where the line of decency was drawn. That story sent the local newspapers into a frenzy. "This is the case that brought things to a head," said Tammy Meade, the Assistant District Attorney. "You won't be seeing three-ways on tape anymore."[20] Nonetheless, the head of the vice unit, Capt. Todd Henry, defended their tactics. "What's the greater good? It may be distasteful to some people, but it's better that we have those places shut down."[21]

Nearly every police department has an official policy in which prostitution arrests are supposed to be made *before* sex has occurred. Then again, that rule is sometimes abused unofficially and those kinds of cases surface from time to time. On the other hand, it's unheard of for a police official to defend his right to have sex with prostitutes. Believe it or not, but the Honolulu Police Department is seemingly the only unit that publicly objected in 2014 when state legislators officially barred police officers from making sexual contact with suspected prostitutes during their undercover operations. The HPD claimed that the new laws would diminish their investigations.[22] In an even more unbelievable twist, the *Associated Press* reported one year later about the HPD's new approach for prostitution investigations. Their officers made several arrests while conducting undercover stings in conjunction with the FBI and the Department of Homeland Security. However, they didn't arrest the women for prostitution. No, they had the audacity to charge those women with sexually assaulting the undercover officers![23] Yes, that's part of how your tax dollars are being spent.

Prostitution laws are a breeding ground for police corruption. A study conducted by researchers at DePaul University found that over half of the pimps they surveyed had paid off police officers to stay in business.[24] Furthermore, several researchers have found that prostitutes are frequently extorted by police officers to give free sex; otherwise, they will be arrested. A study by Steven D. Levitt and Stephen J. Dubner (the famed "Freakonomics" duo) not only confirmed this type of corruption with eyewitnesses, but they also quantified this criminal misconduct. They found that 3% of prostitutes' sex acts were performed for free with police officers.[25]

A separate investigation resulted in as many as 40 NYPD officers facing either criminal or departmental charges from a scandal that involved officers extorting sex from prostitutes in exchange for protection. Ultimately, the internal investigation concluded that this sex scam may have been in place for as many as 15 years.[26] These aren't isolated incidents as news reports of police officers being swept up in prostitution sting operations are relatively common.

This issue is an important element of the personal freedom debate and the enforcement of these laws can be downright absurd. Here's a perfect example. Portland police officials investigated a local woman, Samantha Hess, who made national headlines due to her unique profession. She's a professional "snuggler." For $60 an hour, people pay just to cuddle with her. And the demand for her business is so high that she is considering adding a staff of cuddlers.[27] In the end, the Portland Police allowed her to remain in business.[28] However, a different woman tried to set up a duplicate business model in Madison, WI, "Snuggle House," but the city blocked her from ever plying her trade.[29] Shouldn't we just allow these people to pay for this service if they are this desperate for simple human contact?!?

Where is the line drawn as to what constitutes prostitution? Case in point, Donald Trump's infamous *Inside Edition* tape included his admission that he took a woman furniture shopping in hopes of getting her in bed. Was that illegal activity? Here's another scenario. Jody "Babydol" Gibson, aka "the Hollywood Super Madam," ran an exclusive escort service that catered to the film industry's top stars. Before serving three years in a maximum security prison, she wanted to ask a similar question to the judge, "(I)f I'd have introduced a girl to a guy, and instead of him handing her $1,000, he took her shopping. While there I requested she pick me up a pair of $400 shoes (my cut on $1,000). Would I still be going to state prison?"[30]

What about a "sugar daddy" or a woman who marries a man strictly for money? Apparently, those kinds of relationships are legally sanctioned as long as this sexual arrangement takes place over an extended period. Moreover, there has been a lot of media coverage surrounding a website, SeekingArrangement.com, which hosts 2.6 million "sugar babies," many of whom are college students.[31B]

Our tax dollars are being flushed down the drain in the name of a lost cause. For all intents and purposes, our government addresses prostitution entirely through criminal justice methods. Then again, there are credible government officials who have publicly addressed this flaw. One such individual, Michael S. Scott (the Director of the Office of Community Oriented Policing Services of the U.S. Department of Justice) wrote a report entitled, "Street Prostitution," and came to similar conclusions. He wrote, "Enforcement strategies are expensive; each arrest costs thousands of dollars to process. By themselves, they are ineffective at either controlling street prostitution or protecting prostitutes from harm."[32]

In some instances, the departmental pressure to arrest prostitutes can lead to some officers abusing their power. Norma Jean Almodovar (former LAPD officer and the author of *Cop to Call Girl*) has been documenting the abuses that prostitutes face from the police for several years. She once witnessed an officer of the LAPD intentionally throw a lit flare into a parked car, just for kicks, where a prostitute was seated. That resulted in that woman's leg being badly burned, yet this violent act only led to that officer being suspended for two days.[33] That kind of attitude was par for the course as Almodovar also witnessed that LAPD vice officers basked in tormenting these women. They rounded up groups of prostitutes and forced them to race barefoot in a contest for the officers' amusement. The women who finished last were arrested and those who finished first were let go.[34]

We've seen how the drug war and mandatory minimum sentences have disproportionately affected poor, minority communities. In a similar fashion, 41% of the people arrested for prostitution are black.[35] In fact, the police have implemented enforcement strategies that they wouldn't dare attempt in

---

[B] The anti-trafficking group, Polaris Project, actually wrote a series of blogs loosely conflating these kinds of arrangements with human trafficking.

predominantly white, wealthy communities. Washington D.C., along with other cities, established specific "prostitution-free zones," just like the failed "drug-free zones." Those laws granted police officers the authority to displace or arrest people *believed* to be congregating for the purpose of prostitution. Naturally, such a broad measure has led to systemic harassment of women and transgender individuals in these poor communities. The Alliance for a Safe & Diverse DC has investigated these zones extensively and noted that "interactions as mundane as ID checks were characterized by humiliation, abuse, and extortion" and "(a)lmost one in five people approached by the police indicated that officers asked them for sex."[36] Again, these aren't isolated cases. One Municipal Court administrator in San Francisco explained why over half of the city's prostitution charges were dropped by the District Attorney. He cited the court costs, but also noted that "the police are probably just harassing the people and hoping that they go someplace else."[37]

Most importantly, the police in some cities are combating prostitution in a manner that fundamentally opposes public health. The former Surgeon General, Dr. Joycelyn Elders (a notable advocate for the decriminalization of prostitution), has criticized the way in which many police departments confiscate unused condoms as evidence for prostitution arrests.[38] A report by *Human Rights Watch* covered this issue in New Orleans and found that prostitutes were reluctant to carry condoms specifically due to this police tactic. That is such a disastrous finding considering that the death rate from AIDS in Louisiana is over twice the national average![39]

The right hand doesn't know what the left hand is doing. Most likely, your local police department has this same policy. Meanwhile, your local health department provides prostitutes with free condoms.[40] No one wins with this kind of political tug of war. Then again, there has been some progress recently. San Francisco stopped allowing unused condoms to be used as evidence for prostitution arrests in 2013 and New York City followed suit one year later.[41]

Outreach workers also frequently report being harassed by the police when they try to assist prostitutes. Some hardline right-wingers may regard these workers as part of the "welfare state," but most of these people volunteer for charitable non-governmental organizations (NGOs) that are financed independently of government funding. Besides, it's quite counterproductive to harass outreach workers who have similar goals of reducing prostitution, albeit by different means. NGOs are trying to provide various harm reduction services such as offering free food, access to drug rehab, STD testing, free condoms, etc. They also provide a support system to help them leave the industry with various job programs.

Nonetheless, some of these workers recounted some stunning patterns of police harassment in a study, "Revolving Door: An Analysis of Street-Based Prostitution in New York City," by the Sex Workers Project at the Urban Justice Center. These volunteers were repeatedly pulled over and threatened with false arrest on charges of solicitation of prostitution even though the police knew that they were outreach workers. Remarkably, one such worker reported being threatened with arrest if he so much as left the area to buy a bottle of water. Due specifically to these kinds of encounters, some outreach workers have abandoned public health initiatives involving prostitutes simply out of fear of being arrested on trumped up charges.[42]

Our criminal justice system handles the issue of prostitution in a reactive manner, rather than being proactive by addressing the causes. Building more jails isn't the solution. The issues of prostitution and drug addiction are often interrelated. Studies often find that the majority of street prostitutes are addicted to drugs and/or alcohol. In short, there's no more powerful pimp in the world than heroin, cocaine, and methamphetamine.

As mentioned earlier, harm reduction methods are helpful in reducing the damage from these powerfully addictive drugs. *CNN* once did a story on state-sanctioned heroin injection rooms in Canada titled, "Health clinic helps shoot addicts up."[43] On the contrary, a more appropriate title would have been, "Injection room saves woman from selling her body." The story quoted a woman who no longer needed to prostitute herself. The clinic had removed the black market pricing and she could start to recover in a more dignified setting with much greater access to professional help. Injection rooms shouldn't necessarily represent a standard in drug harm reduction, but they could very well be the type of progressive reforms necessary for *some* addicts.

Those with the "lock 'em up and throw away the key" mentality towards street prostitution are ignoring that the vast majority of these people don't want to be prostitutes. Their basic desire is solely one of survival. Shaming and degrading them with harsh penalties only adds to the cruelty of their existence. Many of the prostitutes who are soliciting in public are doing so because they don't have stable housing. Sixty-five percent of the women in a street prostitution study also self-reported having major mental health disorders. The most common disorders were schizophrenia, severe depression, bipolar disorder.[44]

Nearly every local government isn't currently up to the challenge of reducing street prostitution in a holistic, cost-effective manner. Your local government dedicates a portion of its resources to prosecuting street prostitution while providing next to nothing in social services to help them leave that lifestyle. Meanwhile, there is universal sympathy for victims of sex trafficking, yet most people feel contempt for prostitutes who are selling their bodies in the streets out of sheer desperation. In other words, a prostitute basically has to be a documented victim of coercion from sex trafficking to get help.

Beverly Golston, of the Alternative Sentencing Division of the Las Vegas Municipal Court, has personally witnessed the progress that can unfold by using the carrot, not the stick. Las Vegas has a program, "WIN (Women In Need)," dedicated to repeat prostitution offenders. "I've seen girls go from prostitution to college," says Golston.[45] Likewise, there are two particular prostitution diversion programs (Pawtucket, Rhode Island and Dallas, TX), that have had fantastic results. Unfortunately, comprehensive programs with this fresh approach to an age-old problem are quite rare in the U.S.

The city of Pawtucket experimented by establishing Project RENEW (Revitalizing and Engaging Neighborhoods by Empowering Women), which offers personalized social services for the area's prostitutes in hopes that they will one day leave the sex trade. They provide programs such as detox, mental health treatment, employment services, etc. Also, Pawtucket Police Maj. Arthur Martins has worked in conjunction with RENEW and touts the success of the program. There were roughly 60 prostitution arrests annually in Pawtucket before RENEW was implemented, but that number has been reduced to 10. "There was some skepticism that this program could actually work," Martins said. "But I knew what wasn't working: the revolving door of continuing arrests."[46]

The average person takes their social safety net for granted and doesn't acknowledge the hard choices that some people have to make to survive. Felicia Delgado has worked for this program since the beginning and is quick to defend it. She says, "A lot of women already have what they need inside of them, they just need someone to help them, support them, and not judge them."[47] One of RENEW's success stories involves a woman, "Jennifer," who relapsed into a heroin addiction after seven years of sobriety. This setback ensued after two of her sons died. "I was (back) in the street for a year and a half, and I met Felicia (Delgado), and she saved me," says Jennifer. "She helped get me into a program, and from then it's been another world. It's been a new life for me."[48]

A Dallas Police Sergeant, Louis Felini, also witnessed firsthand the haplessness of relying wholly upon the conventional formula of arrests and jail time. Consequently, he began organizing the Prostitute Diversion Initiative (PDI) in 2007, one of the most unique and comprehensive programs in the nation. What sets PDI apart from other programs is the broad cooperation that it has among various organizations, including drug rehabs, law enforcement, judges, and over 45 different social services. PDI consists of a group that travels in buses filled with various social workers and volunteers. There are also former prostitutes who try to counsel these women with an exit strategy in mind. PDI's "New Life" program is a 45-day program with substance abuse and mental health services. These women are also eligible for transitional housing, job training, and mental health services.[49]

Dallas, TX is the 9th largest city in the U.S. and offers a fantastic sample set for the potential benefits derived from these diversion programs. There were 860 participants within the first five years of the PDI program and fifty-three percent of them completed substance abuse treatment without a subsequent arrest.[50] With that said, that may not seem like an overwhelming success at first glance. However, those outcomes are substantially better than the status quo. Thus, those kinds of positive results would have been next to impossible without this outreach program.

The Dallas PDI program was an offshoot of a similar progressive experiment by the Dallas Police Department. Another Dallas Police Sergeant, Byron A. Fassett, was determined to find a way to help teen prostitutes break away from their pimps. He discovered a notable trend while researching old case files. The vast majority of teen prostitutes had run away from home over four times a year and, in response, he presumed that a new approach (again involving the carrot, not the stick) would be the most appropriate measure. Thus, he initiated the "High Risk Victim" unit to identify those teens most at risk. Granted, any police-operated initiative will usually involve arrests, but Fassett's program made it a point to not brand these youths with the Scarlet letter, i.e. a prostitution arrest. Instead, they charge them with much lesser crimes, such as truancy. Afterward, the teens are sheltered at a sequestered site where they receive various services. And in case you're wondering, it's been an overwhelming success. Roughly 75% of these teen runaways involved in this program quit prostitution and several of them have been willing to testify against their pimps in court.[51]

Incidentally, the fundamental flaw with diversion programs is that their assistance is only available after an arrest. "We really do care about the women," Capt. Dan Harris, head of Houston's vice division, told the *Houston Chronicle* after a prostitution raid in conjunction with the county's narcotics task force. "Even though we're arresting them, we don't want them to go back to that life."[52] Those kinds of sentiments show how it's no longer politically correct for the police to publicly refer to prostitutes as the scourge of the earth. However, this particular police officer is wrong. We shouldn't have to arrest these women for them to get help. His words highlight how you can call diversion programs "voluntary," but that isn't the case because the only alternative is jail time and a criminal record.

We have so much to learn from Portugal's experiment with the decriminalization of drugs in which drug addicts are offered rehab without the threat of prison. Portugal has made tremendous progress with their drug problem and the key takeaway is that people help themselves best when it's on their terms. Thus, these kinds of diversion programs need to be made readily available by outreach workers, not the court system, to maximize the results.

Also, not all prostitution diversion programs are created equally. Specifically, Houston's diversion program has some past participants who attest that it helped turn their lives around, but there are detractors as well.[53] This program is led by a former drug-addicted prostitute with a confrontational approach who often lectures with a "scared straight" tone.[C] The women who enter these programs have various needs such as drug rehab, mental health support, job training, etc. Therefore, it's a waste of taxpayer funds to implement a one-size-fits-all approach. Such a combative atmosphere isn't appropriate for someone who simply needs help finding a job. And that was the case with one woman who publicly uploaded audio from a lecture in which the participants were forced to "confess" that they were no different from rapists and Charles Manson because prostitution is also a crime. After listening to the browbeating from these recordings, it's no surprise that this whistleblower felt the need, for the first time in her life, to seek out a therapist due to the treatment that she received in the program.[54]

With all that said, some prostitution diversion programs can point to a successful track record and that's a step in the right direction. However, facilitating volunteer outreach work would yield even better results. But it's difficult to gain support for this approach with voters from both major political parties due to the stigma surrounding this issue. Then again, those within the conservative group-think, in particular, seem to refuse to listen. To be specific, Carol Leigh, the activist who created the term "sex worker," had a guest appearance on "The O'Reilly Factor." Bill O'Reilly dismissed decriminalization as a "ruse" and disregarded the outreach work that Leigh has performed for decades as though

---

[C] This program's director, Kathryn Griffin, used to be a backup singer for Rick James before her addiction led her into prostitution.

it were hypothetical. "You won't get them. They won't cooperate," he insisted.[55]

Some cities have wised up and are beginning to implement these kinds of rehabilitation programs. Yvette Brooks-Godley, who was mentioned earlier, had graduated from college before she became a prostitute. Drugs sent her life into a downward spiral and she didn't reform her ways until the court system tried something different. She benefitted from a fairly new prostitution diversion program in Chicago, WINGS Court, which manifested from a grassroots campaign by the Chicago Coalition for the Homeless.[56] Consequently, Brooks-Godley received the rehabilitation services that she desperately needed and now she is drug-free, financially independent, and owns a small food company. "Sometimes all we need is somebody to believe in us when we don't believe in ourselves," says Brooks-Godley.[57] In short, the prostitution debate, like so many other issues, tends to be discussed in abstract terms, but her message shows that we need to remember that these policies directly affect real people's lives.

Naturally, many people assume, albeit incorrectly, that liberalizing prostitution will result in law and order falling to the wayside. After all, the general narrative states that we need prostitution laws to protect women from exploitation and human trafficking. However, it is the *criminalization* of prostitution that causes most of the exploitation and coercion in the sex industry. In other words, the criminalization of prostitution is a racket. Those laws are presented as a solution to a problem that wouldn't exist without those laws being in place. This underground market leaves its participants with no legal protections and that makes them a target of thieves, gangs and or pimps who often "tax" them. The prostitutes who work independently from those thugs are labeled "renegades." It's analogous to how independent bookies who operate without ties to organized crime are labeled "renegades" as well.

There certainly will always be violent criminals who look to prey upon the buyers and sellers of sex, but the results from these diversion programs show that a more tolerant approach to prostitution arrests can lead to *less* overall crime. Prostitution isn't a virus that inherently causes more crime; instead, it's the *prohibition* that attracts crime. To demonstrate, there was a 39% reduction in the overall crime rate in the areas where the Dallas PDI program was implemented![58] Also, the local community members of Pawtucket reported an increase in neighborhood quality of life after the RENEW program was put into action. That was on top of the fact that these kinds of harm reduction services are cost-effective; Pawtucket benefitted from a per-person savings of $17,331 in law enforcement costs.[59] In other words, these types of progressive experiments may sound like pie in the sky, but they're actually the most fiscally conservative decisions.

Those results indicate that public safety improves when this vice is liberalized. When prostitution is taken out of the shadows of the black market with decriminalization, it will provide law enforcement agents with the additional evidence needed to convict violent felons. Naturally, a violent predator is much less likely to assault a woman if she has no qualms about contacting the police. That was the case with "the Craigslist Killer," so let's examine the details.

This was a high-profile case that the media covered in depth. However, most news outlets glossed over one important detail. Many prostitutes report crimes after they have been assaulted, but the majority do not. In fact, many even laugh at the suggestion of contacting the police. That's why what happened in this case is quite noteworthy. The Craigslist Killer assaulted multiple women and he attacked one particular woman at gunpoint (a stripper from Craislist.com) in a Rhode Island hotel, but she called the authorities immediately afterward. Former Rhode Island State Representative, David Segal, pointed out that she easily could have faced police harassment for prostitution charges had that happened in any other state. However, the attack took place *before* Rhode Island's indoor prostitution laws had been reversed.[60]

Decriminalization opens up an environment in which more people would feel free to provide tips about possible sex trafficking. Nonetheless, conservative activists successfully pressured Craigslist to shut down their "adult service" ads. These activists have focused exclusively on the fact that Craigslist facilitated prostitution, but they ignored the service Craigslist provided by informing its users about sex trafficking. Craigslist encouraged them to report suspected trafficking or exploitation while providing contacts for law enforcement and rescue groups. Furthermore, their website had technical features that screened and blocked ads for potentially under-aged users. Also, their company forwarded the relevant information to law enforcement.[61]

In the end, the political pressure forced Craigslist to shut down their erotic advertisements. As a result, these activists drastically reduced the information flow for criminal investigations into sex trafficking and under-aged prostitution. FBI agents had credited Craigslist for assisting anti-trafficking sweeps by providing numerous referrals. Bear in mind that Craigslist is a free service, but they specifically added fees to their adult service ads to enable a telephone and credit card fee verification system. This was system implemented at the request of the Attorney General and the National Center for Missing and Exploited Children.[62]

After Craigslist discontinued their "adult service" ads, the online traffic for those services moved to different websites with far fewer protections and regulations in place. "Craigslist was the most equalizing force in the sex industry in generations," lamented Will Rockwell, editor of "$pread" magazine (written by prostitutes). Rockwell, a male prostitute, explained that Craigslist eliminated the need for a pimp and took people off of the streets "into safer working conditions."[63]

Lois Lee, founder and president of "Children of the Night," an organization that provides housing and educational services for sex trafficking victims, points out that the PR campaign to shut down websites like Craigslist or Backpage.com has only pushed the industry further underground.[64] Unlike Lois Lee, many people in the anti-trafficking industry consider the terms "prostitution" and "trafficking" to be synonymous; therefore, they want strong anti-prostitution laws. However, these groups are generally blinded by their ideology and never mention that it would be easier to catch traffickers in a more transparent environment.

Our government has demonstrated poor leadership at the federal level with this issue. It's a waste of federal investigative resources to specifically target madams who haven't violated anyone's fundamental human rights. The FBI is arguably the most capable and competent crime investigation organization in the world, but the bureau has wasted numerous resources pursuing cases of high-end escort agencies that haven't been involved in any fraud, force, or coercion. These investigations reward the actual human traffickers with less interference.

The FBI monitored over 5,000 phone calls by a New Orleans madam, Jeanette Maier, "the Canal Street Madam."[65] Their six-month investigation, in conjunction with the Department of Justice, took place before and *after* September 11, 2001. Obviously, the timing of this case left much to be desired, but the lead prosecutor, Sal Perricone (the former Assistant U.S. Attorney) defended the merit of their investigation. He told the press, "This case represents, I feel, one of the vilest forms of racketeering there is, and that's the exploitation of women for the sake of a buck," he said.[66] That's some powerful rhetoric, but there was no evidence that the Canal Street Madam coerced her employees. Instead, she usually charged her clients $300 an hour and some of the women were making as much as $5,000 to $10,000 a week.[67]

Ultimately, several members of the media criticized the decision to mobilize vast federal resources for such a case when national security should have been at the forefront. In fact, Sen. Patrick Leahy (D-VT) publicly ridiculed that investigation in front of Congress to the sounds of laughter. "I realize it comes as an enormous revelation to the American public that there might have been prostitutes in New Orleans. I mean, who knew," he said.[68]

Oddly enough, this case came about from a tip by a local doctor, Howard Lippton, who was under investigation for committing an estimated $1.3 million worth of Medicare fraud. Lippton had been one of their best clients, having reportedly spent up to $350,000 with them. However, his sentence was cut in half (only 18 months in prison with a $10,000 fine) by snitching on the Canal Street Madam's operation.[69]

The Canal Street Madam case was a bad PR move for the FBI, but the feds continued to pursue high-end escort agencies. Just a few months after the 9/11 attacks, a Miami prostitute contacted the local authorities because one of her clients, a Middle Eastern man, alluded to an upcoming terrorist attack.[70] Hence, the local authorities put her in touch with the FBI. That referral didn't lead to any relevant information regarding terrorism, but the FBI proceeded to tap the phone of that informant's madam, Judy Krueger. Thereafter, the FBI listened to more than 14,000 of Krueger's calls. Ultimately, they discovered that Krueger was part of a national escort agency, "The Circuit," which featured highly-paid call girls earning as much as $1,000 an hour in most major U.S. cities.[71] Again, there was no evidence that any of these women were being coerced in any way. Nonetheless, Krueger received a sentence of 21 months in prison, a stronger penalty than the Medicare fraudster, Howard Lippton's.[72] Moreover, Krueger's sentence would have been 30 months longer if she hadn't snitched on a dozen other people across the country.[73]

These kinds of cases illustrate why prostitutes don't trust the police. Albeit, the female gender as a whole should have trust issues with the criminal justice system. Thousands of rape kits are still untested in various cities across America because rape is a difficult case to prosecute. Therefore, most prostitutes don't even bother to report violent crimes that have been committed against them on account of their fear of the legal system. Oddly enough, police often rely upon prostitutes as criminal informants. "As a rule, whores know more about what's going on in the street than anybody," says one officer.[74] These women are often privy to valuable information and cops have legal leverage over them.

Decriminalization would provide these women their most basic human right, protection against violence. There are several reasons why the American Civil Liberties Union (ACLU), Human Rights Watch, and Amnesty International strongly support the decriminalization of prostitution and this is arguably the most important.[75] We all would hope that the police would respond with an effort comparable to something from an episode of *CSI* if we were ever attacked. Prostitutes, on the other hand, don't expect such basic protections. The fact that prostitutes are reluctant to report any instance of abuse has emboldened some sadistic serial killers.

The Green River Killer, Gary Ridgway, once said, "I picked prostitutes as my victims because I hated most prostitutes, and I did not want to pay them for sex. I knew they would not be reported missing right away and might never be reported missing. I picked prostitutes because I thought I could kill as many of them as I wanted without getting caught."[76] He eventually pled guilty to the murder of 49 different women, most of whom were prostitutes.[77] Thus, December 17th, the date that Ridgway was sentenced, has since been recognized as the International Day to End Violence Against Sex Workers.[78]

Prostitutes have been found to be 18 times more likely to be murdered than all other women![79] Also, their friends and associates are reluctant to contact the authorities afterward due to their fear of the police. That may be why the Long Island Serial Killer was so brazen as to taunt the sister of one of his victims by calling her after the attack with the victim's cell phone.[80] In response, a sex workers' rights organization, the Red Umbrella Project, asked for amnesty for all of the area prostitutes until the killer was apprehended, in hopes that it would lead to more people coming forward with information. However, that clearly didn't happen and those crimes are still unsolved. Likewise, a string of six drug-addicted prostitutes in Chillicothe, OH were murdered or presumed missing over a short span in 2014. You may wonder, "How did the local police react?" Well, there was no olive branch extended. Instead, the police responded by cracking down on the town's section where drugs and prostitution were more prevalent.[81]

Sometimes there is a general malaise by law enforcement unless these kinds of murders get attention in the newspapers. To be specific, the Hillside Strangler had killed several prostitutes, but he didn't become the target of a thorough investigation until *after* he killed a woman who wasn't a prostitute. In like manner, Joel Rifkin killed 17 women and most of them were prostitutes. Nonetheless, those deaths weren't even acknowledged by the NYPD until Rifkin was apprehended in another jurisdiction after another body was found in the trunk of his car during a traffic stop.[82]

One of the most egregious examples involved a string of 43 unsolved murders in the San Diego area from 1985 to 1992. All of the victims were women, mostly transient types or prostitutes. Hence, one unnamed San Diego police officer was quoted by the *Sacramento Bee* in 1990 saying, "These were misdemeanor murders, biker women and hookers. We'd call them NHI's, no humans involved."[83]

Norm Stamper, the Assistant Chief of the San Diego Police at that time, was later assigned to review the Homicide Division's handling of those cases due to the negative media exposure.[D][84] He acknowledged overhearing various officers refer to murdered prostitutes as "misdemeanor murders." An irritated Stamper later wrote in his book, *Breaking Rank: A Top Cop's Expose of the Dark Side of American Policing,* "I wonder how these officers of the law would respond to the murder of forty teachers? Forty homemakers? Forty ER nurses?"[85] Stamper also promoted the idea of decriminalizing indoor prostitution in the chapter, "Prostitution: Get a Room!"[E]

In many instances, the stigma associated with prostitution essentially nullifies the penalties for violence against women. To illustrate, the DOJ's Inspector General released a report in 2015 that revealed that several DEA agents had sex with prostitutes in Colombia six years earlier. Understandably, this was a highly sensational story. Ultimately, most of the media reaction centered on the sexual matters even though one DEA agent smashed a prostitute in the head with a glass bottle. He did so after a verbal

---

[D] It took some time before the "NHI murders" received much press coverage. In fact, only 7 of those 43 victims were even mentioned in the local newspaper at the time of the murders. However, that changed due to one particular murder that pointed to police involvement. Donna Gentile was a prostitute and criminal informant who had been exchanging sex to avoid being arrested. She eventually reneged on this unofficial arrangement by filing an official complaint with the city and later testified publicly about police misconduct. Her testimony resulted in the firing of one officer and another being demoted, although he was promptly re-promoted. Her murder has never been solved and it happened just months after her testimony. Investigators found that her murderer put gravel down her throat while she was still alive. Obviously, some have assumed that it was a symbolic act because of her testimony. One of Gentile's friends, Cynthia Maine (a prostitute as well), had also provided information about the misconduct of many police officers. Likewise, she was reported missing around that same time period and has been presumed dead from homicide since 1986.

[E] After retiring in 2000 as Seattle's Police Chief, he is now a prominent member of Law Enforcement Action Partnership (LEAP), which is dedicated to ending the drug war and criminal justice reform.

dispute about the payment and compounded this behavior by lying to investigators with a claim that she had injured herself falling from a seizure attack. In the end, that agent's violent act was merely penalized with an unpaid suspension for 14 days.[86] Do you think that he would have been punished with, more or less, a vacation if he had assaulted anyone other than a prostitute?

Violent sexual predators can get away with some of the most heinous crimes, as long as their victims are prostitutes. It's essentially a "Get Out of Jail Free Card" for felons and the blame is placed on the victim. "A woman who goes out on the street and makes a whore out of herself opens herself up to anybody. She steps outside the protection of the law. That's a basic and fundamental legal concept," said a Pasadena judge and former police officer, Gilbert C. Alston. He made that statement while dismissing a case against a man who had been accused of raping, sodomizing, and robbing a prostitute.[87] Likewise, a Texas man openly admitted in court to murdering an escort. In fact, he never insinuated that the murder was an act of self-defense. Instead, the woman refused to have sex with him after he had paid her $150. In spite of such an admission, a jury acquitted him of murder because his attorneys successfully argued that Texas state law allows for the use of deadly force to "retrieve stolen property."[88]

Similarly, a Philadelphia judge, Teresa Carr Deni, dropped rape charges against a group of men who gang raped a prostitute at gunpoint. The judge said that she didn't consider it to be a rape case, rather it was a case of "theft of services." The woman initially agreed to sex with two of the men for money. However, they then refused to pay, held a gun to her head, and forced her to have sex with them, along with several other men. In short, Judge Deni felt that her case "minimizes true rape cases and demeans women who are really raped."[89] Deni's judgment was "a throwback to the Middle Ages, when rape was a crime against property, not against a person," responded Carol Tracy, executive director of the Women's Law Project.[90] Yes, this double standard has existed for many years in various cultures. The laws in 13th century China distinguished between the rape of a prostitute (50 demerits), a wife (500 demerits), and a widow or a virgin (1,000 demerits).[91]

The on-the-job violence that street prostitutes face is typically much more frequent and more severe than what indoor prostitutes face. However, only about 10%-20% of prostitutes work in the streets.[92] Nonetheless, several anti-prostitution or anti-trafficking activists use a narrative that overemphasizes street prostitution. They prefer to disregard the data with indoor sex workers because it advances their agenda. That's important to note because there is a diverse hierarchy within the sex industry. Hence, it's ineffective to continue with the same cookie cutter approach for combating a complex issue.

The ideal role for the government is to provide social services for helping women withdraw from prostitution voluntarily. Sixty-nine percent of indoor sex workers in one study reported that they wanted to leave the sex industry eventually, but they had ambivalent feelings due to a lack of other options.[93] This particular segment (basically the majority of the prostitution industry) should not be targeted by law enforcement as long their activities take place without coercion, completely out of the public eye, and as long as no other crimes are committed in the process. This segment of the industry needs to be able to access help from NGOs and outreach workers while not fearing the repercussions from contacting law enforcement. The majority of indoor prostitutes have backgrounds with legal work experience outside of prostitution, but they reported that they didn't earn enough money. Many of them are also making a living by legal means, but they use prostitution to supplement their income.[94]

Although the majority of prostitutes would prefer to leave the business, there is a segment of the industry that personifies the "happy hooker." Obviously, this depends on the individual, but these are generally the women who are making the most money and enjoying high independence. Most of these women enter the industry with an endgame in mind. In fact, a sociologist Lewis Diana found that most call girls or escorts left the industry within five years. He also determined that the majority weren't raised in desperate economic conditions; they were typically brought up in middle-class families. In fact, many of them were college students or had full-time employment elsewhere.[95]

Ann Lucas conducted similar research with call girls and found that they "expressed a clear preference for prostitution...(They) entered their vocation voluntarily and valued the independence, autonomy, and control it offered."[96] Furthermore, Diana Prince conducted a study and concluded that many sex workers are significantly happier than most people would expect. She interviewed 75 streetwalkers, 75 call girls, and 150 Nevada brothel workers. To summarize, ninety-seven percent of call girls reported *increased* self-esteem after they entered the industry. Conversely, those figures were fifty percent for Nevada brothel workers and only eight percent of street prostitutes.[97]

Despite being loathed by most of society, many in the industry are completely unapologetic about what they do. Several prostitutes revel in the adrenaline-filled, fast-paced, quick-money lifestyle. They cite the autonomy of their work and don't want to participate in the corporate rat race. Some genuinely take pride in their work. To illustrate, consider the words from one woman interviewed during a study, "Behind Closed Doors: An Analysis of Indoor Sex Work in New York City." She said, "I find it (prostitution) more meaningful and easier to deal with than restaurant work. I like working one-on-one with people. When it goes well, I feel like I'm giving someone something that is needed and appreciated and makes me feel special."[98] Yes, these choices are highly unconventional, but blocking these people from making their decisions is a perfect example of "the tyranny of the majority."

You'll likely never hear those types of perspectives from the actual people in this line of work because, in general, the right-wing activists have won the PR battle. Again, many alarmists have convinced the masses that there is no difference between sex trafficking and prostitution. They've essentially nullified the existence of free will. Also, these advocates have manufactured some moral panics, including a theory that legalized prostitution would lead to more women being raped.

This theory is utter nonsense. It's nothing more than grasping at straws, but it has been regurgitated by many. That's why it needs to be addressed. More or less, the core belief is that legal prostitution will lead to more men viewing women as sexual commodities and thus it will become a viral force upon society that will incite more instances of rape. To enhance this premise, some of these activists like to selectively choose their statistics to make the case. They focus on Nevada's historically higher than average rate of forcible rape as evidence. Specifically, Nevada had the 18th highest rate of forcible rape in 2011 and the 15th highest rate in 2012. These same people neglect to mention that the rate of forcible rape for Rhode Island was below the national average for 23 of the 30 years in which decriminalization was in place.[99] Indeed, it takes an unusually partisan activist to suggest that the entire female population will be subjected to more sexual violence by legalizing prostitution. In any event, only those within the sex industry would be affected by this kind of new policy and they would be less likely to be assaulted due to their newfound rights.

On the flip side, some liberals casually theorize that legalization would decrease rape by providing men with more sexual options. After all, the previously mentioned academic study, "Decriminalizing Prostitution: Surprising Implications for Sexual Violence and Public Health," noted that rape statistics decreased in Rhode Island during decriminalization. However, this case study didn't prove that the change in prostitution laws *caused* less overall rapes throughout the state. To sum up, there simply isn't a sustainable statistical correlation for either side of this theory based upon examining numerous examples internationally. The simple takeaway is that prostitution policy has no apparent bearing on rape statistics for the entire female population, only the sex workers. Albeit, decriminalization clearly better protects sex workers from violence.

The U.S. Department of Justice funded a study, *Focusing on the Clients of Street Prostitutes: A Creative Approach to Reducing Violence Against Women,* which concluded that only a small percentage of these men, the "johns," are likely to commit violent acts. That conclusion was reached due to the responses of johns to "rape myths." These are questions used to test if someone agrees with concepts that perpetuate rape, such as "women who get raped while hitchhiking get what they deserve." The more "rape myths" that someone agrees with the more likely that person is to commit rape. In the end, their research found that johns didn't agree with "rape myths" at higher rates than other men surveyed. To sum up, their research "may point to the existence to a small population of men who are at increased risk of perpetrating violence against women...and who have access to vulnerable women in isolated settings through prostitution...Interestingly, frequency of prostitution encounters alone was not significantly associated with these disturbing attitudes."[100]

Professor Ronald Weitzer at George Washington University is a leading prostitution researcher and he has come to similar conclusions. He didn't find that johns were more likely to endorse rape myths than other samples of men. Also, his "findings indicate that most clients do not hold views that justify violence against prostitutes, and it is likely that most of the violence is committed by a minority of customers."[101] Moreover, a Canadian group, John's Voice, has conducted similar studies and concurs. Their leading researcher, Chris Atchison, found that "only a small percentage of respondents pose a real problem in terms of violence...My initial findings show that johns shouldn't be painted as uniformly good or evil in efforts to control prostitution...We only need to target a subset of this population."[102F]

America's prostitution laws are blocking programs that effectively prevent violence. Numerous countries support efforts by NGOs to notify prostitutes about dangerous johns by offering their physical descriptions, locations, etc.[G103] These kinds of programs are known as "bad date books" in Canada or "dodgy punters" and "ugly mugs" in the United Kingdom. In fact, there is a free Android smartphone app, "Ugly Mugs," for prostitutes in the UK, Ireland, Canada, Sweden, Norway and Finland. The police

---

[F] It may be hard for some to believe, but a survey of the men who pay for sex found that 20% of them reported being robbed when meeting a prostitute and 4.5% of johns reported being physically attacked by a prostitute.
Ultimately, it will rarely elicit sympathy when men who pay for sex are victimized, but it should also be a concern as violence generally begets a cycle of violence.

[G] A website, myredbook.com, unofficially served this purpose before it was shut down by the FBI in 2014. That website allowed clients to rate their experiences with different prostitutes. Also, prostitutes were able to share information among each other about potentially dangerous clients.

even participate in such programs because most foreign cultures recognize the importance of protecting people from a serial killer or rapist, no matter how they earn a living.

The effectiveness of these harm reduction efforts flies in the face of the radical feminists and evangelicals who assert that legalized prostitution causes rape. Then again, that is the same cast of characters who, beginning in the 1970s, insisted and continue to claim that pornography also causes rape. These scaremongers went so far as to lobby for the creation of "the Pornography Victims Compensation Act of 1992" that would have allowed women to file civil lawsuits against the manufacturers and distributors of pornography. In the end, the bill died mainly due to the lobbying efforts of other feminist groups, such as the National Organization for Women (NOW) and Feminists for Free Expression (FFE).[104]

Decades later, the anti-pornography crusaders have been proven to be indisputably wrong. The frequency of rape has dropped substantially all while the use of pornography has grown exponentially. In fact, recent studies have found that pornography can "reduce the desire to rape by offering a safe, private outlet for deviant sexual desires."[105] Also, numerous studies have concluded that pornography can even cause sexual dysfunction in men.

Once again, pornography offers another example of how liberalizing and regulating these kinds of vices reduces the associated harm to the general public. Pornography is obviously a controversial subject, but there is a common ground. We all can agree that it is something that minors shouldn't be viewing. Therefore, the practical response would be to fully sanction this industry for it to be thoroughly regulated and thereby ensure that minors don't access this material. However, anti-pornography crusaders have vigorously lobbied to establish obscenity laws from state to state in hopes of blocking *everyone* from purchasing this content. As a result, pornographic manufacturers operate within a gray area of the law and the copyrights to their films aren't recognized. Thus, the Internet is flooded with websites pirating their content and offering free unlimited viewing of copyrighted pornographic films in an unbounded market that is completely unregulated.

In other words, these conservative activists tried to block *everyone* from viewing this kind of material, but their efforts sent the industry underground and now *anyone* with an Internet connection can watch this stuff. These advocates have never acknowledged that the most realistic way to decrease pornography usage, in particular with minors, would be if consumers had to pay for their content as a result of pirated pornography websites being shut down. As a side note, pornography is now widely tolerated in American culture while prostitution is extensively stigmatized. Apparently, pornography is not considered to be prostitution because there is a camera in the room. All in all, American culture generally accepts the sex industry as long as it is in a voyeuristic mode.

3

"How many guys do you know want a receipt for a bribe?"
Joe Conforte[1]

Nevada has long been home to libertarian ideals and consequently this state has tolerated prostitution, particularly in mining towns, since its inception. In fact, Mona's in Elko, which has been in business since 1902, is the oldest existing brothel in Nevada.[2] This is the only state that didn't pass wide-ranging prostitution laws, but pandering and street prostitution were outlawed in 1911 and 1913. Nevada's legislators valued laissez-faire principles, but they also implemented some basic regulations by not allowing brothels to be located near churches or schools, nor on main streets.[3] Furthermore, in 1937, Nevada's State Board of Health began requiring prostitutes working in brothels to submit to tests for venereal diseases.[4]

"Block 16," the original red-light district in Las Vegas, had existed ever since the city was established. However, state-sanctioned prostitution was a deal breaker during WWII because federal officials were considering building a nearby military base. Thus, the local authorities naturally compromised and shut down the red-light district in exchange for Nellis Air Force Base being built in their city.[A5] Again, prostitution wasn't illegal in Nevada, but local officials were able to put an end to Block 16 by enforcing "public nuisance" statutes.

This legal issue resurfaced a few years later in Reno when a madam challenged whether the local police had the authority to shut down her business. Ultimately, the judge ruled that the county commissioners and the District Attorney had the right to close a brothel if it was considered a "public nuisance."[6] This also meant that a brothel could operate legally as long as the area's residents weren't bothered by its presence in the community. In other words,

---

[A] The first Las Vegas casino, the Meadows Club, was opened by Tony "the Hat" Cornero in 1931. Over the years it transitioned into a brothel and it was one of the "public nuisances" that was closed down in 1942 to oblige the military.

prostitution was "tolerated." That is also known as de facto decriminalization. Several countries around the world currently have a similar system in which prostitution is technically illegal, but the local authorities generally don't enforce the laws as long as other laws aren't being broken.

Nevada's decriminalized prostitution flew under the radar until the 1970s when a few stand-out stories attracted a national audience. One Nevada madam, Beverly Harrell, had operated her business, the Cottontail Ranch, for several years with no local complaints until a nationally syndicated columnist took issue with her exact location. The reason being, she had technically set up her brothel on land that was leased by the Bureau of Land Management (BLM). Hence, news outlets across the country reveled in reporting that the federal government was a landlord to a brothel! In response to the media controversy, Harrell decided to simplify matters by trying to purchase the property outright because she had signed a 100-year lease with an option to buy. Be that as it may, the BLM was backed into a proverbial corner and refused to accept her payment due to the negative publicity. Nonetheless, Harrell persisted; she was convinced that her business operated legally. Therefore, she took the federal agency to court. Beverly Harrell eventually lost her case, but as a consolation prize, the newfound fame helped launch her campaign run for the Nevada State Assembly. "I think it takes a madam of an honest bordello to show them how to run an honest system," she told the press. In the end, she nearly won in a very narrow decision.[7]

Nevada's brothels operated openly for decades before the current legalized licensing system was established. The man responsible for legalizing prostitution was a particularly flamboyant local brothel owner, Joe Conforte. He reportedly had ties to the mafia and perpetuated that reputation by habitually sporting fur coats and smoking cigars. He was a very influential person in local politics because he controlled a voting bloc of poor immigrants. Conforte owned a trailer park and charged low rent to his tenants; in return, they voted in his favor.[8] More importantly, he had several officials in his pocket, including the local police and politicians.[9] In particular, Conforte had a close ally in the District Attorney of Storey County, Virgil Bucchianeri, whom he helped elect. That was money well spent. Bucchianeri convinced the Storey County Commissioners to license the area's brothels and this fully-sanctioned system went into effect on January 1, 1971.[10]

That turn of events was a long time in the making. Joe Conforte, along with his wife, Sally, began operating their first of many brothels throughout the state, the Triangle Ranch, in 1955. These brothels weren't brick and mortar buildings. Rather, they owned three trailers that were set up in Wadsworth, NV (30 miles east of Reno, NV). That was a strategic location to play a game of cat and mouse with the local authorities because Wadsworth lies at the junction of three counties (Washoe, Storey, and Lyon). Sally and Joe Conforte repeatedly received cease and desist orders from judges based upon "public nuisances" laws, but that had little impact on their bottom line. They routinely thwarted the authorities by keeping their brothels open for at least a month or two while the local officials processed the paperwork. Afterward, they moved the trailers of their business a few hundred feet away and re-opened under a new name, thereby starting the whole process over again.[11]

This was a lucrative business model and he skimmed untold millions of dollars, thereby cheating the IRS out of a small fortune. On the other hand, Conforte understood that he needed to pay "local taxes," i.e. greasing the palms of various Nevada officials. Considering his standing in the community, it would have been prudent for Conforte to maintain a low profile, but he was a very public figure in the Nevada press. He never hid the fact that he paid kickbacks to the necessary people and flaunted his newfound wealth around town and in the local casinos.

Joe Conforte also found out that not every local official was up for sale. He met a formidable foe in, Bill Raggio, then an ambitious, conservative District Attorney of Washoe County, NV. Raggio later became the longest serving State Senator in Nevada. Raggio took pleasure in seeing that one of the Triangle Ranch's trailers was burned to the ground by the police after it was officially designated as a public nuisance. Raggio also saw to it that Conforte was arrested for vagrancy on three separate occasions within his county lines.[12] At that point, Conforte hatched a scheme to ruin his rival. He paid a 17-year girl to meet with

Raggio under the guise that she needed legal advice. Later, Conforte approached Raggio in person. He threatened Raggio with a warning that the young girl would claim that she had sex with him if the vagrancy charges against him weren't dropped. However, Raggio was one step ahead of Conforte; he had a secret recording device running during their interaction.[13]

In 1961 Conforte received a sentence of 3 ½ years for extortion, but this wasn't hard time served in prison. "A guy like me goes to prison and you have it about as good as you can get because I had so much juice (power)," he boasted. "I was running a casino inside the prison and had a cook, a maid and for $3 a week, a guy to fan me while I played bridge."[14]

Sure, that may sound like some wannabe gangster determined to inflate his notoriety, but Conforte wasn't exaggerating. Indeed, Nevada's only state prison at that time had an actual rec room casino, "the Bull Pen." It had existed for decades before he arrived at the prison, but the stakes and variety of games expanded with Conforte's bankrolling. In fact, there are photos in which he is chomping on a cigar at the craps table along with the other inmates. What's more, this casino wasn't even a secretly run operation; various journalists had covered the story. In fact, one of the wardens bragged about the trustworthiness of the games to a reporter. "If someone was caught cheating, they'd stick a shiv in their ribs," he said.[B15]

[B] Conforte's life further became something befitting of a Hollywood script soon after prostitution was legalized. In fact, Joe Pesci portrayed him in the film *Love Ranch*. His most famous brothel, the Mustang Ranch, burned to the ground in 1975 in what was a suspected arson. He immediately rebuilt his business, but a famous murder took place in the parking lot one year later. One of Conforte's bodyguards shot a notable professional boxer, Oscar "Ringo" Bonavena. He had been managed by Joe Conforte's wife, but the two men had been feuding because Bonavena openly stated that he wanted to take over the Mustang Ranch.

Conforte was later convicted on multiple counts of tax evasion and fled the country in 1980. However, the FBI tracked him down in Brazil and offered a deal to return to the U.S. Conforte saw his tax debt forgiven ($18 million) and had four years shaved off his sentence in exchange for his testimony in a bribery case against a federal judge, Harry Claiborne. Conforte testified that he bribed Claiborne in hopes that his charges would be dropped, but the jury

While in prison, Conforte heard through the grapevine that business was booming for a brothel owned by one of his competitors, the Mustang Ranch. He then purchased the Mustang Ranch after being released from prison. Only months after being licensed by Storey County, Conforte pressed his luck by trying to open another brothel on the outskirts of the Las Vegas city limits.[16] And things were looking good for him. After all, he had already corrupted a few of the necessary county commissioners and some local polls at that time showed that Las Vegas residents were in favor of legal prostitution.[17]

However, the casino industry was concerned about the impending media circus had Conforte opened a licensed brothel just outside of Sin City. To be clear, the casino industry didn't have a moral objection to legal prostitution; it's an open secret that Nevada casinos have provided prostitutes for their high roller clients.[C18] Instead, this flashy pimp with a felony record was a

---

didn't buy his story. Claiborne's case resulted in a hung jury, but he was later convicted of tax charges. Harry Claiborne became the first sitting federal judge to be sentenced to prison.

After leaving prison, Conforte returned to the Mustang Ranch, along with his old ways. He continued skimming millions of dollars. By 1990, the IRS finally seized the Mustang Ranch and put the business up for auction. However, Conforte briefly re-acquired the Mustang Ranch at a bargain price through a shady deal arranged by the Storey County Commissioner at that time, Shirley Colletti. Colletti, a former madam at the Mustang Ranch, misled potential buyers by claiming that the brothel wouldn't be licensed in order to drive down the price. Ultimately, a sham company that was secretly-run by Conforte acquired the Mustang Ranch, but the charade didn't last long. After more criminal tax charges were filed against Conforte, he later escaped the country again and fled to Brazil where even today, as a fugitive, he still stays in the public eye. The Mustang Ranch is now under new management after another public auction. The property was purchased on eBay for $145,100.

[C] The SEC investigated the Del Webb Corporation, which owned a number of Vegas casinos. They uncovered that the company paid $178,294 to escorts for their casino's high rollers between 1969 and 1976. There will always be a connection between prostitution and Las Vegas casinos, but the obvious presence of prostitutes in Nevada casinos has decreased over the years as the industry has become more regulated, corporatized, and family-friendly. Those regulations have forced casinos to adjust their unofficial policies. For instance, the Palms was fined $1 million in 2013 after undercover police

public relations nightmare for the gambling industry at a time when several mobsters were being run out of the business.

The casino industry reacted by lobbying for a statewide ban on prostitution. In the end, the state legislators passed a compromise bill. They upheld the rights of Storey County to maintain their legalized system, but their bill also appeased casino lobbyists by banning licensed prostitution in counties with populations over 250,000, which at that time only applied to Clark County (Las Vegas).[D19] That law now applies to only Reno and Las Vegas.

In effect, that law indirectly opened the door for legalized prostitution everywhere in Nevada, *except Las Vegas*. Then again, that conclusion didn't come about immediately. A legal battle manifested a few years later and it involved a less flashy brothel owner who also wanted to set up his business just outside Las Vegas. A former truck driver, Walter Plankinton, sued the county for the right to operate his brothel, "the Chicken Ranch," after the local authorities of Nye County shut it down as a "public nuisance."[20]

If the name Chicken Ranch sounds familiar, it is in reference to the actual brothel that inspired the film and musical "The Best Little Whorehouse in Texas."[E21] Nevertheless, the police weren't protecting the sensibilities of the locals when they raided Walter Plankinton's brothel. That decision was invoked by a competing brothel owner in the area, Bill Martin, who relied upon the good ol' boy network to weed out his opposition. Bill Martin later took matters into his own hands with some brass tacks because Plankinton was resolute about remaining in town. Specifically, Martin arranged for the Chicken Ranch to be burned down and nearly killed 14 people in the process. That fire, along with a series

---

officers were provided access to cocaine and escorts by a host manager at the casino.

[D] That number is now 400,000.

[E] The real life brothel that inspired "The Best Little Whorehouse in Texas" was located just outside La Grange, TX and had reportedly been in operation for 129 years. The shutdown order came from the Governor's office in 1973. Incidentally, that brothel was also the inspiration behind the ZZ Top song "La Grange."

of other violent acts, which were detailed in the book *Nye County Brothel Wars*, illustrated that a change needed to be made. Nevada's system of "toleration" was primarily benefitting corrupt cops and the people with the deepest pockets to dish out kickbacks.[22]

A lawsuit against Nye County was Walter Plankinton's only legal recourse to operate his business. This case dragged on for years, but it eventually culminated in a Nevada Supreme Court ruling in his favor in 1978. That case established the legal precedent for the licensed brothels that currently operate throughout the state. Prostitution was already licensed in one other county. Therefore, the court ruled that this issue could be determined by each separate county with a population less than 250,000.[23] As a result, legalized prostitution is sanctioned in eleven counties, which host a total of 19 licensed brothels in the state.[24] In contrast, there are five counties that prohibit prostitution and one county, Eureka, neither bans it nor issues licenses.[25]

It's difficult to get unbiased, factual information about these brothels due to the controversial nature of the business. Also, some of the industry's most prominent critics are wholly committed and demonstrative with their activism. One of the most bizarre critics of these licensed brothels has been John Reese, the former president of a small group known as "Nevadans Against Prostitution." He is a born-again Christian who admittedly used to patronize the area's brothels. Despite his past, he is a passionate man who has pulled some publicity stunts in hopes that these efforts might scare patrons away from doing business with these establishments.

For instance, he once broke the window of his car and left the engine running near the parking lot of Joe Conforte's Mustang Ranch. The police saw the bloodstains and naturally assumed that a murder and or kidnapping had occurred. Multiple officers searched for the missing man, but Reese was spotted ten days later in California. Afterward, he admitted that it was all a ploy and, in the end, he was only fined $8,761 for the cost of the search, a light penalty considering all of those police man-hours wasted.[26]

That wasn't this moral crusader's first publicity stunt and it wouldn't be his last. He once chained himself to the Nevada Health

Board building in hopes that the media coverage would help his cause. In addition, he attempted to prey upon homophobic fears by publicly applying for a license to open the first gay brothel in Nevada. Albeit, he wasn't serious about operating the brothel and, as a formality, he was turned down for a license. Likewise, Reese also spent $35,000 of his money to pay for highway billboards which read "Warning: Brothels Are Not AIDS Safe." However, he discontinued the ad campaign after being threatened with a lawsuit because those were libelous claims.[F27]

John Reese has been merely a local nuisance for the Nevada brothels. On the other hand, Melissa Farley, a psychologist and longtime anti-prostitution researcher, is the most notable critic of the industry. Nevada's licensed brothels were portrayed as havens for human trafficking by Farley, but there is a wide divide between Farley's conclusions and the actual number of documented arrests for this crime. According to Farley, she passed on her information to the FBI, yet there have been no known trafficking prosecutions related to her information.[28] Long before her investigation, there were a handful of cases in the late 1990s. A few pimps were convicted of pandering women through licensed Nevada brothels.[29] Otherwise, documented cases are hard to find because there is an abundance of regulations in place intended to prevent trafficking. For example, prostitutes must pass FBI background checks and be fingerprinted before working in Nye County.[30]

Farley wrote her book, *Prostitution and Trafficking in Nevada: Making the Connections*, in which she interviewed 45 women from Nevada brothels and several brothel owners. Her conclusions were vastly more negative and sensational than any other researcher who has examined this industry. It's patently obvious that Farley has an agenda. To illustrate, she doesn't use the terms prostitute or sex worker; instead, she says "prostituted woman."[31] Likewise, she takes issue with the fact that conditions are safer with indoor prostitution than outdoor prostitution. In turn,

---

[F] Reese claimed that state officials were intentionally withholding information about the state's venereal disease testing. He also told reporters that he took a job as a courier with a medical testing firm so that he could verify the frequency and the quality of testing at the brothels, but he has never offered any proof of his suspicions.

she analogized street prostitutes to be plantation slaves working in the fields and indoor prostitutes as "house n****s."[32]

These kinds of biases undoubtedly shape her research. Hence, the aforementioned professor at George Washington University, Ronald Weitzer, has long criticized Farley for her "ideological blinders." Weitzer, who is known for research on prostitution and trafficking, has explained that the studies she conducted were "deeply flawed methodologically" with "sampling biases" and "procedural problems" that aren't addressed "because that might undermine her sweeping claims."[33]

Farley's credibility as an "expert witness" was belittled in a landmark prostitution case that overturned Canada's prostitution laws, Bedford v Canada. The judge, Susan Himel, found that the "expert witness" testimony from Melissa Farley didn't meet the standards set by Canadian courts. Not to mention, Himel concluded that Farley's evidence was "problematic" because "her advocacy appears to have permeated her opinions." Himel also felt that "Dr. Farley's choice of language is at times inflammatory and detracts from her conclusions." In particular, she took issue with how "some of (Farley's) opinions on prostitution were formed prior to her research, including, 'that prostitution is a terrible harm to women, that prostitution is abusive in its very nature, and that prostitution amounts to men paying a woman for the right to rape her.'"[34]

Thirty percent of the research for Farley's book was funded by the U.S. Department of State Office to Monitor and Combat Trafficking in Persons. Many would consider that to be a conflict of interest, but Farley was clearly going to write a complete condemnation of the Nevada brothel industry, with or without any financial assistance. She already had a lengthy and outspoken record as an extreme abolitionist. After all, she founded an organization, "Prostitution Research & Education," which has a stated mission to "abolish the institution of prostitution."[35]

According to Farley, "In prostitution, the conditions which make genuine consent possible are absent: physical safety, equal power with customers, and real alternatives."[36] In addition, she has written, "To the extent that any woman is assured to have freely chosen prostitution, then it follows that enjoyment of rape and domination are in her nature..."[37] That type of rhetoric renders every prostitute as a trafficking victim and it clearly shapes the interpretations of her research.

It's important to recognize these biases because there hasn't been much in-depth press coverage about this industry and it usually errors on the melodramatic side. On the other hand, Barbara Brents, the foremost expert on Nevada's licensed brothels, has come to very different conclusions about the state's most controversial industry. Brents is a professor of sociology at the University of Nevada, Las Vegas (UNLV) and she, along with her colleagues, have over 15 years of field research studying Nevada's licensed brothels. Brents, the co-author of *The State of Sex: Tourism, Sex, and Sin in the New American Heartland* describes those brothels in a very practical and academic style. To her credit, Brents has the temperament to cover such a risqué topic properly. She says, "(W)hen you shed the light, you find out that it's not at all what you thought it was — it's neither dangerous nor awful, nor is it as titillating."[38]

The safety of Nevada's brothels is one of the main elements highlighted by Brents and other researchers. Brents found that 84% of the women that she interviewed felt safe. They mentioned that the law was on their side and they had the option to call the police if necessary.[39] That's an important point of comparison when we know for a fact that prostitution is much more dangerous in Las Vegas.

To reiterate, prostitution is illegal in Las Vegas, never mind the national perception. It's hard to believe that the city's marketing campaign, "What happens here, stays here," isn't intended to partially include prostitution. Certainly, there is a bit of a charade. The city clearly caters to tourists and prostitution is part of that draw. Yet, the Las Vegas Metro Police prosecute prostitution more aggressively than most cities. Despite those efforts, with nearly 3,000 prostitution arrests in Clark County, NV (Las Vegas) every year, the U.S. Department of Justice has named Las Vegas as one of the 17 cities in America with the highest risk for human trafficking.[40]

The policy in Las Vegas is a worst case scenario. Criminal penalties haven't reduced the supply and demand of prostitution.

In fact, prostitution is ubiquitous throughout Las Vegas to such an extent that street vendors and taxi drivers hand out flyers with advertisements for the local escort agencies. With prostitution so rampant, some tourists may assume that prostitution is legal in Las Vegas. Meanwhile, no tax revenues have been raised, there are no disease control efforts, no public safety measures have been implemented, and police resources have been wasted.

Despite the murky details behind its creation, Nevada's system of legalized prostitution improves upon public safety much better than the status quo that is present throughout America. The women are in control of who they have sex with and what types of acts they perform. That's especially relevant because johns, other than at a legal brothel, sometimes react violently if they're denied specific sexual services. Therefore, most of the brothels have rooms equipped with panic buttons in case the client gets out of hand.[41]

Oddly enough, this public safety factor was indirectly illustrated by the media coverage of Lamar Odom's near death; he is the former NBA star and ex-husband of Khloe Kardashian. The brothel's employees didn't hesitate to call 911 when Odom was found unconscious in his room after a late night drug bender.[42] Think about it, "What are odds that someone from an illegal brothel would have risked going to prison to call 911 under the same circumstances?"

Nevada's brothels operate within a regulatory framework that has an undeniable track record. The women in this industry must, of course, be legal adults to be licensed, with a minimum age of 21 years in most counties. However, in some counties, they can work if they are 18 years old. Not to mention, the revenues from the licensing system account for up to 25% of the budgets for some counties.[43] To be specific, Lyon County has only 50,000 residents, but it raises $300,000 to $500,000 per year from the local brothels. According to Geoff Arnold, the owner of two brothels in Wells, NV, "There are only 500 families in that town," he says. "The two brothels pay more in fees than every other business combined."[44]

A former UCLA professor conducted a study and found that STDs were basically nonexistent in the licensed brothels.[45] Venereal disease testing has been mandatory since 1986, although roughly three-quarters of the women took the tests voluntarily before then. Now, the women must release their medical records, pass a background check, and everyone is tested for all STDs. According to the Nevada Board of Health, there has yet to be a single licensed woman who has tested HIV positive. Granted, there have been 26 past applicants who have tested HIV positive, but they've all been banned for life.[46] In comparison, the Las Vegas police have arrested over 500 HIV-infected prostitutes![47]

Nevada's licensed prostitutes are examined weekly and submit to monthly blood tests to the State Health Department. Hence, their health cards are suspended if an STD is detected, but their license can be reinstated if a physician certifies that the disease has been cured. Predictably, the rates for other diseases, such as chlamydia, syphilis, and gonorrhea, are far below the national average.[48]

The brothels are legally liable if a client contracts HIV from one of their workers. Thus, the procedures within the brothel maximize safety.[49] The women are trained to recognize visual signs of venereal disease and they make an inspection by shining a halogen light on the client's genitals before any sexual contact is made. Also, condoms are mandatory and the women leave no room for debate as they place the condom on the men every time. In fact, Alexa Albert, author of *Brothel: Mustang Ranch and Its Women*, can attest to that. This former Harvard medical student spent months living on location for her research. After every sex act, she literally inspected every condom to verify if they were being used and to check for breakage, which was negligible.[50]

The topic of legal prostitution typically evokes images of the garish, mega-brothels of some European red-light districts. However, the regulations within Nevada force these businesses to maintain a low profile in the community. There are basic zoning rules and, as a result, brothels can't be located within 400 yards of a church, school, or on a principal business street. In fact, the sign in front of the brothel must not be larger than 24 square yards, nor can it include the words "brothel" or "house of prostitution." On top of that, the sign must not display more than three 200 Watt red lights.[51] In other words, you really have to be determined to find these businesses.

The brothels are blocked from advertising as well. In response, the ACLU contested that they have the right to commercial speech in 2010, but the U.S. Supreme Court ultimately upheld the ban one year later.[52] Nonetheless, the leader of the Nevada Brothel Association, George Flint, pointed out that they didn't market aggressively before it was prohibited. They obviously feared that too much attention would harm the industry. "Aggressive marketing frightens us all...and make(s) legislators very nervous," said Flint.[53]

Most Congressmen from Nevada have avoided taking a firm stance on the issue of legalized prostitution as it is truly a state matter. Then again, former Sen. Harry Reid (D-NV) stated in 2011 on the U.S. Senate floor, "The time has come to outlaw prostitution." That was an odd remark by Reid considering that he grew up in Searchlight, NV where prostitution was tolerated. He had a tough upbringing in a dirt-poor family that indirectly relied upon the sex industry to survive. In his memoir, he mentioned that his mother earned a living doing laundry for the local brothels. These businesses even extended hospitality; he learned how to swim at a brothel as a youth.[54] Think about it. These people did nothing more than lend a helping hand. And that's how Harry Reid thanked them, by proposing to lock them up.

According to Reid, his sudden attention to this issue had been raised by a business owner who decided not to open a business in Storey County, NV because of the brothels. "Nevada needs to be known as the first place for innovation and investment — not as the last place where prostitution is still legal," responded Reid.[G][55] But here's the catch: either Reid was mistaken or it was all a ruse because that specific business owner *did* set up his business in Storey County.

It turns out that business owners don't seem to care about the brothels. As noted by Rob Hooper, the executive director of the Northern Nevada Development Authority, the topic of legalized prostitution "hardly ever does come up and if it does come up it's just a point of interest and it just goes away."[56] And if Harry Reid is still looking for "innovation and investment," there is nothing

---

[G] He was asked about the prostitution issue again in 2014. "The legislature, they're all a bunch of cowards," said Reid.

more cutting-edge than Tesla Motors' lithium-ion battery factory at the Tahoe-Reno Industrial Center in Storey County, Nevada. Tesla Motors decided to make their $5 billion investment even though the Mustang Ranch is located only eight miles away. As a matter of fact, Lance Gilman, the owner of the Mustang Ranch, is also the Director of the Tahoe-Reno Industrial Center. Despite this connection to prostitution, the Tahoe-Reno Industrial Center is one of the largest industrial parks in the world and hosts several major corporations, including Walmart, Dell Computers, Toys R Us, etc.[57]

Oscar Goodman, the former mayor of Las Vegas (an advocate for licensing prostitution in Las Vegas), publicly rebutted Reid's claim that businesses have been scared away by the state's licensed brothels.[58] Indeed, Las Vegas hasn't witnessed its Sin City reputation diminish outside investment. In fact, Las Vegas had the third-highest growth of any city in America during the last decade.[59] Furthermore, Las Vegas remains one of the most popular cities for business conventions.

Most researchers have come away with an overall positive assessment of the Nevada brothel industry, but there are fair criticisms and some specific reforms need to be made. The legal brothels provide a certain level of protection against violence, but their house rules still exploit women financially just like a pimp. The women earn an income that is far above average (potentially over $1,000 a day), but those wages must be split 50/50 with the house. The women are hired as independent contractors, which means they receive no benefits and have very few labor rights. To add insult to injury, any cab driver who brings a client to the brothel receives a 20% commission of whatever price is negotiated because the brothels can't advertise; whether the cab driver actually referred the client is irrelevant.[60]

There are also various regulations that severely limit the workers' basic freedoms. They are required to stay in the brothel 24 hours a day for the length of their contracts, which are usually for three weeks at a time. Many brothels only allow the worker to leave for a doctor's appointment and an escort is required at her expense. Understandably, rules must be in place to prevent prostitutes from doing business outside the brothels, but many of the regulations are excessive and seemingly attempt to re-establish antebellum social standards. The rules deviate from county to county, but Lenore Kuo, a former Professor of Women's Studies at California State University, Fresno provided some excellent examples. In her book, *Prostitution Policy: Revolutionizing Practice Through a Gendered Perspective*, she noted that some counties require prostitutes to use a side entrance in restaurants and maintain a 5 P.M. curfew when they're not working. Furthermore, some counties require the woman, along with her children, to leave town once the contract is over.[61]

In conclusion, the Nevada brothel system shines a light on a common weakness among legalized prostitution models--all prostitution outside the licensed brothels is illegal. The Nevada system, like most legalized prostitution, often forces the prostitute to trade her pimp for a legal one. The regulations in place have little to do with empowering the workers and more to do with enriching their employers. Legalized prostitution models aren't inherently exploitative, but once tax revenue is raised from prostitution it can be a corrupting force that overlooks the workers' fundamental rights. Furthermore, a prostitute should have *the choice* to enter into a licensed system while not facing criminal penalties as long as her activity takes place between consenting adults behind closed doors. Therefore, the ideal prostitution policy is a hybrid of legalization and the decriminalization of indoor prostitution. New Zealand has a similar type of system and it will be examined in the next chapter.

4

"Refusing to offer him this service would be a violation of his human rights."

Ideally, our government would examine the best aspects of various models worldwide when developing its own policies. Unfortunately, that is virtually impossible in the U.S. with the issue of prostitution because it sparks such intense emotional reactions. No perfect prostitution model exists, but that doesn't mean that we can't create a better model. Many European nations have implemented various harm reduction methods while addressing this issue purely as a social problem. Some of the methods even go above and beyond. To illustrate, in some Swiss brothels, the employees are trained to use a defibrillator in case someone has a heart attack.[1]

For the sake of perspective, it's interesting to note how differently some nations view prostitution. First of all, several international organizations no longer use the term, "prostitute." Instead, "sex worker" is unofficially considered the politically-correct terminology. As a side note, there certainly was a need for some level of political correctness in our country due to our history with racism, sexism, etc. However, most Americans would agree that the PC movement has gone too far and taken on a life of its own. This liberal over-reaction with political correctness is even more apparent internationally. You might even think that some actual news reports from around the world were written by the satirical publication *The Onion*. For example, the U.K.'s *Daily Mail* reported in 2010 that a social worker authorized a 21-year-old man to travel to Amsterdam to visit the red-light district, all financed with taxpayer money. The caseworker defended the decision because the young man has learning disabilities and was an "angry, frustrated, and anxious" virgin. "Refusing to offer him this service would be a violation of his human rights," said his social worker. The social worker added, "Who says he can't do what he wants? We can't place restrictions on a young man who wants to experience the world."[2]

That has to be a one-of-a-kind report, right? No. Various departments within the Danish and Australian governments also subsidize these types of services for the disabled. "What we've got is a longstanding policy based around the principles of human rights that people with disabilities have the same rights as anyone else in the community and are entitled to be assisted to exercise those rights," said Michael Plaister from the Australian Department of Health and Human Services in the Australian state of Tasmania. "Sexual frustration can be a major problem for the disabled, and in some cases the last solution is to visit a prostitute," said Stig Langvad, the chairman of the Danish Association for the Disabled. "Politicians can debate whether prostitution in general should be allowed, but if it is, why should the disabled be the only ones prevented from having access to it?"[3]

The majority of countries worldwide, particularly first world nations, have some form of legalized or decriminalized prostitution, with the Netherlands as arguably the most recognized. What may best demonstrate the Dutch tolerance for prostitution is the fact that Amsterdam's red-light district, which has existed for 700 years, has an actual "Prostitution Information Center" for tourists.[4] That includes a store, De Wallenwinkel, which also provides tours of the area.

Prostitution was officially legalized in 2000, thereby requiring brothels to be licensed and inspected. The sex trade had been technically illegal for decades prior, but the laws were sparingly enforced. Also, street prostitution is permissible in certain zones, "tipplezones," as of 1983.[5] These zones are located away from schools and churches and these areas restrict the hours in which prostitution can take place. Some of these decriminalized zones also include car parks with walls and privacy screens. They were built so sex could take place inside the client's car without visibility from the outside.[6]

Obviously, American taxpayers would never support such an initiative, nor is it recommended, but the Dutch rationalized such an unusual policy to maximize public safety. There are security cameras present to monitor for any potential violence and NGO outreach workers are usually on site to provide harm reduction assistance, such as free condoms. Consequently, ninety-five percent of sex workers in these areas reported feeling safer. In hindsight, federal officials have also supported this experiment, including the Dutch foreign ministry, who noted that "the introduction of these zones has significantly increased the safety of street walkers."[7] Likewise, the residents of these areas reported a reduction in other crimes.[8]

There certainly are positive takeaways from the Dutch model. A Dutch prostitute must be at least 21-years-old. They can choose to be self-employed and only have to register with the tax authorities.[9] Dutch prostitutes have the same rights and benefits that all other professions receive, such as health insurance. In fact, the government publishes booklets for sex workers and their employers, advising them as to their legal rights and benefits.[10] As a result, there is a Dutch labor union for sex workers. Likewise, the legalized aspect has facilitated volunteer outreach work.[A][11]

Germany, like the Netherlands, had tolerated prostitution with de facto decriminalization and allowed numerous brothels to operate openly. Their country further liberalized this activity when the Berlin federal court ruled in 2000 that prostitution is not immoral activity. That decision led the way to the formalization of a legalized model of prostitution one year later.[12] Germany has since completely commercialized prostitution and their country hosts corporate chains of brothels. Thus, European sex workers, particularly those from Eastern Europe, have immigrated to Germany in large numbers and this country now hosts the most prostitutes per capita in Europe. In total, as many as 400,000 prostitutes are working in Germany's €15 billion industry.[13]

Germany's prostitution policies are determined at the local level due to the federal government removing its prostitution laws in 2000. Several small towns prohibit prostitution, but it is quite visible in the larger cities. Just how visible? There are about 500 brothels in Berlin.[14] Roughly 80% of Germany's sex industry operates indoors, but some cities have conducted unique

---

[A] Only 6% of the cities reported that they had programs in place to help sex workers find different work. The city of Eindhoven developed a unique program in which sex workers were given vouchers after each step that they take towards leaving the industry. Those vouchers could be used to buy things like professional clothing.

experiments to deal with street prostitution.[15] Essen and Cologne have the same style "drive-ins" as in some Dutch cities.[16] Whereas, the city of Bonn spends $116,000 a year for a private security company to guard the red-light district. In return, the street walkers can work from 8:15 p.m. to 6 a.m. as long as they purchase a ticket from a street meter for a nightly fee of six euros.[17] If a sex worker is caught working without a ticket, that person can be fined up to 130 euros. To sum up, such a brazen policy would obviously be abhorred in America, but a German spokeswoman for the city praised the system while asserting that it would remain in place. In particular, she noted the revenues generated from the meters (250,000 euros) are far higher than the cost of providing security.[18] Other German cities have a similar system in place, but only Bonn uses automated street meters.

Legalization has partially reduced the traditional taboos of prostitution, but it certainly hasn't eliminated the stigma. Granted, that is not a realistic goal. Legalization doesn't force society to welcome this behavior. Specifically, a prostitute was the most successful contestant on Germany's version of "Who Wants to Be a Millionaire?" She won 500,000 euros, but some exasperated viewers notified the show's producers about her occupation.[19] Likewise, one official with the Dutch National Bank received her termination notice in 2014. She was fired for something unrelated to her on-the-job performance; she violated their code of conduct because she had worked as a dominatrix in her off hours.[20]

On paper, Germany's laws are very similar to the Netherlands, but their government hasn't implemented the proper steps to improve the rights and safety of sex workers. German prostitutes are entitled to receive health insurance, pension, and social security benefits. Despite these benefits, almost every prostitute in Germany has refused to register with the government. Remarkably, as of 2013, only 44 out of roughly 400,000 prostitutes have registered with the proper authorities![21] Again, many sex workers don't want to register due to the stigma related to prostitution. However, the primary reason is that the German government often charges them for 5-10 years of back taxes after registering.[22] More important, German prostitutes also have the choice of working independently or in a brothel just like in the

Netherlands, but their actual labor rights are notably ambiguous. The courts have sided with German brothel owners in cases of violations of labor rights.[23] Essentially, this industry has been commercialized, but the workforce hasn't been legitimized.

One of the primary purposes of legalization is to enact practical regulations, but these two countries have missed the mark. Generally speaking, most countries with legalized prostitution tend to over-regulate the industry and, consequently, force the industry underground. The laissez-faire approach has its positives, but Germany and the Netherlands have taken that mentality too far. Neither country requires their sex workers to be tested for STDs.[24] Also, the managers of the brothels are licensed, not the prostitutes.[25] By granting licenses to the brothels, and not the prostitutes, it takes power away from individual workers. The management of a brothel has to pass a criminal background check and face periodic government inspections, but, in several cases, figures within organized crime have been the ones truly operating these businesses. The two countries have taken steps to crack down on abuses, but it's an ongoing battle. In fact, the top court in the European Union ruled that brothel owners must speak the same language of their workers to prevent abuses, in particular, human trafficking.[26]

Critics of legalization tend to point to Germany and the Netherlands because of their association with sex trafficking. That reputation is both somewhat deserving and rather unfair. Both nations obviously have an established rule of law and certainly value human rights. However, both countries, particularly Germany, have imported much of Europe's sex trade, yet they haven't taken enough measures to regulate the industry properly. That's an astonishing set of circumstances because both nations' economies are firmly rooted in socialist values with heavy regulations for business owners and more negotiating power for the labor force. Somehow the sex industries, particularly Germany's, operate in the exact opposite manner. We've all heard the horror stories of sex trafficking associated with brothels. Therefore, these governments have a responsibility to monitor this industry more thoroughly.

The prostitution debate is often dominated by generalizations. One of which is a sweeping claim that legalized prostitution leads to more human trafficking. However, the official data is far from conclusive because there is no consistent trend. To be specific, the number of documented victims of sex trafficking in the Netherlands increased after legalization with there being 341 victims in 2000 and 419 victims in 2009.[27] On the contrary, the number of human trafficking victims in Germany decreased after legalization. In 2011, ten years after legalization was implemented, there were nearly 33% fewer cases of sex trafficking.[28]

The example from the Netherlands and Germany should not be a condemnation of the legalized model. Nevada's licensed brothels demonstrate that this industry can be properly monitored. Nevada is a state with strong libertarian values, yet prostitution is thoroughly regulated because of this particular danger. In fact, Nevada's legal brothels have never been mentioned in the State Department's annual Trafficking in Persons Report, the most comprehensive worldwide investigation into this issue. Suffice it to say, that contradicts the views of some anti-prostitution activists who state empirically that legalization leads to more sex trafficking. They're discounting the fact that the transparency from legalization clearly makes it easier for the authorities to identify these kinds of cases.

In the case of Germany and the Netherlands, the connection between legalization and sex trafficking centers upon how to properly regulate the industry. Both nations, along with many other countries with legalized models, have received the best rating (Tier 1) from the U.S. Department of State for their efforts to reduce human trafficking. Bear in mind, the U.S. State Department officially supports the criminalization of prostitution and tries to steer other nations in that direction.

Regardless of their ideology, the U.S. State Department acknowledged a significant factor leading to high numbers of sex trafficking victims in these two countries and it isn't related to legalization. Both Germany and the Netherlands have appropriate maximum penalties for human trafficking, but their overly-liberal court systems have an appalling record when it comes to punishing human traffickers. In the Netherlands, convicted human traffickers are punished with an average of only 21 months in prison![29] The U.S. State Department report stated, "Local police complain that low sentences for traffickers continued to result in the reappearance of the same offenders and thus the continued exploitation of trafficking victims within the regulated commercial sex sector."[30] Such weak penalties won't deter the brothel owners, i.e. the people who profit the most from ignoring signs of human trafficking.

Germany's courts have met human traffickers with an even softer touch. The U.S. State Department reported that "the majority of convicted labor and sex trafficking offenders (in Germany) were not required to serve time in prison, raising concerns that punishments were inadequate to deter traffickers or did not reflect the heinous nature of the offense."[31] In fact, most of the convicted traffickers have received suspended sentences![32] That's particularly astounding because sex trafficking is one of the most harrowing crimes imaginable as it combines rape, slavery, assault, and kidnapping.

Australia, on the other hand, has legalized prostitution, but considerably less sex trafficking occurs in their country. In fact, the State Department found that the Australian authorities only identified 14 potential victims of sex trafficking in 2014.[33] Harsher penalties seem to be a factor as human traffickers in Australia can face 12 to 25 years in prison and fines of up to $152,000.[34] Another leading factor that helps Australia minimize sex trafficking is beyond the control of Germany and the Netherlands. Often undocumented women are the victims of sex trafficking and roughly half of the sex workers in Germany and the Netherlands are foreigners. In essence, these countries have imported their sex industry, but the logistics of illegal immigration are much more complicated in Australia.

Prostitution was a states' rights issue in Australia and it was first legalized in Victoria in 1984. Then Queensland followed in 1990, the Australian Capital Territory in 1992, and eventually New South Wales in 1995.[35] The Labor Party of Australia had much to do with this change.[36] As a result, brothel owners must now be licensed, have local permission to operate, and conform to restrictions on the size of their businesses. Prostitutes must also submit to regular health checks.

The laws vary by territory. Western Australia (Perth) prohibits all forms of prostitution, but the capital city of Melbourne (Victoria Territory) is the country's most commercialized region. For one thing, a legal brothel in Melbourne, Daily Planet, made international news in 2003 when it became the first publicly traded brothel on a stock exchange.[B][37] However, the regulations in this region restrict workers' rights far more than in other territories. The licensed brothels in Nevada would be a fair comparison. Hence, most of the sex workers choose to work outside the legal sector in this region. In contrast, New South Wales (Sydney) has a more liberalized form of decriminalized prostitution. Street prostitution is even tolerated as long as it doesn't happen near or within view of a home, school, church or hospital.[38]

The states are the laboratories of democracy and, thus, the differing policies within Australia offer opportunities for credible case studies. Basil Donovan of the National Centre of HIV Epidemiology and Clinical Research at the University of NSW conducted research with sex workers across the country. He concluded that regardless of the model in place it had "little or no impact on the size of the industry."[39] Most importantly, Donovan found that the lowest rates of STDs among sex workers were in the territory which is fully decriminalized, New South Wales (Sydney).[40]

A report by the United Nations, "Sex Work and the Law in Asia and the Pacific," confirmed these conclusions and strongly supported decriminalization. Those researchers found that HIV transmission among sex workers in this region of Sydney was "extremely low or non-existent."[41] That's particularly remarkable because New South Wales (Sydney) has by far the highest rate of HIV relative to population size.[42]

How were the sex workers able to stay relatively free of STDs in this particularly dangerous environment? That may seem remarkable at first, but those results make a lot of sense. One of the primary reasons is that sex workers in Sydney were the most

---

[B] The Daily Planet hired Heidi Fleiss as a consultant, which also provided a great deal of publicity.

likely to have contact with a health worker and receive support services, such as free condoms and STD testing. On the other hand, outreach workers have restricted access to sex workers where it's prohibited. By the same token, a legalized model with overly burdensome regulations pushes many workers out of the legal sector and that negates potential harm reduction efforts as well.

The general fear that legalized or decriminalized prostitution will wreak havoc upon society in the form of venereal diseases isn't based on the available information. Despite one of the most commercialized models of prostitution in the world, Germany has one of the lowest rates of HIV in the world. Only 0.1% of German adults are infected with this disease, as opposed to the rate of 0.6% in the U.S. In fact, almost every first world nation with legal or decriminalized prostitution has a lower rate of HIV than the U.S. The CIA World Fact Book designates 33 nations as "developed countries" and 24 of them have legal or decriminalized prostitution.[C] Remarkably, only two of the 24 developed countries, Estonia and Portugal, have a higher HIV rate than the U.S![43] (A table is provided in the notes) In a similar vein, some Americans would be flabbergasted to find out that a country such as Brazil has an estimated rate of HIV (0.3%), less than the U.S. Let's take into account that Brazil is a country with a notably lower average income, a more sexually open culture, and legal prostitution.

Most Americans are blind to the fact that liberalized prostitution policies protect public health. Numerous international organizations widely endorse this point of view. As a matter of fact, the world's most renowned international health agencies publicly support the decriminalization of prostitution, including the World Health Organization (WHO), the Global Commission on HIV and the Law, the Joint United Nations Program on HIV/AIDS (UNAIDS), among others.[44] These organizations endorse decriminalization because it presents more opportunities for reducing STDs, such as free condoms, safe sex literature, venereal disease testing, etc. The results speak for themselves. One such study, "Global epidemiology of HIV among female sex

---

[C] Countries with the Swedish model should be considered as a prohibition model, not decriminalization. The Swedish model will be detailed later in this chapter.

workers: influence of structural determinants," was published by *The Lancet* (one of the most prestigious peer-reviewed medical journals). It concluded that new cases of HIV among prostitutes would be reduced by 33% to 46% over the next decade through decriminalization![45]

New Zealand created one of the most liberalized forms of decriminalized prostitution in the world and it has enhanced the public health and safety of the entire country. New Zealand has one of the lowest rates of HIV infection in the world (0.1%). And that has been facilitated by reversing some of the inefficient policies that currently take place in the U.S.

Prostitution was illegal in New Zealand in 1987, but their Department of Health made a bold decision. They selected the New Zealand Prostitutes' Collective to operate a non-confrontational HIV prevention outreach program. Just like in the U.S, the police opposed this program. They confiscated condoms and safe sex literature provided by the outreach workers and used it as evidence for prostitution arrests. Fortunately, over time, these intimidation tactics lost favor and by 1993 police were officially instructed to no longer confiscate condoms or safe sex literature.[46]

Ten years later, the Prostitution Reform Act of 2003 was passed. As a result, brothels now operate openly and legally. Most importantly, the owners of these businesses do not have the overbearing control that exists with many legalized models. This is why New Zealand's model is the one most supported by sex workers worldwide. Likewise, this system maximizes the rights of workers and public health without laying the foundation for an ultra-commercialized sex industry.

It turned out that those with fire and brimstone forecasts couldn't have been more wrong. The government of New Zealand reported that decriminalization didn't lead to more street prostitution, nor did it lead to an increase in the overall number of sex workers.[47] Independent research by the Christchurch School of Medicine and Victoria University's Crime and Justice Research Centre also came to the same conclusion. In fact, prostitution is less visible to the public eye because fewer women are working in brothels now that they can legally work independently.[48] Up to four prostitutes can set up collectives as equal partners; if there are five or more workers they must register with the authorities.

New Zealand's sex workers now have the same occupational health and safety laws as all other workers. Reports by New Zealand's Parliament and the Ministry of Justice found that decriminalization created better work conditions. Likewise, independent researchers have found that sex workers were less susceptible to coercion and labor conditions had improved.[49] Prostitutes are now more aware of their legal rights and more likely to report violations of their rights.[50] One very symbolic case illustrated that point in which a prostitute successfully filed a sexual harassment claim against a brothel operator.[51]

As was the case in the decriminalized region of Australia (New South Wales), that same UN report stated that HIV transmission among New Zealand's sex workers was "extremely low or non-existent."[52] That's not because decriminalization created a utopian society. Instead, their government chose the most realistic policy for reducing the harms to society from this issue. To be clear, many of New Zealand's sex workers report that men continue to ask for sex without a condom. They are required by law to use a condom, which made that uncomfortable situation easier, thereby increasing safe sex practices. In fact, a few men have since been arrested for removing their condoms during sex acts, something that would have never occurred before decriminalization.[53]

New Zealand is a unique example. Several nations have a form of decriminalized prostitution, but they differ from New Zealand. Those countries typically have a variety of prostitution laws on the books, but those laws aren't widely enforced. That system is best described as de facto decriminalization. Let's explore a few examples.

Prostitution isn't illegal in the United Kingdom per se, but there are 25 related crimes such as street prostitution, solicitation, and pimping. The sex trade is out in the open. As a matter of fact, the British trade union, GMB, even allows prostitutes to join their organization.[54] Generally, the enforcement of prostitution laws in the U.K. is largely dependent upon citizen complaints. In some cases, juries have been reluctant to convict brothel owners as long as there are no related crimes. In one such case, Claire Finch ran a brothel from her home, but she stressed the importance of how her business insured the safety of the four women who worked there. And, in the end, the announcement of her acquittal was met with loud cheers in the courtroom.[55]

Commercial sex is prohibited, but it is unlikely for a prostitute to be arrested as long as she works alone indoors. Predictably, the U.K.'s model has far fewer negatives associated with prostitution than in the U.S. Specifically, a British study found that 78% of indoor workers had never experienced violence. Moreover, a study in Belgium, a country with similar laws, found similar results with 77% of indoor workers who never experienced violence.[56] That is, of course, in stark contrast to reports in the U.S. from indoor prostitutes. They experience a rate of violent assaults twice as high as their European counterparts.[57]

There is, however, one glaring weakness with the U.K.'s prostitution model. Their government created several well-intentioned pimping laws, but the language is quite vague and open to broad interpretation. As a result, those laws prevent women from working together to ensure their safety because their coworkers could be arrested for human trafficking. Then again, the U.K. deserves credit for creating some of the most uniquely protective human trafficking laws. Men can be criminally prosecuted if they pay for sex with a woman who has been trafficked, even if the man is unaware that she is a trafficking victim. Also, men who pay for sex *knowingly* with trafficked women can be charged with rape.[58]

France closed its state-sponsored brothels in 1946, but their government has maintained their version of de facto decriminalization for indoor sex workers. There is a very fine line and subjective nature to the language of France's prostitution laws as was illustrated when the former head of the International Monetary Fund (IMF), Dominique Strauss-Kahn, was arrested for "aggravated pimping." Paying for sex in France isn't illegal, but Strauss-Kahn was accused of organizing orgies with prostitutes, which is illegal. He never denied participating in these sex parties, but he claimed ignorance that the women were prostitutes. As a side note, it was a laughable defense that Strauss-Kahn believed that this group of young, statuesque models engaged in an orgy with a larger group of senior citizens simply for kicks. On the other hand, this case certainly had the look of an underhanded political prosecution because Strauss-Kahn was a strong contender to win the presidency of France. In the end, he was acquitted, along with most of his co-defendants, and Straus-Kahn has remained as a popular candidate to become a future President of France, despite his lifestyle.[59]

France is renowned for tolerating prostitution, but a tide has slowly been turning for some time. Former President Nicolas Sarkozy led a new wave of conservatism and in 2002 the French National Assembly passed more stringent street prostitution laws, including "passive solicitation" laws. Those laws granted the police the authority to arrest a woman if her style of dress or attitude gave them the *impression* that she is a prostitute. Naturally, those laws reduced the visibility of street prostitution, but those statutes were overturned in 2013 because they opened the door to police corruption and civil liberty abuses. Street prostitutes merely sidestepped the law by dressing in a less risqué manner.[60] Nonetheless, the French still enforce street prostitution laws, but there has been a trend in which more legislators want the police to focus on the buyers of sex and less on the prostitutes. That is known as the "end demand" model.

Like France, Canada had a similar system with de facto decriminalization of indoor prostitution. Prostitution wasn't illegal per se in Canada, but there were various prohibitions, including laws against public communication for the purposes of prostitution. With this in mind, the constitutionality of Canada's prostitution laws was challenged by a small group of sex workers. Bedford v Canada resulted in an Ontario Judge, Susan Himel, overturning those laws in 2010 by ruling that they violated sex workers' constitutional rights to "life, liberty and safety." Himel ruled, "By increasing the risk of harm to street prostitutes, the communicating law is simply too high a price to pay for the alleviation of social nuisance."[61] She added, "I find that the danger faced by prostitutes greatly outweighs any harm which may be faced by the public."ᴰ⁶²

Based on the Bedford v Canada ruling, many assumed that prostitution would be fully decriminalized as in New Zealand. However, the Canadian Parliament passed contentious legislation in 2014, which made it illegal for someone to pay for sex.⁶³ This "end demand" policy mimics the Swedish model that has gained political traction in recent years. The Swedish model decriminalizes prostitution for the women who sell sex while criminalizing their clients. This approach has been marketed as a feminist initiative that protects women from the woes of the sex trade, but much evidence shows that it fails to achieve its goal. In particular, a report by a Vancouver NGO, Pivot Legal Society, strongly opposed Canada's new direction. Their report stated, "The evidence from Sweden and Norway indicates that prohibiting the purchase of sexual services does not result in increased safety and protection for sex workers, nor does it eliminate prostitution. In fact, violence and stigma against sex workers increases."⁶⁴

The Swedish model came about in 1999 when their government formed an official policy based on a philosophical belief. According to the Swedish government, prostitution is not consensual activity. The Swedish viewpoint presumes that prostitutes have no free. Therefore, every act of prostitution is automatically an act of violence against women. As a result, Sweden decided that prostitutes shouldn't face criminal penalties and all of the penalties for prostitution are applied to the men who purchase sex. They face a fine of $1,000 to $2,000 and possibly six months in jail.⁶⁵

The Swedish model has reduced the visibility of street prostitution for obvious reasons. Regardless, a report in 2007 by the Swedish National Board of Health and Welfare found that it was impossible to draw any conclusions about the overall level of

---

ᴰ That decision had to have been influenced by a Vancouver serial killer, Robert Pickton. He admitted to murdering 49 women, most of whom were prostitutes or drug addicts. He was arrested as early as 1997 for murdering a prostitute, but the charges were dropped. Evidence shows that law enforcement ignored crucial leads given by other prostitutes that could have brought Pickton to justice much earlier.

prostitution in Sweden. Thus, the industry most likely has transitioned underground.[66] Therefore, the Swedish model needs to be recognized for what it is -- a more effective prohibition model, rather than what it is not -- a truly feminist model.

Certain Swedish officials have trailblazed an effort to export their "end demand" model worldwide, including Gunilla Ekberg, the former Swedish government special adviser on prostitution and trafficking. She openly acknowledged that part of her job was to travel internationally to influence other countries to copy their model.[67] Their government essentially labeled their experiment as a success long before it could truly be determined. Thus, adverse results from Sweden's venture have been glossed over because the motivations behind the Swedish model were more symbolic, rather than a response to the conditions on the ground.

The sex trade wasn't rampant in their country before the "Swedish model" went into effect. Prostitution was then decriminalized for both the buyers and sellers. The reason behind such a small sex industry is simple. Sweden has one of the highest standards of living in the world, with a per capita income higher than the U.S., along with a strong social safety net. Nevertheless, this public relations campaign has been effective. Finland, Iceland, and Norway established a model similar to Sweden's.[68] Hence, some now call this the Nordic model.

The Swedish model has become a trendy and politically correct crusade for those who believe this will advance feminism. Albeit, it's difficult to consider this a feminist policy when there is absolutely no inclusion of the women who are directly affected. Pye Jakobsson, the most high-profile Swedish sex worker activist, resents the patronizing tone of her government. By the way, that's not her real name. The fact that she feels compelled to use a pseudonym illustrates the fact that the Swedish model hasn't exactly been "liberating." Jakobsson clearly doesn't agree with the notion "that no prostitution is prostitution out of free will." She says, "It means that everybody is a victim. If you scream and shout that you're not a victim you are suffering from a false consciousness. And if you try to convince them that you're not even suffering from a false consciousness, they will say, 'Well you're not representative.'"[69]

At face value, the Swedish model certainly seems to offer compassion to female sex workers by not throwing them in jail, but, in reality, that doesn't negate the fact that criminalizing the sex trade still punishes prostitutes directly and indirectly. Yes, that contradicts much of what you've probably heard in the American media, but the truth is out there for anyone who chooses to look. Case in point, a Swedish sex workers rights group, the Rose Alliance, conducted the largest survey of the industry. They found that thirty-six of their respondents had been assaulted by a john, yet only nine of them had been comfortable reporting the crime afterward. Furthermore, only two of those nine women said that they would be comfortable reporting a crime committed against them in the future due to the treatment they received from their government.[70] How could this be the case when, in theory, the Swedish model is protective of sex workers?

Again, prostitution is automatically an act of violence against women, according to the Swedish model. Therefore, the government now enforces incredibly expansive laws in which anyone can be arrested for pimping if the person benefits in *any* possible way from prostitution. Hence, sex workers can't live with anyone, not even family members because their loved ones will benefit from their work.[71]

In fact, landlords must kick them out of their apartments or else face sex trafficking charges. This is one of the worst aspects of the Swedish model and it has been mimicked in other countries. Amnesty International documented a four-year law enforcement investigation in Norway, "Operation Homeless." Several sex workers were evicted and left homeless after the police threatened their landlords with arrest.[72]

As a result, sex workers living under the Swedish model have reported being extorted for higher rent due to the legal risk from offering them housing. Likewise, the expanded interpretation of these prostitution laws denies sex workers the right to hire a security guard. Nor can prostitutes work in pairs for safety reasons.[73]

In theory, the Swedish model views prostitutes as victims, but they can be stripped of their parental rights by the government. An international news story brought that issue to the forefront after a

Swedish sex worker and political activist, Eva-Marree, was murdered by her ex-boyfriend during a visitation to see her daughter. Unfortunately, she was put in that position by her government when they granted custody of her daughter to her ex-boyfriend, a man with a history of violence. Ultimately, her activism, which "romanticized prostitution," prompted those officials to take away her child.[74]

The lives of the most vulnerable prostitutes are now much more challenging as a result of the Swedish model. Many streetwalkers say that the ban has pushed away otherwise law-abiding clients; primarily, the more dangerous and perverted customers are still available. These new laws created a change in the supply and demand, thereby, forcing sex workers to have less negotiating power. That means that they're less likely to use condoms and more likely to feel compelled to perform sex acts that they would be otherwise unwilling to do. Also, with the more police on the lookout, these women have less time to assess the safety risk of their potential clients. To provide a visual effect, consider what happened when similar penalties were put in place in Milan. Street prostitutes began wearing sneakers to chase after the cars.[75] All in all, the Swedish model hoped to reduce the exploitation of women, but it has resulted in more street prostitutes using pimps for protection.[76]

Dr. Jay Levy from the University of Cambridge, author of *Criminalising the Purchase of Sex: Lessons from Sweden*, spent several years in Sweden conducting field research. "Empirically speaking...outcomes of (the Swedish model) are certainly not positive and it fails to achieve its ambition," says Dr. Jay Levy.[77] In fact, the lives of Swedish sex workers were less stigmatized when prostitution was truly decriminalized before 1999.

Despite not facing criminal penalties, sex workers are still investigated by police officers to obtain evidence to arrest their customers. "How do you think (police) find the clients? By following random men around? No, they target us," says Pye Jakobbson.[78] These women don't have much of a defense against harassment because there are several other laws that the police can selectively enforce to gain leverage for their investigations. In fact, the National Board of Health and Welfare reported that the new policy resulted in sex workers feeling less trust for social authorities, police, and the legal system. In turn, that made them less likely to take advantage of social services intended for exiting prostitution or harm reduction, such as free condoms or HIV testing.[79]

How could such a policy have been pioneered in a country that strongly supports feminist causes? When examining Swedish politics, it is quite easy to find the openly radical feminist contingent. The Left Party's leader, Gudrun Schyman, once insisted that the oppression from Swedish men is similar to that of the Taliban.[80] Clearly, that's a ridiculous suggestion because Sweden is the most gender neutral nation in the world. Sweden's Left Party made international news when they proposed a law to force every man to pay a tax in retribution for all past crimes that have been committed against women. The "man tax" wasn't passed, yet the Left Party's leader, Gudrun Schyman, ironically was later convicted of tax evasion.[81] Nevertheless, the Left Party waited several years and unveiled an even more controversial and symbolic proposal. This motion, along with others, was detailed in an article by *Euronews*, "Has Swedish feminism gone too far?"[82] They proposed a law that would require all men to sit down to urinate in a public toilet.[E]

An award winning Swedish television documentary, "The Gender War," visually demonstrated that Swedish politics have been influenced by a dangerous faction of radical feminists. The documentary had numerous stunning revelations about ROKS, a powerful Swedish organization that shelters abused women and is subsidized by the government. ROKS also happens to have been the leading lobbying group for criminalizing only the buyers of sex. They began pioneering that policy as early as 1987.[83]

"The Gender War" profiled the leaders of ROKS who were fairly open about their extreme views. The film's director took issue with their organization's positive review of *SCUM Manifesto*. To put it briefly, *SCUM Manifesto* ("Society for

---

[E] In fairness to the author of that proposal, Viggo Hansen, he has never stated that the law was intended as a gesture to humiliate all men. Instead, he cited medical reasons and the desire for more cleanliness in bathrooms. But, at a minimum, it is clearly overly authoritarian.

Cutting Up Men"), is a lengthy diatribe by a radical feminist, Valerie Solanas. Her work appeals only to the fringes of society and she would likely have remained as a relative unknown if not for being the person who shot Andy Warhol. To describe this book as anything other than hate speech is quite difficult, yet the director of ROKS unflinchingly supported such literature during this documentary.[F][84] But don't take my word for it. Her manifesto included several revealing anecdotes, such as, "To call a man an animal is to flatter him, he is a machine, a walking dildo…the male is, by his very nature, a leech, an emotional parasite and, therefore, not ethically entitled to live…"

Gunilla Ekberg was interviewed for this documentary because she was closely connected and mentored by the leaders of ROKS. As mentioned earlier, Ekburg was the former Swedish government special adviser on prostitution and trafficking who has been a preeminent international supporter of this model. However, Ekburg's interview came to an abrupt end when she stormed out because she didn't like the line of questioning. At the conclusion of the documentary, Ekberg threatened the film's director. When Ekberg thought she was no longer being recorded, she told the director, "Don't ever expect any help at a women's shelter (even if you were to become a victim of violence)." Ekberg warned her, "That's what happens when you betray us."[85] Generally speaking, you can learn a lot about the power structure of a country by examining how a government responds to its political scandals. In this case, despite this awkward exchange being broadcast all over Swedish television in 2005, Ekberg kept her lofty position in the Swedish government.

[F] ROKS is strongly influenced by a Swedish professor, Eva Lundgren, who received Swedish government grants for research into many feminist issues. For many years, Lundgren warned about a network of Swedish satanic pedophiles who perform sacrificial slaughters of young females. Despite thorough investigations by the Swedish police that have found no evidence of this kind of abuse, Lundgren still claims that they're abusing young women in widespread numbers. Lundgren also claims that these men have magic pills that can make a fetus spontaneously combust and erase the victims' memories of their abuses.

The "end demand" and anti-prostitution agenda within Sweden has resulted in some predictable results. The U.S. State Department has criticized the Swedish government's anti-trafficking efforts because they're "overwhelmingly oriented toward the combating of sex trafficking to the exclusion of the growing trend of individuals exploited for labor in the country."[86] On the other hand, in fairness to the Swedish government, their anti-trafficking efforts received a Tier I ranking by the U.S. State Department. Also, the Swedish National Police Board estimates there are 400-600 sex trafficking victims in their country, which is low by international standards.[87] And that seems to be a fair assessment, but Sweden wasn't considered a major destination for sex trafficking before the new laws were put in place.

The Swedish model clearly has flaws in combatting sex trafficking. In March of 2010, the Swedish National Police Board openly challenged the popular notion that sex trafficking had been reduced after the Swedish model went into effect. The press release stated, "Serious organized crime, including prostitution and trafficking, has increased in strength, power and complexity during the past decade. It constitutes a serious social problem in Sweden and organized crime makes large amounts of money from the exploitation and trafficking of people under slave-like conditions."[88] The National Police Board has also openly criticized the new policy because it is now more difficult for them to prosecute sex traffickers. They used to be able to get information from johns, but now the men are no longer willing to cooperate from fears of prosecution.[89] To sum up, the end demand or Swedish model fails in the most important aspect, which is preventing coercion and exploitation. Nonetheless, this policy has become the least controversial, or most "safe," model to support in an increasingly PC world. However, that wouldn't be the case if their most ardent activists would acknowledge insight from the people who are most directly affected by these laws.

5

"I remember talking to U.S. officials who were confused that there could be voluntary prostitution."

The United States squanders vast resources pursuing criminal prostitution cases between consenting adults. The same resources would be better utilized in the fight against sex trafficking and child prostitution. There are roughly 100,000 prostitution arrests every year, yet those cases result in discovering an astonishingly low number of sex trafficking victims.[90] In fact, only 459 confirmed sex trafficking victims were aided by law enforcement cases over a two and half year period (January 2008 to June 2010).[91]

Under the current prohibition model, the police could have a noticeable impact on sex trafficking simply by screening every prostitute for signs of human trafficking after an arrest. That should be a mandatory police procedure, but it rarely happens. A study conducted by the Sex Workers Project, "The Use of Raids to Fight Trafficking in Persons," firmly illustrates this point. They interviewed several sex workers, eleven of whom were trafficking victims. These women had all been previously arrested for prostitution (most of them on multiple occasions), but only one of them had actually been screened for trafficking by the local police. These oversights even occurred in cities that included human trafficking task forces.[92] The main reason behind such negligence has to do with the conflicting mission to crack down on this vice. "The local police agencies are familiar with traditional crimes, like prostitution, but human trafficking requires officers to look through a different filter at a situation they once thought they understood," offered one police officer.[93]

The stigma involved with prostitution clouds some obvious truths. Case in point, if an adult has sex with a minor, no matter if the minor is a prostitute, that act is statutory rape. "Under federal law, a child under 18 years old is considered a victim when there is child trafficking involved. On the local level, however, you are charged with child prostitution," says Tina Frundt, director of Courtney's House, a non-profit organization dedicated to aiding victims of sex trafficking.[94] Tina Frundt is an expert on this topic as she became of victim of sex trafficking at the age of 13 and was arrested for prostitution two years later. Ultimately, she received no rehabilitative services from the government after completing a one-year sentence in juvenile detention.[95] With the odds stacked against her, Tina Frundt eventually broke that cycle and went on to found her charitable organization. She did so despite the trauma of jail, abuse, and being labeled a teenage prostitute.

Human trafficking is an issue that can't be addressed solely by law enforcement. After all, many of these victims have obvious trust issues with the police. In fact, Alexandra Lutnick, author of *Domestic Minor Sex Trafficking: Beyond Victims and Villains*, has conducted numerous interviews with teen prostitutes and has found that they overwhelmingly report more abuse, both physical and sexual, at the hands of police officers, instead of from their clients, family, etc. Lutnick referenced an instance when a teen prostitute was arrested by an undercover officer. The girl was fondled by the officer in his car for roughly five minutes before he made the arrest. Afterward, she asked, "If I'm a minor and he's a police officer, isn't that not supposed to happen?"[96]

It's now time for a more victim-centered approach to this issue. And, on a positive note, Los Angeles became the first major city to pioneer a new way of addressing this matter. The County Sheriff, Jim McDonnell, ordered his deputies in 2015 to refrain from arresting underage prostitutes.[97] One year later, a scandal involving the Oakland Police Department made this particular issue a national news story. It unfolded after investigators discovered a suicide note left by one of their officers. He mentioned in the letter that he had been in a sexual relationship with a teenage prostitute. Three police chiefs subsequently resigned over the course of nine days as the details developed. The young girl referenced in the suicide note is known by a pseudonym, Celeste Guap. According to Guap, she had sex with 31 different cops in the San Francisco Bay Area. They served in a variety of offices (Richmond, Alameda County, Contra Costa County, San Francisco Police, Livermore, and Stockton).[98]

As a side note, this wasn't the Oakland Police Department's first run-in with corruption. Their department had been under federal oversight for thirteen years in relation to a prior scandal involving a group of officers who called themselves "the Rough Riders." The city was forced to pay a $10.5 million settlement because these officers had beaten, robbed, and planted evidence on 119 individuals. All of those victims were black, except for one.[99]

To get back to the subject at hand, our prostitution laws allowed these officers to extort this young woman for sex. During an interview, Celeste referred to those cops as "one less officer that's gonna arrest me."[100] In fact, some of them even provided her with specific information to avoid undercover sting operations. Most of these officers had sex with her after her 18th birthday, but that's merely the difference between extorting an adult or a minor. In fact, a few of them had sex with her while she was underage. And her age wasn't a secret because they nicknamed her, "Juve," which is short for juvenile.[101] There is a pending civil suit against the city, so more disturbing details are sure to follow.

Pedophilia is a crime that is usually punished quite harshly by the justice system, unless, of course, the defendant is wealthy and powerful. It would be difficult to find a man with a more impressive Rolodex than Jeffrey Epstein whose personal friends include Bill Clinton and Prince Harry. The Palm Beach Sheriff's Office began investigating this billionaire hedge fund mogul in 2005 because they received a tip from a mother who believed that her 14-year-old had been paid to have sex with him. Law enforcement eventually identified over 30 underage girls whom Epstein had paid for sex, but undoubtedly there were more young women who were never identified by the authorities.[102]

Epstein's investigation eventually became a federal matter because he had frequently engaged in this same pattern on his 72-acre, private island of the U.S. Virgin Islands, Little Saint James. Some of these underage victims were flown in from other countries against their will.[103] Suffice it to say, anyone other than Epstein would have been buried underneath the prison, but he had a modern-day dream team of defense attorneys, including Alan

Dershowitz and ironically...Ken Starr. Epstein faced a mandatory minimum sentence of 20 years, but a life sentence would have been more likely. However, federal prosecutors ultimately dropped their case and granted Epstein a confidential plea deal.[104]

He was only convicted of two state prostitution charges and the details of his 18-month sentence were even more staggering. He served 13 months and it took place in a vacant wing of the Palm Beach County Stockade. He was even allowed to return to his home for 16 hours each day as part of a work release program.[105] By the way, Donald Trump nominated the former U.S. Attorney who was responsible for this plea deal, Alexander Acosta, to be the Secretary of Labor.[106]

Epstein's case highlighted another aspect of human trafficking. He paid his staffers and a teenage girl to recruit teenagers for their sexual services. Victims of trafficking often view the people who introduced them into the sex trade as their friends. In other words, not all sex trafficking cases involve the Hollywood narrative with shackles and chains. That's partially why respected independent parties, such as the GAO, have criticized our federal government's primary approach for identifying victims of trafficking (both minors and adults). It comes by way of law enforcement raids. Notably, Luis CdeBaca, the human trafficking "Czar" has stressed the importance of a fresh approach. He advocates providing awareness training for the appropriate government personnel, such as police and child protective workers, who come into contact with people at risk for human trafficking. CdeBaca insists that we need to help victims "instead of, as all too often happens, arresting the women and prosecuting them for being prostitutes."[107]

Human trafficking raids still need to be conducted but in a very different manner. The police refer to these operations as "rescue missions," but in many cases it's difficult to discern the difference between sex trafficking raids and any other SWAT raid. One sex trafficking victim described how she tried to escape during one such raid but was knocked unconscious by an officer who struck her in the back of the head with a gun.[108]

You would assume that these victims are "set free" after being "rescued," but victims of sex trafficking are rounded up, cuffed, and detained as any other criminal suspect. They also can be subjected to hostile interrogations with threats of incarceration while in police custody.

These victims are usually coerced by the authorities without anyone noticing a hint of irony. Police officials typically attest that prostitution laws need to remain intact for legal leverage and, as a result, victims generally don't receive any assistance unless there is a trade-off. Thus, they remain in custody unless they're willing to testify against their exploiters.[109]

The kind of terror that a trafficking victim faces in the most extreme cases is downright unimaginable. One young woman told her story of running away from a group home where she had been violently and sexually abused. She was picked up by a pimp in Times Square at the age of 12 and by the age of 15 she had been beaten and raped on the job. She even sat in on a "family meeting" where her pimp forced her and the others to watch another girl tied to a chair be burned to death because she hid some of her money from the pimp.[110] It's unrealistic to expect anyone who has experienced such trauma to immediately cooperate with the authorities after an arrest. Shouldn't our government just offer help without strings attached?

We're all familiar with these kinds of stories, but our current model shows little mercy for someone who has been convicted of prostitution. This prohibition model only reinforces the authoritarian dynamic of the pimp/prostitute relationship when a pimp bails a woman out of jail. That same scenario also adds to a psychological condition known as Stockholm syndrome in which victims tend to develop feelings of sympathy for their captors as a coping mechanism.

There are a number of conflicting messages with the public perception of sex trafficking. American media outlets have thoroughly warned about this issue, including many exaggerated accounts. Nevertheless, there seems to be no country more obsessed with pimp culture than America. After all, these vermin receive vast representation from the music, television, and film industries. This disconnect between the perception and the reality must be, in part, formed as a rebellious response to our nation's prostitution laws. In fact, the term "pimp" is often affectionately used as an adjective to describe something as "cool" or synonymous with being a "ladies' man," rather than accurately defining someone who often beats, rapes, manipulates, and intimidates vulnerable women for all of their money.

It's clearly quite difficult to accurately assess the extent of this problem due to the nature of the crime. Unfortunately, several NGOs and governmental agencies have conflicts of interest that encourage them to exaggerate their estimates. By doing so, it opens the door to millions of dollars from the federal government. As a result, determining the extent of the sex trafficking problem has been highly contentious among polarizing opposition.

Highly-credible, independent groups, such as the GAO, have challenged the widely-cited estimates. In particular, the GAO took issue with one particular assessment by the State Department, a declaration that 600,000 to 800,000 persons are trafficked across international borders annually. In their report, the GAO exposed terrible flaws in the State Department's research. They stated, "The accuracy of the estimates is in doubt because of methodological weaknesses, gaps in data, and numerical discrepancies. For example, the U.S. government's estimate was developed by one person who did not document all his work" and the country data wasn't "available, reliable, or comparable."[111]

Is it harmful to cite exaggerated trafficking statistics even if that leads to more funding to fight this crime? Yes. There are unintended consequences from inflated sex trafficking statistics. First of all, overstated estimates force the government to overreact with their law enforcement resources, rather than to create comprehensive, proactive solutions. For instance, Congress passed the Trafficking Victims Protection Act of 2000 (TVPA) in a bipartisan manner in reaction to estimates that 50,000 human trafficking victims were entering the United States every year.[112] Instead of addressing the needs of the victims, the federal government dedicated its resources to police task forces because of the alarming trafficking estimates. Due to our prohibition model, the federal government doesn't adequately address the root causes of sex trafficking. As the saying goes, if all you have is a hammer, everything looks like a nail.

You would think that a bill titled, "The Trafficking Victims Protection Act" would prioritize the needs of actual trafficking victims, but that hasn't been the case. This is quite similar to the drug war. We'll spend billions of dollars each year to lock up drug dealers, but we don't have enough money budgeted for rehab or detox services. Several years have passed since the Trafficking Victims Protection Act (TVPA) went into effect, yet our government often still fails to provide even the most basic assistance for these victims, i.e. shelter and services. To demonstrate, after being let down by the federal government, a survivor of human trafficking in Florida needed to contact the Polaris Project (a human trafficking NGO) in order to find basic shelter. Consequently, the Polaris Project followed up with an investigation (twelve years after the TVPA was passed) and concluded that there was still a resounding shortage of housing shelters for these victims across the country.[113] Even the Department of Health and Human Services, which is responsible for assisting these people, has acknowledged this breakdown. Their report stated, "While much progress has been made since the passage of the TVPA and the availability of federal funding to provide effective services to victims of human trafficking, the evidence of this progress remains for the most part anecdotal in nature." [114]

America's strong anti-prostitution laws have created such a stigma that 30 states have yet to pass laws that remove prostitution arrests from the record of anyone documented as a sex trafficking victim.[115] That should be a non-controversial issue, but then again, in some cases, our government doesn't even follow its own advice. Trafficking victims in the U.S. face undue pressure from the police to testify against their abusers. Nevertheless, the U.S. State Department has expressly advised Germany to "consider granting residence permits for trafficking victims that are not reliant on the victim's willingness to testify at trial."[116] Unfortunately, in some cases, sex trafficking victims in America didn't receive the help they needed and were deported only to be re-trafficked.[117] On the other hand, Dutch authorities have a more progressive policy. They grant victims a three-month reflection period, in addition to immediate care and services, while they determine if they want to cooperate with law enforcement.[118]

It is counterintuitive to some people, but prostitution laws are actually inhibiting sex traffickers from being brought to justice; the primary reason being that prostitution laws naturally create a barrier between sex trafficking victims and the police. Hence, a study by the Department of Justice found that officers replied that "victims' distrust" of law enforcement was by far the most difficult challenge in their investigations, as opposed to a lack of resources, lack of training, etc.[119]

Prostitution laws are blocking the flow of vital information to the proper authorities. As of now, only thirty percent of criminal trafficking investigations are prompted by tips from concerned citizens.[120] Clearly, more people would feel free to contact the police with this kind of information if prostitution were decriminalized. You can't understate the value of community outreach with this particular issue. After all, there is a common misperception that the police provide the only means of escape for victims of sex trafficking. Look no further than the research provided by the Sex Workers Project after interviewing service providers for trafficked victims. They found that the majority of victims had not been identified as a result of police raids. Furthermore, a supervisor from one such organization said, "Ninety percent of our cases are not from raids, not even law enforcement identified."[121] Therefore, the police should rely less on intimidating potential witnesses and coordinate more with volunteer outreach workers. Additionally, some members of the sex industry would be a fantastic resource for combating sex trafficking, but our prohibition laws have negated that potentiality.

The federal government's efforts to address this issue have become somewhat of a boondoggle. Steven Wagner oversaw millions of dollars that were distributed to various anti-trafficking organizations while he served as the Director of the Human Trafficking Program for the Department of Health and Human Services. "Those funds were wasted," Wagner said. "Many of the organizations that received grants didn't really have to do anything. They were available to help victims. There weren't any victims."[122] To clarify, he didn't literally mean that there weren't *any* victims. Instead, the number was very low. Additionally, the former Inspector General of the Department of Justice, Glenn A. Fine, found that these organizations and task forces had significantly overstated the number of victims that they had helped by as much as 165%.[G][123]

We have to be careful to not paint the entire anti-trafficking industry with a broad brush because some of these organizations do great, innovative work. Some NGOs are providing seedy hotels in suspect areas with free bars of soap in which the packaging is labeled with the National Human Trafficking Hotline Number.[124] However, the federal money spigot tends to attract opportunists and Michael Horowitz, a religious leader and pioneer of the anti-trafficking movement, has lamented that many of these organizations have more cynical goals. "Now it's just one big federal entitlement program, and everybody is more worried about where they're going to get their next grant and whether they are going to get it," says Horowitz.[125] Hence, Norma Jean Almodovar (author of Cop to Call Girl) has popularized a term, "victim pimps," to describe the unethical individuals or groups involved in this movement.

Anne Elizabeth Moore, an investigative journalist, wrote a scalding report of the anti-trafficking industry for *Truthout*, "Special Report: Money and Lies in Anti-Human Trafficking NGOs." She found that the top 50 anti-trafficking organizations received $686 million in funding, not including their federal funds. Yet, those groups failed to provide adequate resources for these victims as a whole, despite receiving on average over $300,000 per person! "The U.S. anti-trafficking movement seems to be one of the few reliable growth areas in the United States' post-recession economy besides low-wage service work," wrote Moore.[126] Hmm…that sure sounds like a racket.

[G] There can also be a cultural mismatch with the recovery process. One example of this dynamic resulted in an ACLU lawsuit against the U.S. Conference of Catholic Bishops (USCCB). The USCCB received government grants to fund services for trafficking victims. However, due to religious beliefs, they denied victims from receiving information and access to condoms or abortions, even if the pregnancy was a result of a rape.

Many of these organizations are operated by former police officials, which helps to explain their penchant for cracking down on prostitution, rather than prioritizing preventive measures. Many of these organizations deflect criticism by highlighting their efforts to "raise awareness" for human trafficking. In fact, one public relations firm, Ketchum, received a federal government contract for $11 million for those services.[127]

Americans are well aware that sex trafficking takes place in this country, yet most are shocked to hear about labor trafficking crimes committed within our borders. Prostitution clearly has a disproportionately high rate of human trafficking, but there is a commonality among the industries with high rates of human trafficking -- criminal statutes and stigma. The industries that are notorious for labor trafficking (agriculture, restaurant, construction, domestic work, etc.) have a large workforce comprised of illegal immigrants and that makes them vulnerable to exploitation. All in all, the solutions to these problems are much more complicated than declaring a "war on trafficking." Just as a matter of perspective, there is understandably no call for a "Swedish model" or "end demand" with domestic work. In other words, no reasonable person thinks it should be a crime to hire a domestic worker even though that industry is disproportionately associated with human trafficking.

Sex trafficking is clearly a pervasive problem, but it represents a relatively small portion of the overall human trafficking issue. To be exact, the International Labor Organization estimated that sex trafficking victims comprise 22% of the world's forced laborers.[128] As you may recall, it was mentioned in the last chapter that the U.S. State Department criticized the Swedish government because their anti-trafficking efforts were "overwhelmingly oriented toward the combating of sex trafficking to the exclusion of the growing trend of individuals exploited for labor in the country."[129] However, our federal government makes the same mistake. To be exact, the DOJ brought 208 human trafficking cases to court in 2014 and 190 of those cases (91%) were for sex trafficking primarily, as opposed to labor trafficking. Granted, some cases involved both types of exploitation.[130]

Even the issue of modern day slavery can be highly politicized. There were two competing versions of the "Trafficking Victims Protection Act of 2000" bill. The late Sen. Paul Wellstone (D-MN) sponsored a bill that addressed all forms of human trafficking. To be brief, the Wellstone version was supported by Human Rights Watch and it didn't prioritize sex trafficking over any other type of human trafficking. The DOJ also supported this proposal and had direct input by making sure that there was specific language in the bill to include "force, fraud, or coercion."[131]

The other version, which was sponsored by Rep. Chris Smith (R-NJ) and Sen. Sam Brownback (R-KS), focused entirely on sex trafficking. Those Congressmen willfully ignored labor trafficking and a vocal group of conservative feminists and religious leaders were the prime supporters of that version of the bill.[H] Keep in mind, this was one year after the Swedish model went into effect and they lobbied for prostitution to automatically be considered human trafficking.[132] Despite pressure from these activists, the Wellstone version of the TVPA passed in a bipartisan manner by including all forms of human trafficking and it didn't include "voluntary prostitution."[133]

There were 1,362 victims of human trafficking identified in the seven years after Congress passed the TVPA.[134] That is certainly a worthy cause and a bona fide present danger, but the official figures have been significantly less than what was expected by various groups. Hence, a number of lawmakers compromised their integrity to appease political pressure. In other words, organized activists tried to "juke the stats" by lobbying to make voluntary prostitution a federal crime, equivalent to human trafficking. In response, some members of the House obliged their wishes and wrote an amendment to the TVPA in 2008 (H.R. 3887) to redefine all prostitution as trafficking, even in cases without any evidence of force, fraud, or coercion.

[H] To his credit, Rep. Chris Smith (R-NJ) eventually addressed labor trafficking. In 2011 he co-sponsored H.R. 2759: Business Transparency on Trafficking and Slavery Act. The bill died in committee, but it would have forced U.S.-based multinational corporations to publicly disclose proof that they're not using forced labor overseas.

Luckily, cooler heads prevailed. The DOJ strongly opposed this amendment by noting that their department had already funded numerous human trafficking task forces. The DOJ also asserted that a change in the definition of trafficking would be a drain on federal resources and "a diversion from Federal law enforcement's core anti-trafficking mission."[135] Likewise, the Fraternal Order of Police and the National District Attorneys Association publicly opposed H.R. 3887.[136] "There is something deeply wrong with our government when the answer to the desperate problem of human trafficking is to change the definition of the crime so we can claim we're doing something about it," said Melissa Ditmore, a health and human rights scholar who specializes in prostitution-related issues.[137] In the end, this fringe group of activists who conflate prostitution with human trafficking managed to get their pet project passed in the House, but it never made it out of committee in the Senate.

The trafficking issue is often addressed in very black and white terms, but the background of those in the sex industry often falls into a gray area. The debate surrounding this topic ultimately leads to examining the three "C's" of consent, i.e. choice, circumstance, and coercion. The "coercion" category applies to victims of sex trafficking. On the other hand, the individuals within the "choice" category represent the people with the most autonomy, the highest earners who truly have several career options but choose to work in the sex industry. However, the vast majority of sex workers fall into the "circumstance" category. It's difficult for them to work in a more conventional industry due to their background, i.e. lack of education, abuse, family history, drug addiction, etc. These people voluntarily made a choice to work in this business, yet several anti-trafficking activists like to describe them as trafficking victims.

Many of these activists like to say, "No one ever grew up dreaming of becoming a prostitute," to assert that every prostitute is automatically a victim of human trafficking. However, that really isn't an intellectually honest argument because you could substitute thousands of other jobs into that statement. Moreover, most people don't have careers that they truly cherish. It's a patronizing viewpoint to assume that people from poor or disadvantaged circumstances can't make their own choices in life. "In fact, the anti-trafficking lobby tends to reduce women to the level of children constituting them as innocent, easily duped girls. And this is actually quite strange if you consider the fact that the anti-trafficking world is made up, to a large extent, of people who describe themselves as feminists and as far as I know feminists have traditionally fought for women to be regarded as autonomous, free-thinking individuals, not as clueless victims," says Nathalie Rothschild, freelance journalist.[138]

The media fuels much of the panic surrounding sex trafficking by flooding the airwaves with assertions that prostitution and sex trafficking are rapidly increasing. However, that claim defies logic. It simply isn't true. Prostitution has drastically declined over the past decades and it is directly related to women's increasing economic and social power. Nonetheless, this type of tabloid journalism skews public opinion because prostitution is now more visible on the Internet, but that doesn't mean that more people are entering into the sex trade.

Robert Stutman, former head of the DEA's office in New York City, once described crack cocaine in the 1980s as the "hottest combat reporting story to come along since the end of the Vietnam War."[139] At the present time, sex trafficking has taken its place. For example, a broadcast by ABC's "Primetime" told of an Arizona teen who was kidnapped by pimps in front of her suburban home while wearing Sponge-Bob pajamas. Debbie Nathan, an independent journalist, decided to fact-check the story by consulting with the local police. It turned out that the young lady hadn't been kidnapped; she was a runaway who was ultimately brutalized by a pimp.[140] What happened to her was inhumane and deplorable, but, as is often the case, the media exaggerates and intensifies this genre for that extra tug on the heartstrings.

One of the more exploitive media representations of sex trafficking was a reality TV series, "8 Minutes," produced by A&E. This show was high on drama but offered very little reality. It was a disservice to the volunteers who are actually working to help people leave the prostitution industry. TV viewers seemingly witnessed a former cop turned preacher who posed as a john in hopes of "rescuing" these women from the industry. A&E's

camera crew surrounded the hotel and alerted this man when "the victim" was arriving.

This show was certainly compelling to watch, but there were, however, red flags that raised suspicions. For some odd reason, within moments of meeting this man in his room, these women began telling the horrible details from their personal lives rather than looking to conduct business. Ultimately, *Buzzfeed*, along with some other alternative media outlets, discovered that the show's producers had met the women before they went on camera. In other words, the program was staged. In fact, the producers paid the husband of one of the women to pose as her pimp and walk around the hotel in a menacing manner. In the end, these women decided to expose this charade because they felt that they had been exploited -- not by some pimps, but at the hands of the show's producers! The women weren't granted the basic courtesy of having their faces blurred out and that subsequently led to a first-time prostitution arrest for one of the cast members.

The negative publicity surrounding the show forced the producers to cancel "8 Minutes" after only a few episodes. In fact, they never made good on their promise to provide the women with various services, such as shelter, job assistance, and drug rehabilitation. As a matter of fact, the only support these women received came by way of various sex worker activists.[141]

The modern 24-hour news cycle has led several media outlets to favor speed over accuracy. Consequently, many of them casually cite estimates for human trafficking that are completely unrealistic. Often these farfetched "statistics" are derived from organizations that receive significant federal grants. You've probably heard various "experts" warn that staggering numbers of sex trafficking victims will come to the area of the Super Bowl. In the months leading up to Super Bowl 2014, an op-ed in *The Dallas Morning News* actually stated that "in Houston alone, about 300,000 sex trafficking cases are prosecuted each year."[142] Whoa, that would mean that *one out of every seven people* in Houston, TX is prosecuted for sex trafficking every year! Naturally, those figures were later retracted.

Likewise, some groups have claimed that as many as 38,000 under-aged victims and a total of 100,000 sex trafficking victims would be brought to the host city of the Super Bowl.[143] In other words, that's more people than can actually fit in the football stadium. This kind of yellow journalism defies reason, but so many people buy it hook, line, and sinker. That's why in 2011 an NFL spokesman, Brian McCarthy, adamantly struck down such a notion. He said, "This is urban legend that is pure pulp fiction. I would refer you to your local law enforcement officials."[144] Well, some journalists have followed up on that advice with sound fact-checking, but these reports haven't been widely disseminated.

Phoenix hosted the Super Bowl in 2008 and the city's police aggressively targeted prostitution arrests. However, Phoenix police spokesman, Sgt. Tommy Thompson, told reporters, "We did not notice an increase or anything out of the ordinary."[145] The following two Super Bowls had prostitution arrest numbers that fall in line with a typical major city. Tampa was the host in 2009 and a police spokeswoman said there were only 11 prostitution arrests for the entire week of the Super Bowl. In 2010 in Miami there were 13 prostitution arrests for the week of the Super Bowl.[146]

However, the media's call to arms eventually helped launch a much more coordinated and focused effort to curb prostitution in 2011. It included U.S. Immigration and Customs Enforcement (ICE), Homeland Security, and a task force of 17 local, state and federal agencies. Also, flight attendants and hotel staffers were trained to recognize signs of trafficking. Ultimately, there were 105 arrests for the metro area over the two week build up for the Super Bowl. Mind you, several of those arrests included men who tried to pay for sex with an undercover officer. Nonetheless, from those arrests, authorities were able to help identify eight victims of sex trafficking, by far the highest number discovered for a Super Bowl.[147] Obviously, it's a positive result whenever the government can free someone from sex slavery, but those arrest statistics point to more of a zero-tolerance roundup of all prostitutes in sight, rather than evidence of epidemic levels of human trafficking. In fact, the FBI's top agent in Dallas surmised, "In my opinion, the Super Bowl does not create a spike in those crimes (human trafficking)."[148]

The same type of multi-agency law enforcement effort was launched for the 2012 Super Bowl in Indianapolis. No stone was left unturned as there was an increased awareness effort with over 600 volunteers; nearly 3,400 people received human trafficking training, and close to 3,000 different educational materials were distributed throughout the city.[149] In short, over that two week period, there were 68 prostitution arrests that uncovered four sex trafficking victims.[150]

Dr. Annalee Lepp (Associate Professor, Chair, and Undergraduate Advisor of Women's Studies at the University of Victoria) has lectured at length that there isn't a link between trafficking and major sports events, such as the Olympics and the World Cup. She has pointed out what should be obvious to everyone. Independent researchers have found that large numbers of fans who travel to sporting events do so to simply *watch the games*.[151]

The World Cup took place in Germany in 2006 and some groups estimated that there would be 40,000 sex trafficking victims. "A huge sporting event like that creates a significant hazard. The number 40,000 is not outlandish in my mind, at all," affirmed Mark P. Lagon, former director of the State Department's Office to Monitor and Combat Trafficking in Persons during the George W. Bush administration.[152] However, the German police raided 71 brothels in Berlin but found only five victims of trafficking.[153]

Substantial evidence suggests that the demand for prostitution during the 2014 World Cup in Brazil actually *decreased*. A research group associated with the Federal University of Rio de Janeiro wrote, "The Observatory of Prostitution," and conducted over 2,000 hours of field research. They found that only 16 out of the 279 brothels in Rio de Janeiro had an increase in the number of sex workers and tourists before the World Cup. They reported, "All of the other (brothels) in the city are practically empty, with women complaining about the loss of clients and income during World Cup."[154]

There is a nearly universal rebuttal by activists from these anti-prostitution organizations after they are presented with evidence that some estimates are wildly exaggerated -- "One victim is one too many." Yes. Obviously, one victim is one too many, but brazen exaggerations are the enemy of sound policy making. Examining the extent of the problem isn't a denial of the problem; it is intended to reduce the damage from propaganda. Casual skeptics who haven't thoroughly researched this issue may believe that this has all been some media-contrived hoax, which isn't the case. There is a verifiable sex trafficking problem in the United States. The DOJ convicted 113 sex traffickers in 2013 alone and clearly there were more who went unpunished.[155] On the other hand, when parents hear an irresponsible claim, such as 300,000 American children are forced into sexual slavery every year, they will naturally assume that it would be irresponsible to allow their children to even leave the house.

Inflated human trafficking "statistics" set back the fundamental human rights of prostitutes. Human trafficking propaganda often serves as the justification for increasing penalties for consensual adult prostitution, domestically and internationally. That's why Nikki Adams from the English Collective of Prostitutes confronted a former member of the British Parliament, Denis McShane, on the *BBC* program *Newsnight*. He had cited estimates that 25,000 women were trafficked into the U.K. every year. As a result, the British Parliament expanded their trafficking laws similarly to Sweden and those changes now deter independent prostitutes from working with their peers for safety reasons. "I thought that you were coming on the program to apologize because the claim is so clearly ludicrous and this *Guardian* article does begin to uncover the truth to what is actually going on," said Nikki Adams.[156]

Adams referenced a fact-finding report in 2009 by *The Guardian* in London, which detailed the results from the most thorough sex trafficking investigation in the history of the U.K. Fifty-five different police forces, along with some NGO's, coordinated in a six-month sex trafficking crackdown known as "Operation Pentameter Two." They raided 822 brothels, homes, and massage parlors across the U.K. and it resulted in 406 arrests. However, as is typical with most law enforcement operations, they like to focus on arrest figures, rather than divulging in great detail the type of arrests that were actually made. Operation Pentameter resulted in a high number of arrests, but most of them were for drug charges. Ultimately, fifteen people were convicted as sex traffickers because it's illegal in the U.K. to transport a person for the purpose of prostitution, even if that person is a willing worker. However, in the end, not a single person was convicted for the actual definition of trafficking, which must entail force, fraud, or coercion. To sum up, this report from *The Guardian* didn't deny that trafficking exists, but it clearly stated that the extent of the problem had been exceedingly overstated.[157]

The U.S. has been down this road before with the White Slave Panic. Above all, what's happening now is also eerily similar to the buildup of the drug war. Career-minded politicians have found an apt substitute for the drug war by using the issue of human trafficking to anoint themselves as "tough on crime." Hence, forty-two states and Washington D.C. passed 236 of these types of bills in 2014 to 2015 alone![158]

These new laws are typically marketed as "anti-trafficking," but they can be more accurately described as tougher prostitution laws. What happened in Colorado with SB 85 is fairly typical. The bill passed without a single word of formal debate on the floor because SB 85 was described as an anti-trafficking effort. This "end demand" legislation increased the fines for the buyers of sex to a minimum of $2,500 and a maximum of $5,000. However, distressingly, none of those funds are forwarded to the victims of trafficking. Instead, every dollar goes to a fund for the police to conduct more prostitution investigations.[159]

A North Dakota blogger, Rob Port of SayAnythingBlog.com, wrote a post supporting legalized prostitution after his home state had passed similar "anti-trafficking" or "end demand" legislation. One of the State Attorneys contacted him by email the next day and provided the exact language from existing prostitution laws and compared it to the new "human trafficking law." They were quite similar except for the fact that the new trafficking bill "converted a number of routine prostitution cases to Human Trafficking Class A Felonies." The State Attorney also noted that it is "trendy" for politicians to write human trafficking proposals even though these laws have been on the books for decades. "It just didn't have the same scary headline grabbing name of 'Human Trafficking.'"[160]

Alaska caved in to the political pressure and passed some absurd sex trafficking laws in 2012 that removed "force, manipulation, and coercion" from the definition. As a result, the police were able to make a number of arrests due to the wider reach of the law, but there were no real, tangible results. After two years, there wasn't a single arrest for sex trafficking in which there were any of those three factors involved. Just like in Sweden, the expanded definition of trafficking meant that prostitutes were discouraged from common sense safety measures, such as working together in groups, because that could lead to sex trafficking charges. In fact, some Alaskan women have been accused of "trafficking" themselves.[161] In essence, the state artificially manufactured a new social problem and appeased the prison industrial complex in the process.

Tara Burns of the University of Alaska has conducted the most thorough analysis of the new policy and she concluded, "In none of the documents I've examined since the law's inception has it been used to benefit a victim."[162] She found that prostitutes are still terrified of contacting the police if they are victims of a crime. In fact, according to Burns' survey, the police only filed reports 20% of the time in which a prostitute reported being the victim of coercion; the others were either threatened with arrest or arrested.[163]

"I really never thought that in my career, opposing people who exploit other people, I would actually be advocating against a (human trafficking) law, but I am," said John Vanek, former head of the San Jose Police Department's human trafficking unit.[164] Well-intentioned California voters passed Prop 35 in 2012 in a widely bipartisan manner even though credible authorities, such as John Vanek, opposed the bill. In particular, his chief complaint was that the fines from these arrests benefit the police and anti-trafficking NGOs, instead of those funds assisting the actual victims through restitution.[165] He acknowledges that sex trafficking laws are usually "feel good" bills for voters, but warns that these proposals shouldn't be rubber stamped because they need to be in "the best interests of the victim."[166]

California's Prop 35 increased the penalties for sex trafficking, but that bill also included overly broad, expansive, and ambiguous language in which virtually anyone voluntarily working in the sex industry could be prosecuted as a trafficker and sex offender. These laws have created the same scenarios as in Sweden in which the government tears sex workers apart from their families. As noted by Maxine Doogan, the founder of ESPLERP (the group challenging prostitution in the federal courts of California), her son could technically be convicted as a human trafficker because he benefits from her wages.[167]

Prostitution is ubiquitous in several regions of the world (particularly poor countries) and the main culprit is economics, not criminal traffickers. This complex issue has been oversimplified for too long and that has enabled our State Department to pressure other countries (often reliant on U.S. foreign aid) into changing their prostitution laws. Our government needs to be cautious when making such recommendations because not every nation has a strong human rights record or a visible rule of law. In many cases, these new anti-prostitution laws are empowering already corrupt police forces. In particular, Cambodia passed tougher anti-trafficking laws in 2008 due to pressure from the U.S State Department. In a brave act, a group of 200 Cambodian sex workers publicly organized chanting, "Save us from our saviors."[168] They were protesting because they had been abused en masse by the police after the new laws were passed.[169]

It should have been patently obvious that the Cambodian police wouldn't suddenly relish their newfound "rescuer" role as their pattern of abuse had been detailed in a prior report by USAID. Two years earlier, one thousand Cambodian sex workers participated in that survey and roughly half of them reported being beaten and gang-raped by police officers.[170] Human Rights Watch conducted a thorough follow-up investigation in 2010 and found little evidence that the new laws had an impact on trafficking. Instead, *every* sex worker that they interviewed reported having been forced to pay a bribe to a police officer. Also, Human Rights Watch documented that police officers were physically abusing sex workers upon detention and extorting them for free sex.[171]

Ben Svasti is the executive director of a Thai organization that coordinates services for trafficking victims, TRAFCORD. He says, "I remember talking to U.S. officials who were confused that there could be voluntary prostitution."[172] Again, many members of faith-based NGOs don't acknowledge the traditional definition of trafficking, which includes force, fraud, or coercion. That's concerning because some of these organizations are funded by our government and they coordinate prostitution raids with local law enforcement agencies worldwide.

Noy Thrupkaew of *The Nation* extensively investigated sex trafficking throughout Southeast Asia and she warns against the potential "collateral damage" from overly aggressive anti-prostitution efforts. She acknowledges that law enforcement is a necessary part of combating human trafficking and has saved many victims, but there needs to be a distinction between those who chose to participate in this industry and those who don't. Thrupkaew reported about a particular "rescue" facility in Thailand, where women were held against their will after a police raid. Some of the detainees tied sheets together to climb out of an upper story window in order to make their escape. Another woman pushed out an air conditioning unit and jumped out the window. Another tried to burn down the building.[173]

These kinds of reports aren't unique and various international organizations have recognized the kinds of abuses that sex workers face with rescue missions. The World Health Organization once wrote that sex workers in Indonesia and India were being physically assaulted during these raids and "coerced into having sex by corrupt police officials in exchange for their release."[174] Likewise, a report, "Sex Work and the Law in Asia and the Pacific," by the United Nations Development Programme also documented that several police "rescue" missions have forced women involuntarily into "rehabilitation" or "re-education" facilities. These institutions often appear just like prisons with barbed wire fences. This report also noted that these women are often subject to abuse in these facilities and exploited for cheap or free labor, particularly in China, India, Sri Lanka, and Myanmar.[175] In other words, they're forced from one form of trafficking, sex trafficking, to a less stigmatized one, labor trafficking.

Anne Elizabeth Moore, an investigative journalist (she was mentioned earlier for her work with exposing the conflicts of interest in anti-human trafficking funding), has detailed this same scenario in Cambodia. She spent several years there and found that some of the anti-trafficking NGOs exploited the local women. After they were "rescued," these NGOs put these women to work in sweatshop garment factories. On top of that, Moore revealed that these women are paid below market value. That's particularly appalling as many of them worked in the sex trade to escape the low pay and poor treatment in garment factories, Cambodia's primary industry for female workers.[176]

Thomas Fuller of *The New York Times* detailed the "misery tourism" in the orphanages of Cambodia in which children are coached to look pitiful when potential donors visit. Donors are obviously well-intentioned, but a government study found that 77% of the children in these orphanages aren't orphans. The orphanages often recruit and coerce parents to give up their children; meanwhile, many of the orphanages are solely focused on raising money. Consequently, the children live in deplorable conditions and sexual abuse is fairly common, yet overlooked.[177]

Fuller's investigation seemed to be sparked by Simon Marks' report for *Newsweek*, "Somaly Mam: The Holy Saint (and Sinner) of Sex Trafficking," which discredited one of the most highly-regarded activists in the anti-trafficking movement. According to Somaly Mam's bestselling book, she was forced as a child by her grandfather to work in a brothel for roughly a decade. Her story helped raise millions of dollars for the cause, earned her the adoration of numerous A-list Hollywood celebrities, in addition to accolades such as one of *Time Magazine*'s 100 most influential people.

Newsweek looked into her background and found her story to be fraudulent. Several of her classmates and teachers contradicted her claim that she was sold into sexual slavery. In addition, her ex-husband Pierre Legros insisted that Somaly Mam had, in fact, been a prostitute as a young adult when they first met in 1991, but not a victim of human trafficking. According to Legros, she was working independently of her own free will in various nightclubs, as opposed to the torturous conditions of the brothel that she described in her book.[178]

Somaly Mam and her ex-husband, Pierre Legros, co-founded their organization, AFESIP, in 1994. She, being the more photogenic and naturally charismatic, was the obvious choice to become the face of their charity. In the process, she helped raise millions of dollars, but too many of Mam's media appearances have turned out to be complete hoaxes. For instance, she once claimed that a gang of sex traffickers abducted her daughter as a form of retribution due to the impact her organization had on their bottom line. They even sent a video of her daughter being gang raped, according to Somaly Mam. However, her ex-husband and an official from their charity assert that her account was entirely bunk. The young girl was never kidnapped nor assaulted, she simply ran away with her boyfriend.[179]

Likewise, two of the young women from Mam's organization who were widely profiled in the international press later admitted that their personalized, gut-wrenching tales of sex slavery were entirely fabricated. One of the women, Long Pross, is missing an eye. That added credibility to her story in which she told reporters that a pimp had poked her eye out. In actuality, that was a lie. She had her eye surgically removed at age 13 because of a malignant tumor. Also, she had never been part of the sex industry. Furthermore, another woman whom Somaly Mam had trotted out for the media, Meas Ratha, admitted that her tale of sex slavery was also a complete concoction. In fact, Ratha had rehearsed her story under the supervision of Mam. She actually had to audition for Mam, along with a group of other girls.[180]

Despite these kinds of revelations, many have defended Somaly Mam because her lies benefitted a good cause, right? Well, yes and no. She certainly helped coordinate some brothel raids and provided a number of young women with food and shelter. Though, many of the people closest to Mam, including workers from her organization, say that she abused her power. They described being threatened by Mam in the workplace and even accused her of forcing the trafficking victims in her charity to perform her personal chores.[181] In fact, as millions of dollars were pouring into her charity, various insiders say that she purposely understaffed and underequipped her organization. Moreover, some staff members claimed that she flagrantly misappropriated funds, including purchasing various properties for herself. In the end, Somaly Mam resigned from her organization in 2014 in response to the *Newsweek* article, but she started a new group one year later with the backing of a New York-based PR firm.[182] Obviously, Somaly Mam isn't the emblematic anti-trafficking crusader as portrayed in the media, but these kinds of abuses can occur when this issue is oversimplified and sensationalized.

Another name, Chong Kim, falls into this category. Her tale of survival as a teenage sex slave was the basis behind the movie, *Eden (Abduction of Eden)*. This award-winning, critically-acclaimed film was "based on a true story." The graphic portrayal of her life story included a scene in which she was abducted in Dallas, TX by Russian mobsters and then transported to a Las Vegas warehouse.

Chong Kim made her way around the talk-show circuit while receiving personal accolades. She captivated listeners with several horrific details, including an accusation that one of her traffickers was a consultant with the FBI.[183] She also began working to raise funds for various sex-trafficking charities, including one called Breaking Out. The founder of Breaking Out, James Barnes, came to an ethical crossroad after meeting Chong Kim because he had many suspicions about the authenticity of her backstory. It clearly would have been financially advantageous to bury those thoughts. Undoubtedly, he was essentially handed a winning lottery ticket and could have ridden the gravy train from the donations that were sure to follow. However, he listened to his instincts, followed up on his suspicions, and concluded that her backstory was a hoax. That included a story about why she now walks with a cane. She claimed that her traffickers had inflicted that injury, but Barnes found that she had developed a debilitating condition at the age of seven. To make matters worse, Barnes uncovered that Kim had been convicted a few years earlier for theft-by-swindle. In this case, Kim used her celebrity status as "sex slavery survivor" to persuade an actual victim of human trafficking to hand over her life savings![184]

Like Somaly Mam, this kind of exposure hasn't ruined her career. She continues to work as a consultant and public speaker. Both women have survived their scandals and resurrected their careers in the same field. In what other industry is that possible? As always, their supporters will defend them with the notion that they're "raising awareness" about sex trafficking, but those efforts are to the detriment of the less-examined and more widespread issue of labor trafficking.

The vast majority of Americans don't realize that many of the foods we eat and the goods we purchase are derived from forced labor, both domestic and abroad. For one thing, Thailand is the world's largest exporter of shrimp, but it's well-documented that a significant percentage, thousands of those fishermen, are victims of human trafficking.[185] Likewise, many of our electronic devices are dependent on an obscure mineral, coltan. Unfortunately, a large percentage of coltan exports come from Central African and South American nations where warlords and paramilitary groups terrorize and force laborers against their will.[186] In short, there are several seemingly innocuous goods and services that are immersed in vast human suffering.

There is a divide between the U.S. federal government's anti-trafficking rhetoric and its actions. For starters, our government should no longer provide diplomatic immunity to foreign diplomats who have violated human trafficking laws while visiting the U.S. Sure, it sounds like something from the plot of Lethal Weapon II, but these are real life occurrences. Typically, these cases involve domestic workers who've been forced to work excessive hours for pennies on the dollar of their promised wages, in addition to threats of violence if they leave the residence. This is by no means a widespread issue, but the fact that it has *ever* been allowed is a travesty. Traver Riggins with the International Consortium of Investigative Journalists found that the U.S. State Department files a report every year covering all of the cases that have invoked diplomatic immunity, but those reports remain classified. Therefore, we don't know the exact extent of this problem.[187]

George W. Bush announced a "zero tolerance" policy for human trafficking during a United Nations speech in 2003. He urged for more nations to join in the fight against human trafficking, but there was a much bigger issue that needed to be addressed. The U.N. officially opposes human trafficking, but there is a heartbreaking and repetitive theme in which U.N. peacekeeping troops have been involved in numerous forms of sexual exploitation such as rape, child prostitution, and human trafficking. For good reason, Sen. Bob Corker (R-TN) once remarked that he would be on the first plane back home to protect his wife and kids if the U.N. troops were in his neighborhood.[188]

Several war-torn and impoverished nations have been the setting for such cruelties, including Bosnia, Mozambique, Sudan, Haiti, Liberia, Burundi, East Timor, the Democratic Republic of the Congo, Kosovo, Sierra Leone, Guinea, Cambodia, and the Ivory Coast.[189] Worst of all, these violent attacks at the hands of U.N. peacekeepers have often been swept under the rug with very few repercussions. A U.S. ambassador to the U.N., Isobel Coleman, once read part of an internal U.N. report to the Senate Foreign Relations Committee. In particular, she mentioned that some children described their abuses as "rape disguised as prostitution." Peacekeeping troops raped the girls but provided them afterward with small amounts of money or rations of food "to give the rape the appearance of a consensual transaction."[190] That report dates back to 2005, but few U.N. leaders have been willing to hold their soldiers accountable. In fact, a whistleblower who worked in the United Nations' human rights office leaked documents detailing similar abuses to the press to no avail. No actions were taken and that whistleblower resigned from his position in disgust.[191] As Americans, we can't look the other way and deny any responsibility. By all means, the U.S. government is the top financial contributor to U.N. peacekeeping missions.

Obviously, George W. Bush wasn't aware of the human trafficking atrocities committed by our government officials when he made his U.N. speech. The U.S. corporate media rarely covers such stories, but some of the worst offenders have worked as defense contractors. This is a group deeply embedded with the political power structure and they're part of a more prominent issue, the vast corruption enmeshed within the Pentagon.

We're going to veer slightly off-topic for a moment and loop back, but this detour will unveil more about the issue of human trafficking. Former Rep. Cynthia McKinney (D-GA) once interrogated Donald Rumsfeld during a House Armed Service Committee meeting. She wanted to know if there had been any progress with the $2.3 trillion that was missing from the Pentagon accounting records![192]

That's the moment when Donald Rumsfeld's life had gone full circle. Rumsfeld, as an Illinois Representative, had been one of the most outspoken members of Congress in response to the profiteering of the Vietnam War. In 1966 he referred to the no-bid contracts that companies like Brown and Root (a future subsidiary of Halliburton) received as "illegal by statute." He also urged for investigations into the company's political contributions to the Johnson administration. Nonetheless, over the decades, Brown and Root's multi-million dollar, no-bid contracts swelled into multi-billion, no-bid contracts for Halliburton by the time of the Iraq War. Albeit, this time around, Rumsfeld served as the most notable cheerleader for privatizing as many military functions as possible to these kinds of defense contractors.[193]

Let's return to Rumsfeld's testimony in 2005. In case you're wondering, no, that $2.3 trillion figure isn't a misprint. That is a mind-boggling amount of money and that just so happens to be the most serious accounting scandal in the history of the world, over 50 times the size of the Bernie Madoff scandal. Yet, not one person involved with this fraud has been charged with a crime! Worst of all, a report by *Reuters* in 2013 found that nothing has changed. Pentagon staffers are routinely pressured to falsify figures to cover for any missing funds.[194] Meanwhile, the Pentagon has received $8.5 trillion since 1996, the first year in which all government agencies were required to submit to audits. Notwithstanding, none of that money has been audited by an independent party, thereby making the Pentagon the only federal government agency that has refused to allow outside audits![195] It's difficult to find more incontrovertible evidence to show the galling lack of accountability for the military industrial complex, but the human trafficking aspect may just do so.

During that same House Committee hearing, Rep. Cynthia McKinney also confronted Rumsfeld about DynCorp. To be brief, DynCorp is a privately-run defense contractor with tremendous political connections, including executives and board members who served in the Reagan and Clinton administrations. As a reminder, DynCorp was mentioned in *The Drug War: A Trillion Dollar Con Game*. This company is the top recipient of anti-drug contracts in Latin America to the tune of billions of dollars and has earned a fortune from the wars in Iraq and Afghanistan.

Putting aside DynCorp's history of overbilling the government, Rep. McKinney asked Rumsfeld why DynCorp has continued to receive contracts even though the company had been involved with human trafficking.[196] After all, don't we have a "zero tolerance" policy? He answered, "I'm advised…that it was not the corporation that was engaged in the activities you characterized, but I'm told it was an employee of the corporation and it was some years ago in the Balkans that that took place."[197] To clarify, the company's executives weren't directly involved with trafficking, but they decided to figuratively kill the messenger once they were made aware of their employees' heinous crimes.

A couple of DynCorp employees, Ben Johnston and Kathryn Bolkovac, blew the whistle by informing their supervisors that some of their co-workers were actively trafficking minors into sexual slavery. The whistleblowers reported that their coworkers were so audacious about their activities that they would brag about where to find "really nice twelve-to-fifteen year olds" and they purchased them outright from various brothels.[198] They actually imported the girls into Bosnia with help from the Serbian mafia. In fact, one of the supervisors had a homemade video in which he filmed himself raping multiple women whom he had purchased beforehand. He even circulated that video among his coworkers.[199]

After an Army CID investigation, DynCorp fired the employees who were involved in this inhumane activity. The corporation never faced any penalties, nor were any of their employees prosecuted in the U.S.[200] In their defense, you could say that a corporation shouldn't be punished for the actions of a few employees, but that doesn't hold water because the company tried to cover up these horrific crimes. Ultimately, those who faced the most severe consequences from this scandal were, in fact, the *whistleblowers themselves*, who were wrongfully fired for their honorable actions.

Regardless of what happened in Bosnia, DynCorp hasn't forfeited their lucrative contracts, particularly those involving the drug war. In fact, the company was contracted to protect Hamid Karzai in Afghanistan, along with other high Afghan government officials. However, WikiLeaks later released reports detailing that DynCorp employees hired "dancing boys" or "bacha boys" (child prostitutes) for various Afghan officials. Prior reports had surfaced that DynCorp had been transporting prostitutes from Kuwait to Baghdad using armored vehicles. Those reports only added to revelations that some DynCorp employees were killed while using non-armored vehicles to perform dangerous duties.[201]

This issue of "bacha boys" made national headlines in 2015 when a Green Beret, Sgt. Charles Martland, was discharged after beating up an Afghan militia commander who had a boy chained to his bed as a sex slave. Martland, along with other soldiers who have encountered similar situations, was told by his commanding officer to ignore these abuses. In many cases, the local Afghan police or militia leaders are guilty of this reprehensible crime. It is similar to the issue of drug trafficking in which our government overlooks the crimes of our military allies. The Pentagon has denied that soldiers are instructed to overlook these abuses, but *The New York Times* quoted U.S. Army Colonial Brian Tribus who acknowledged that U.S. troops were not required to report such crimes.[202] Thankfully, Sgt. Charles Martland was reinstated in 2016, but this issue of "bacha boys" remains visible in Afghan culture.[203]

Blackwater is another highly-compensated military contractor with vast political connections and the company has been notorious for its scandals as well. For instance, a State Department official received a death threat by a manager of Blackwater while investigating the company in 2007. He was reportedly told that he could be killed and "no one could or would do anything about it as (they) were in Iraq." In the end, the investigation was discontinued and Blackwater remains as a favored contractor.[204]

Some ex-employees of Blackwater have alleged that workers from their company openly engaged in child prostitution. In addition, they claim that Blackwater kept a Filipino prostitute on the company payroll and even billed the government for her services. Allegedly her salary was categorized as "Morale Welfare Recreation" expenses.[205] Nonetheless, Blackwater continues to receive generous no-bid contracts for the drug war from the Pentagon.[206]

To sum up, the U.S. government hasn't truly taken a hard stance to prevent sex trafficking, particularly when it involves corporations with deep pockets. Meanwhile, there is an astonishing number of labor trafficking victims who have worked on America's military bases worldwide. Believe it or not, our government has enabled this kind of abuse. Most likely you've never heard of these cases because this aspect of human trafficking is rarely covered by the U.S media. Therefore, we need to explore why this is happening.

First, our military now needs to outsource, via private contractors, a variety of non-warfare work functions, such as food services, because enlistment numbers have dwindled over the years. Generally speaking, these private contracting companies hire migrant laborers from various third world nations (as many as 70,000 in 2011) to staff our military bases abroad.[207] With so many of these services being outsourced, there is much less governmental oversight and that has led to widespread accounts of human trafficking.

"This is the only form of human trafficking where the taxpayer directly pays the human trafficker," says Sam McCahon, a former federal prosecutor who is now the foremost whistleblower confronting this issue.[208] To fulfill their staffing needs, our nation's defense contractors often subcontract to foreign companies that deal directly with third-party recruiters or agents from various third world countries. Unfortunately, these "agents" are often nothing other than human traffickers who have posed as legitimate business people. They lure desperate, unsuspecting laborers with a web of lies, particularly promises of lucrative jobs. Remarkably, our military is intent upon "spreading democracy" across the world, but it doesn't thoroughly examine whether its third-party workers are being deprived of their human rights. Many of these people have been forced into this work through debt bondage, coercion, threats, and other abuses.

These victims usually enter into a labor agreement voluntarily, but that is about all that is truly voluntary. Everything from then on is a nightmare. Typically, the workers had to pay massive upfront fees of thousands of dollars to the agent in order to get the job. However, these people usually don't have that kind of money so the agent lends it to them at loan shark rates. However, the traffickers only pay these workers a portion of their promised wages. In many cases, they are warehoused for months at a time with no wages in deplorable conditions while their debt continues to mount. Furthermore, the workers have had their identification confiscated, thereby stripping their means for an escape. Ultimately, they're transported to war-torn countries where they never agreed to go. It's very similar to the type of indentured servitude that we're all familiar with from our history textbooks.[209]

One well-documented case involved a group of thirteen men from Nepal who were deceived into this type of hellish agreement. They were told they would be working in luxury hotels in the peaceful Middle Eastern nation of Jordan. However, upon arrival they were confined in a dark room, threatened, told that they would only receive a percentage of their promised pay rate, and their passports were stolen. They were later transported from Jordan, against their will, into Iraq to work for Kellogg, Brown, and Root (KBR), a former subsidiary of Halliburton. Ultimately, twelve of the men were captured en route by terrorists and beheaded publicly. The only remaining man from their group managed to avoid being captured by the terrorists, but he was still brought to an army base in Iraq where he worked for 15 months before returning home.[210]

This wasn't an isolated incident for KBR. In another example, KBR subcontracted with a company, Najlaa International Catering Services, which lured close to 1,000 Southeast Asians to Iraq with promises of high pay and then confined them in warehouses with atrocious living conditions, no work, and no pay for months at a time. To put it another way, these people were stored like commercial goods until they could be further exploited for their labor. In the aftermath, some journalists discovered, through Freedom of Information Act requests, that the U.S. government was aware of those conditions. Outrageously, KBR continues to receive government contracts.[211]

The U.S. embassy in Iraq symbolizes America's military might and it's the largest embassy in the world (104-acre compound), but credible reports demonstrate that the facility was also built with trafficked labor.[212] In fact, an American whistleblower testified before Congress that he witnessed a group of those workers held at gunpoint before their flight to Iraq.[213] Those Filipino workers had agreed to work in Dubai, but they were physically abused, threatened, and were forced to work in Iraq under inhumane living and working conditions. Meanwhile, the primary company responsible for the construction of the embassy, First Kuwaiti General Trading & Contracting, profited handsomely to the tune of a $592 million contract without facing any legal repercussions.[214]

"Nobody's ever disputed that this (human trafficking) is going on. Everyone knows it's happening. The thing is no one is taking responsibility to stop it," says Sam McCahon.[215] Naturally, those words spark the obvious questions such as, "Can this be prevented?" and "What are the causes?" Yes, many of these labor trafficking abuses could be prevented, but, as is often the case, too many companies are solely focused on the bottom line. In fact, an executive from a company that specializes in these types of contracts replied, "It's not our problem," when questioned by Sam McCahon about the measures they're taking to eliminate human trafficking by their subcontractors.[216]

It would all be so simple if the government held its private contractors accountable. President Obama signed an executive order in 2012 that proclaimed "zero tolerance" for companies that are guilty of such crimes, but actions speak louder than words.[217] History has proven that our leaders refuse to hold defense contractors accountable for fraud, waste, abuse, etc. There is a serious lack of leadership if $2.3 trillion can go missing from the Pentagon's budget and no criminal charges have been filed, nor has anyone been fired. There's only one explanation for such an outrageous scam against the taxpayers -- the revolving door between the Pentagon and the private sector. These private companies are notorious for offering lucrative positions to high-level government officials (particularly ex-generals) and receiving sweetheart deals in return.

On the bright side, we can remove some of the financial incentives that indirectly lead to this particular form of human trafficking. We must make it more profitable for our defense contractors to hire their workers directly, rather than use subcontractors. The reason being that these companies gain plausible deniability in regard to labor issues for every subcontractor that they use. According to Sam McCahon, one way to prevent defense contractors from using subcontractors is to no longer offer "cost-plus" contracts.[218]

Cost-plus contracts actually provide an incentive for these companies to rack up as many expenses as possible. This is one helluva racket. The government pays these companies a fixed percentage profit above all of their expenditures. In other words, these contractors would much rather make a 4% fee on $100,000 of expenses as opposed to $10,000. Hence, working on a cost-plus basis prompts contractors to use several subcontractors because those companies charge fees for their services, thus adding more costs. If you've seen the documentary *Iraq for Sale: The War Profiteers* then you're familiar with the concept. That film contains footage of Halliburton employees intentionally setting new $80,000 trucks on fire after a tire went flat. They did so because it was much more profitable to bill the government for a new truck rather than a tire.[219]

All in all, this military outsourcing system has wasted $15 billion for U.S. taxpayers, according to Sam McCahon.[220] Bringing attention to this particular issue is our best course of action. After all, the exploitation and enslavement of thousands of third-world workers never captured the hearts and minds of our journalists. However, combining those facts with the multi-billion dollar price tag may just be the ticket to kick-start our elected officials into action.

To state the obvious, the "zero tolerance" rhetoric on the part of the U.S. government with human trafficking has proven to be an unofficial policy of zero accountability.[221] Very few politicians have tried to prevent U.S.-based multinational corporations from profiting with modern-day slave labor overseas. In fact, official audits have uncovered that the U.S. government exercises less oversight than most American retailers when outsourcing with foreign countries! For instance, more than $1.5 billion a year is spent by our government on clothing made in foreign factories, which often have sweat shop conditions. For all of the "zero tolerance" rhetoric, there is no federal law to block the government from buying clothes produced overseas under unsafe or abusive conditions.

A standout piece by *The New York Times*, "U.S. Flouts Its Own Advice in Procuring Overseas Clothing," revealed the atrocious conditions these factory workers are faced with. Some factories had child labor, physical abuse, and illegal pay cuts. There were even cameras monitoring inside the bathrooms. Furthermore, employees felt compelled to soil themselves rather than stop working due to the restrictions on bathroom breaks. Most important, the work conditions in some factories were alarmingly hazardous and led to some workers' deaths.[222] Sure, our government has a severe debt problem, but this isn't the solution. Our politicians always promise to find inventive ways to bring manufacturing jobs back to the U.S., but somehow they haven't addressed this issue?!?

To sum up, this is an incredibly important, yet complex issue. The average American has been completely misled. And to compound the issue, modern-day slavery attracts opportunists within the media, government, and charitable organizations. What we need is sound, compassionate policies intent upon maximizing human rights to overcome these atrocities, not overly simplistic, politically-correct pandering to uninformed voters.

6

"The feminist analysis of prostitution says that men are using money as power over women. I'd say yes that's all the men have. The money is a confession of weakness."

Prostitution is often referred to as a feminist issue even though there isn't a clear consensus within the feminist community. In fact, the viewpoints are quite polarizing. "When the sex war is won prostitutes should be shot as collaborators for their terrible betrayal of all women," says Julie Burchill.[1] To the contrary, Nikki Roberts insists, "The feminist movement has failed the prostitute, and failed her badly."[2] Abolishing prostitution was the primary objective during the Progressive Era, but there are now far more points of view available for debate among feminists. Some feminists label their positions as sex positive, liberal, conservative, religious, radical, among others.

Today's abolitionists usually support keeping prostitution laws in place as part of a socially conservative and/or religious belief system. There is also a large contingent of abolitionists who have a radical feminist ideology. Both conservative and radical feminists adamantly oppose prostitution, but radical feminists differ in that they rarely condone criminal penalties for the women. They generally prefer the Swedish model. That policy falls in line with a traditional belief among leading radical feminists that prostitution is nothing other than rape. They also describe prostitutes as "unconscious as women" or "brainwashed." Consequently, many radical feminists, along with conservatives, have a theoretical view that women can't consciously consent to prostitution.

The obvious criticism of radical feminists is that they are swayed by a belief system, in particular about sexuality, which only fringe elements of society hold. Sheila Jeffreys, one of the most notable modern radical feminists, once wrote, "The act which men commonly perform on prostituted women is penis-in-vagina sexual intercourse. There is nothing 'natural' about that act."[3] She has numerous other controversial quotes about sexuality including,

"When a woman reaches orgasm with a man she is only collaborating with the patriarchal system, eroticizing her own oppression."[4] According to Catherine MacKinnon, rape and intercourse "are difficult to distinguish...under conditions of male dominance."[5] In her book, *Intercourse*, Andrea Dworkin wrote, "Intercourse remains a means or the means of physiologically making a woman inferior: communicating to her cell by cell her own inferior status, impressing it on her, burning it into her by shoving it into her, over and over, pushing and thrusting until she gives up and gives in--which is called surrender in the male lexicon."[6] All in all, these particular women, along with a number of other prominent radical feminists have strong academic backgrounds, but it is their world view that is in question.

Modern radical feminists differ significantly from their predecessors. Some of the most historically recognized feminists were labeled as "radicals" in their days, such as Victoria Woodhull and Emma Goldman. Woodhull has a unique place in history as one of the most influential supporters of suffrage rights. In fact, she was the first woman nominated for a Presidential race in 1872 by the Equal Rights Party. Keep in mind, her presidential campaign took place decades before women had the right to vote! She and her sister, Tennessee Claflin, were the first women to open a brokerage on Wall Street. They were also the first women to write a news publication, Woodhull & Claflin Weekly.[7]

Neither of these women, Woodhull and Goldman, supported socially conservative restrictions upon women. In fact, they were both strong advocates of free love. Woodhull asserted that women have the right to enjoy sex with whomever they choose. At the present time, few people bat an eye at such statements, but those kinds of assertions were quite bold in the late 19th century. Furthermore, she advocated for women's rights to divorce, birth control, and abortion. Because of those views, the press labeled Woodhull a "prostitute." Nonetheless, she supported legalized prostitution. She also scoffed at the hypocrisy of those laws by alluding to the fact that lobbyists were known at that time to supply politicians with prostitutes. Woodhull said, "I say it boldly, that it is the best men of the country that support the houses of prostitution!"[8]

Like Victoria Woodhull, Emma Goldman was another historic feminist who truly broke the mold. Goldman was a radical in almost every sense of the word. She was an anarchist and an aggressive union organizer. She led labor strikes and was accused of inciting riots. As a matter of fact, J. Edgar Hoover considered her to be the "most dangerous woman in America" and tried to have her deported.[9] She was arrested in 1919, along with roughly 5,000 other subversives, during the Palmer Raids. These raids were conducted by the FBI in which they rounded up anyone with even the slightest hint of a connection to communism. The Bureau's tactics at that time were overly aggressive and unconstitutional as these people were held without charges for months. Given these points, the Palmer Raids represent one of the lowest moments in the FBI's history.[10]

Emma Goldman's liberal view of sexuality differed greatly from today's radical feminists. In fact, Goldman was arrested in New York in 1916 for distributing pamphlets on birth control. The man responsible for such a law was the moral crusader Anthony Comstock. He lobbied Congress in 1873 to pass the "Comstock Law," which made it illegal to send an "obscene" letter through the mail. In other words, he made it a federal crime to send anything even remotely controversial through the mail as the word "obscene" can be widely interpreted. This clear invasion of privacy included love letters that were too dicey for Comstock's standards or even literature that pertained to contraception, abortion, prostitution, gambling, etc. Comstock anointed himself the government's top busybody. Also, like Joseph McCarthy, he abused his power and instigated criminal investigations into anyone who publicly criticized him.

One of Comstock's targets was Emma Goldman, whom he unsuccessfully tried to have imprisoned for her unconventional writings about "the white slave trade."[11] Indeed, Goldman was one of the few public figures who challenged the assertions in the newspapers at that time surrounding the white slave panic. She was truly prophetic when she described that movement as a "toy" that "serves to amuse the people for a little while, and it will help to create a few more fat political jobs--parasites who stalk about the world as inspectors, investigators, detectives, and so forth."[12]

Goldman rejected the Progressive Era abolitionists who wished for prostitutes to be sent to reform schools or institutions for the feebleminded. One such activist, Maude Miner Hadden, said, "These girls have not been, except in rare instances, physically enslaved; but through the loss of freedom and of action, they have been bound to prostitution. Their demoralization of character has constituted moral enslavement."[13] In contrast, Goldman insisted, "To the moralist prostitution does not consist so much in the fact that the woman sells her body, but rather that she sells it out of wedlock."[14] Goldman was, instead, more concerned about society's indifference to the main cause of prostitution -- economic and social conditions.

As a side note, Goldman tried to work once as a prostitute to help raise money for her fellow anarchist and lover, Alexander Berkman. He was well-known for shooting one of the robber barons of their era, Henry Clay Frick. Goldman said, "I felt no nervousness at first, but when I looked at the passing men and saw their vulgar glances and their manner of approaching the women, my heart sank...I wanted to take flight, to run back to my room, tear off my cheap finery, and scrub myself clean." Her first and only customer recognized how uncomfortable she was. He simply paid her $10 and told her to go home.[15]

As of today, the abolitionists are again affecting our nation's response to sex trafficking. Laura Agustín, author of *Sex at the Margins: Migration, Labour Markets, and the Rescue Industry*, strongly opposes the abolitionist view and adamantly disputes the expansive definition of trafficking within the conservative feminist community. She has researched this issue worldwide for nearly two decades and challenges the broad generalizations. "The other idea that is inherent in this kind of feminism is that if you have sex without love it's a complete disaster. If you are abused somehow then you are damaged for life, that you will not be able to recuperate...There is a general expectation that (men) will surmount obstacles and there is no such assumption about women," says Agustín.[16]

Liv Jessen is a recipient of the Human Rights Award from Amnesty International for her work as the head of a national organization for sex workers in Norway. She challenges the oversimplification from abolitionists that women don't "choose" prostitution. She acknowledges that many women enter into this industry from an inferior socioeconomic position. "Some are extremely unhappy with what they are doing, become deeply troubled, and need years of good support to repair the damage. Some seem to sail through it without a problem," says Jessen. However, as Jessen notes, only the "repentant sinners" are embraced by the abolitionists. Hence, she describes this as an "oppressive and fundamentalist attitude."[17]

Liberal feminists are focused on the human rights of sex workers and want to improve their work conditions and individual freedoms. "Rather than take it upon themselves to tell other women which professions to choose, feminists should defend every woman's workplace rights," says Stacy Reed.[18] Sex workers believe that they're entitled to the same rights and protections as any other worker from exploitation, assault, rape, workplace violence, etc. "A woman has the right to sell sexual services just as much as she has the right to sell her brains to a law firm where she works as a lawyer, or to sell her creative work to a museum when she works as an artist, or to sell her image to a photographer when she works as a model or sell her body when she works as a ballerina," says Dolores French, one of the more prominent activists of the sex workers' rights movement. "Since most people can have sex without going to jail, there is no reason except old fashioned prudery to make sex for money illegal."[19]

There is a general impression, albeit mistaken, that the radical feminist ideology speaks for the majority of feminists. It demonstrates that whoever yells the loudest tends to get the most recognition. In essence, they get a heckler's veto. The National Organization for Women (NOW) was formed in 1966 (before sex worker activists organized in large numbers) and one of their early platforms was to liberalize prostitution laws. NOW passed a resolution in 1973 that supported the decriminalization of prostitution.[20] This is a particularly relevant point because NOW is currently the largest active feminist organization, by a wide margin, with over 500,000 members. Therefore, you could easily describe NOW as the most mainstream feminist group.[21]

With that said, NOW no longer has an official platform that addresses prostitution and several of their members have a conservative stance on this issue. Obviously, there isn't a consensus with every member of NOW, but some members continue to publicly support the decriminalization of prostitution. For example, in 2009, the Rhode Island chapter of NOW (RI NOW) lobbied to keep indoor prostitution decriminalized. One of their written statements included this assertion. "RI NOW believes that these women need rehabilitation NOT imprisonment and penalties."[22]

Camille Paglia, a "dissident feminist" with libertarian leanings, even contests the belief that prostitution is a form of male domination. "The feminist analysis of prostitution says that men are using money as power over women. I'd say yes that's all the men have. The money is a confession of weakness. They have to buy women's attention. It's not a sign of power; it's a sign of weakness," says Paglia.[23] Accordingly, some sex workers suggest that prostitution is empowering. Bella Robinson is one of the more prominent sex worker activists to do so. She is the Executive Director of Call Off Your Old Tired Ethics (COYOTE) in Rhode Island and serves on the Board of Directors for the Erotic Service Providers Legal Education and Research Project (ESPLERP). Robinson declares that prostitution has been an "empowering" force because she only needs to work four to five hours a week. That enables her to dedicate most of her time, roughly 40-50 hours a week, for her real passion, which is volunteer work at a domestic violence center/youth shelter.[24]

Shannon Bell believes that prostitutes are sacred healers or goddesses and hold "lineage to the ancient sexual, sacred, healing female body."[25] Likewise, Cosi Fabian holds those same beliefs and considers the term "whore" to be a "noble title" because the root word *hora* relates to ancient divine prostitution. She proudly advocates the benefits of her work. She once wrote, "Rather than inviting rape and murder by being overly sexual, my anonymity offers men a rare chance to be vulnerable, receptive, grateful – what some might call 'feminine.'"[26]

Some sex workers have taken the empowerment belief to an extreme. A group of sex workers from the Canadian Organization for the Rights of Prostitutes (CORP) expressed their contempt towards abolitionists during an interview. One member even asserted that they were "realistic feminists." She said, "A prostitute is a realistic feminist as opposed to an idealistic, hypocritical, shadowy feminist who doesn't want to confront the facts of life, the facts of her own negotiating and trade-off in the marriage situation, the fact that the male is her brother and not the enemy and the fact that she's afraid of sex." CORP also emphasized that they were "tired of (radical) feminists treating (johns) like they're not (people too)...He may just need to be held, he may just need you to act out some fantasy." Obviously, some of their beliefs certainly don't fall in line with the majority of women. Nevertheless, another member of CORP upped the ante by arguing that they "are the only feminists around" because they're the only ones listening to men.[27]

Most feminists would audibly scoff at the belief that sex workers "are the only feminists around," but that interview illustrates the long-running tension between abolitionists and sex workers. No one appreciates receiving a lecture from people who ordain themselves as morally superior. Plus, the lack of input from the prostitute's perspective in the feminist debate isn't lost on them. Indeed, this icy relationship between both sides didn't improve during a meeting that took place in Manhattan in December of 1971. It was seemingly a first-of-its-kind conference between feminist reformers and prostitutes. Tensions were high and some of the prostitutes hissed during one reformer's speech. The emotions within the conference eventually erupted and an actual brawl unfolded.[28]

After the melee, one of the prostitutes said, "They're trying to butt into everything, grab the publicity and wreck our business. How many of them can make $1,000 a week lying down?"[29] Another woman pointed out that prostitution is "degrading and sexist, but so are a lot of things."[30] With that said, a similar conference took place in Canada in 1985 without any violence. However, one reporter on hand, Laurie Bell (author of *Good Girls/Bad Girls: Feminists and Sex Trade Workers, Face to Face*), noted that one prostitute aptly asserted that "feminism is incomplete without us."[31]

Self-labeled "sex-positive feminists" generally believe there shouldn't be some universal, cookie-cutter guideline for all women's sexuality. As one sex worker and activist, Teri Goodson, said, "Some non-sex worker feminists seem to understand that the stigma and oppression of female prostitutes is used to uphold the double standard and is limiting to all women's sexual freedom."[32] Those thoughts capture the essence of the liberalized women of the 1920s who shattered several cultural boundaries. In fact, these women were reverently labeled as "flappers," a term popularized by F. Scott Fitzgerald in reference to these women. Mind you, the term "flapper" had previously been primarily associated with prostitutes.[33]

Historians have widely acknowledged that prostitution, regrettably, was one of the few ways women could gain financial autonomy in our nation's earliest years. However, prostitutes have rarely been considered the leaders of the women's rights movement. Thaddeus Russell, historian and author of *A Renegade History of the United States*, asserted that prostitutes blazed the trail for many women's rights issues. He wrote, "In the nineteenth century, a woman who owned property, made high wages, had sex outside of marriage, performed or received oral sex, used birth control, consorted with men of other races, danced, drank, or walked alone in public, wore makeup, perfume, or stylish clothes - and was not ashamed - was probably a whore. In fact, prostitutes won virtually all the freedoms that were denied to women but are now taken for granted."[34] The last sentence is quite controversial, but, in fairness, Russell brilliantly detailed some overlooked aspects of history. His book thoroughly documents how rebellious people throughout history have expanded social freedoms.

There have long existed unwritten and written boundaries for women's behavior intent upon keeping them virtuous. Nearly all of these uptight restrictions on women's fundamental rights involved the faintest hint of sexuality. For one thing, it was illegal in some states for women to smoke a cigarette in public until the 1920s because it was assumed that she would be a prostitute.[35] One particular report by a Progressive New York reform organization, "Committee of Fourteen," truly epitomized this disconnect between prudish perceptions and reality. The committee's vice investigator witnessed a group of "twenty unescorted women" in a speakeasy during the prohibition era. He assumed they were prostitutes because...*(brace yourself)*...they smoked cigarettes, socialized with various men, exchanged phone numbers, "and some of them appeared to be under the influence of liquor." He even tried (unsuccessfully) to arrange to pay for sex with a few of those women, but he still labeled them as "probable prostitutes."[36]

Glenna Matthews, author of *The Rise of Public Woman: Woman's Power and Woman's Place in the United States, 1630-1970*, noted the distinctly different connotations between the terms "public woman" and "public man." A "public woman" referred to prostitutes or "streetwalkers," which clearly demonstrates women's clear lack of social freedom. To the contrary, "public man" has very positive associations with someone who is a noble statesman.[37]

One very notable case perfectly demonstrated this dichotomy. A young woman, Elizabeth "Lizzie" Schauer, was charged with prostitution in 1895 in New York City. The arresting officer witnessed her talk to two different men late at night, but she insisted that she was merely asking for directions. This same officer later admitted that he didn't actually hear what she said, but he arrested her nonetheless. Notwithstanding, the judge assumed the worst of her character and convicted her stating, "No respectable woman should be on the streets at night unaccompanied."[38]

Lizzie's case was unusual for a few reasons. The fact that the newspapers covered her story at all was abnormal. Also, the local press covered her story sympathetically, which was a sign of social progress. If not for this news coverage, she likely would have had to serve her full sentence in jail. However, the judge ultimately dropped the charges against her on appeal, but that didn't happen until a doctor physically inspected her and found that she was a virgin and disease free.[39]

The early 20th century marked the end of the Victorian era. This was a time of significant social changes when various prudish social restrictions were lifted as they were no longer automatically associated with prostitution. As an illustration, this was when it became generally acceptable for a woman to wear makeup in public. By 1927, a survey found that 50% of women then wore rouge.[40] Again that wasn't always the case. Karen Halttunen, author of *Confidence Men and Painted Women: A Study Of Middle-Class Culture In America, 1830-1870*, noted that "(a)dvice books, fashion magazines, and etiquette manuals cautioned young women against emulating the arts of the painted woman, sometimes a prostitute but more often a woman of fashion, who poisoned polite society with deception and betrayal by dressing extravagantly and practicing empty forms of false etiquette."[41]

The only place where "dirty dancing" occurred before the early 20th century was in brothels or dance halls frequented by prostitutes. Until then, ballroom dancing was the only acceptable kind of dancing and it was basically only for the upper class.[42] One of the first sexually suggestive dance crazes of the early 20th century was known as "tough dancing" and it originated in the brothels of San Francisco.[43] Likewise, the tango originated in Argentine brothels. This dance craze was widely practiced on the east coast during the same time that tough dancing was popular on the west coast.

In reaction, many cities set up undercover vice investigations into dance halls. One investigator noted, "What distinguishes this dance is the motion of the pelvic portions of the body, bearing in mind its origins."[44] However, some of these vice investigators were clueless in deciphering which women were or weren't prostitutes. They couldn't tell the difference because so many of them began to dress like "fancy ladies," a euphemism for prostitutes. One investigator quoted a waiter who said, "The way women dress today, they all look like prostitutes."[45] Keep in mind, prudish standards were the norm at that time as ankle length dresses were customary.[46]

Brothels were also one of the few places where sex among different races was somewhat tolerated. After all, miscegenation laws, which banned interracial sex and marriage, weren't overturned in many states until the 1960s! Likewise, American red-light districts, which were generally located in highly ethnic areas, were called "segregated districts" and the two terms were synonymous.[47] Ironically, the draw of this particular vice, along with others, resulted in the social interaction between various races. In fact, the California Commission of Immigration and Housing in 1917 named the red-light district in Los Angeles as "the most cosmopolitan district" of the city.[48] Likewise, Gary Krist, author of *Empire of Sin: A Story of Sex, Jazz, Murder, and the Battle for Modern New Orleans*, wrote, "Early Storyville, in fact, was arguably the most racially integrated square mile in the entire American South."[49]

It's an unfortunate aspect of history, but Thaddeus Russell's observation was correct. Many of the freedoms that modern women take for granted partially came about due to prostitutes who refused to accept society's norms. Obviously, the women's rights movement has since made tremendous progress. Meanwhile, the issue of prostitution is still considered a feminist issue, as it should be. But shouldn't the real maxim of feminism be to let each individual decide for themselves due to the variety of perspectives within the feminist debate?

7

"The Lord told me it's flat none of your business."

Voters in most secular nations don't care about the sex lives of their elected officials and having an extramarital affair doesn't always end a political career. The political climate is, of course, very different in America. Accordingly, many lawmakers portray a public image of conservative values even if they lead very different private lives. To make this point clear, former Seattle Police Chief Norm Stamper once wrote that it was "common to find in a prostitute's little black book the names of prominent locals--businessmen, elected officials, judges, athletes, cops."[1] That's not a surprise as there are numerous examples of politicians who have legislated with intolerance while behaving as if they were exempt from the same laws. Time and time again, the hypocrisy of these moral crusaders is exposed. That is to say, the prostitution debate only seems to resurface into the mainstream culture after a politician ends up in a prostitution scandal. Then again, that happens fairly often.

Our nation's capital is ironically home to many political prostitution scandals despite the fact that Washington, D.C. now has some of the most stringent prostitution laws and "prostitution-free zones." Whenever these scandals occur the details flow in a manner as if these events were written by hack fiction writers. You simply can't make this stuff up. Take for example the incident in which several agents of the White House's Secret Service paid for prostitutes in Colombia. That story certainly received a lot of media coverage and, consequently, the federal government went into damage control mode. As a result, the Department of Homeland Security conducted an internal investigation, but the lead investigator needed to resign because he had been caught months earlier paying for sex with a prostitute in Florida![2]

You should be skeptical of people who present themselves as moral authorities, particularly when it involves sexuality. Charles Keating was a well-respected attorney turned banker who leveraged his money and power to become the face of the anti-pornography movement during the 1960s and 1970s. If his name isn't familiar, this staunch conservative was portrayed in the film *The People vs. Larry Flynt*. According to Keating, pornography was part of a "communist conspiracy" and he founded an anti-pornography group, Citizens for Decent Literature.[3]

In response to the zealous efforts by Keating and other advocates, Congress authorized a Presidential Committee on Obscenity and Pornography in 1967 to thoroughly study this topic.[4] LBJ appointed an independent group with varied professional backgrounds including doctors, lawyers, religious leaders, etc. However, Richard Nixon differed from his predecessor and he shared Charles Keating's belief that the Committee on Obscenity and Pornography was "dedicated to a position of complete moral anarchy."[5] Hence, Nixon was determined to stack the deck by appointing, none other than, Charles Keating to the committee.

Despite this kind of heavy-handed influence, the majority of the group concluded that pornography resulted in very little harm to society and certainly wouldn't result in more sexual assaults. Did Nixon adjust his platform accordingly? No. Much like what happened with the Shafer Commission Report that suggested decriminalizing marijuana, Nixon also "categorically rejected" the "morally bankrupt" recommendations of the Committee on Obscenity and Pornography to decriminalize pornography. "So long as I am in the White House, there will be no relaxation of the national effort to control and eliminate smut from our national life," proclaimed Nixon.[6]

Charles Keating certainly enjoyed the view from the moral high ground for many years until he became the unofficial face of the Savings & Loan scandal of the 1980s, an ironic destiny for someone who financed an anti-pornography propaganda film, "Perversion for Profit."[7] His name is now synonymous with corporate fraud and corruption because he duped investors with fraudulent accounting and looted millions of dollars from the company for his personal benefit. In the end, Charles Keating's Lincoln Savings and Loan was bailed out by the taxpayers to the tune of $3.4 billion, the largest bailout from the Savings & Loan scandal.

Keating was eventually convicted of 90 counts of fraud, racketeering, and conspiracy.[8] During the buildup to his trial, investigators found that Keating had called in favors from five U.S. Senators, "the Keating Five," who together, received over a combined $1 million in campaign contributions. In return, those Senators intervened on his behalf to stymie various banking regulators from punishing him. Keating even sued an especially effective regulator, William K. Black, and hired private investigators to dig up dirt on him.[9] And yet with all of this information in the public eye, this man still had no qualms about perverting and corrupting our political system. Reporters asked Keating if he thought that his political contributions had bought him influence and he replied, "I want to say in the most forceful way I can: I certainly hope so."[10]

On a similar note, Eliot Spitzer's name was at one time floating in some circles as a potential presidential candidate. Time Magazine's "Crusader of the Year" in 2002 developed a much-deserved reputation because he was the rare breed who pursued much-needed cases against major Wall Street firms while serving as New York's Attorney General. However, Spitzer also targeted petty vice crimes such as gambling and prostitution, which he referred to as "modern-day slavery."[11] In fact, as New York's Governor, he signed human trafficking legislation that increased the penalties for the buyers of sex from a misdemeanor to a felony. He did so despite feedback from sex worker rights organizations. They warned that those penalties do more harm than good because they inhibit people from coming forward with valuable information.[12]

Those factors only added to the surprise when he resigned from the Governor's office after a federal wiretap recorded him paying for sex with an escort. In fact, he paid the woman's travel expenses to cross state lines, which violated the Mann Act. Spitzer was let off the hook by the DOJ, but the bizarre backstory is worth examining. Oddly, the investigation that led to Spitzer's downfall was prompted by the PATRIOT Act. IRS agents found that Spitzer had sent thousands of dollars (reportedly $80,000) over the course of months to a suspicious shell corporation, QAT Consulting Group, which was later confirmed to be a high-end escort agency,

Emperor's Club VIP. After receiving permission from the U.S. Attorney General, the FBI then proceeded to investigate Spitzer's transactions to see if these payments were made to hide bribe money. At least, that's the official story.[13]

The more likely explanation is that the operators of the Emperor's Club VIP were caught in the middle of a politically-motivated prosecution. It's difficult to believe that federal investigators were unaware of the true nature of the shell company, QAT Consulting Group, connected to this escort agency. Court records show that the FBI's investigation took place over a year *after* law enforcement officers were informed about the "QAT Consulting Group." A prostitute who worked for the Emperor's Club VIP cooperated as a confidential informant in exchange for immunity. She documented the inner workings of the business, including their front company.[14]

Spitzer ruined his political career by violating state and federal laws, but he was most guilty of hypocritical behavior. The DOJ never charged him with any crimes, but the same laissez-faire treatment wasn't afforded to the operators of the Emperor's Club VIP who served time in prison. Even the two women who simply booked Spitzer's appointments were convicted of felonies.[15]

Two weeks later Wall Street's favorite madam, Kristin Davis, was arrested. Her interaction with the criminal justice system was quite different and the appearance of selective punishment wasn't lost on Davis. "I spent five months at Riker's Island from which I returned penniless, homeless, and forced to take sex offender classes for five months with pedophiles and perverts while he returned to his wife in his Fifth Avenue high rise without ever being fingerprinted, mug shot, remanded or charged with a crime under the very law he signed," said Davis.[16]

By now American voters should have learned the lesson of caveat emptor or buyer beware when choosing candidates who present themselves as a "family values" conservative. Those same politicians gripe about the "nanny state" of government while they impose religious doctrine upon the entire population with "tough on crime" penalties for various consensual activities, such as pornography and prostitution. Consequently, there is nothing slimier than witnessing one of these RINOs (Republican In Name Only) when they get caught in a sex or prostitution scandal.

It's impossible not to laugh at some of these stories. The character portrayed by Burt Reynolds in *Striptease* was a loosely based representation of former Congressman, Rep. J. Herbert Burke (R-FL). Burke was once arrested for disorderly intoxication and resisting arrest at a Florida strip club due to his belligerent behavior. What an odd place that was for Burke to spend his evening. He had supported the very same zoning laws that opposed those types of businesses before entering Congress when he served as the Broward County commissioner. Being kicked out of a strip club must have been embarrassing enough, but he decided to dig a deeper hole. Burke refused to admit that he was guilty of such conduct and claimed that he was actually conducting an undercover surveillance investigation at that bar. According to Burke, he witnessed what he believed was an illegal drug deal in progress and he followed the suspects to the strip club. In his mind, that must have sounded like a plausible excuse. After all, he was serving on the House Select Committee on Narcotics Abuse and Control at that time. However, Burke later pleaded guilty to the original charges and witness tampering because he tried to manipulate the bar's manager to lie under oath to help his defense.[17]

Do you remember former Congressman "Duke" Cunningham from *The Drug War: A Trillion Con Game*? He's the same man who advocated for the death penalty for drug dealers, yet he used his influence (including crying in front of a judge) to get his son's drug trafficking sentence reduced. That incident was hardly even a speed bump in his political career, but things changed in 2007 when Cunningham was convicted of various corruption charges, including accepting over $2.4 million in bribes from defense contractors. It turned out that he had demanded regularly scheduled envelopes of "maintenance money" and received sex from prostitutes in exchange for rewarding those security companies with lucrative contracts.[18] For that reason, Duke received an eight-year sentence, one of the longest sentences in history for a member of Congress.

He decided, as a mea culpa, to hold a tear-filled public apology/press conference before heading to prison. It appeared to be a humble moment, but a leopard can't change its spots. This was all a ruse and Duke hadn't changed his ways at all. Reports later surfaced that he had tried to stash some of his dirty cash before heading to prison. He literally threw a duffel bag filled with money from his car window onto his wife's driveway on the night before that press conference.[19]

Cunningham was quite chummy with a Greek businessman, Thomas Kontogiannis, who had twice been convicted for bribery. In one instance, Kontogiannis traveled to Saudi Arabia with Cunningham and Rep. Ken Calvert (R-CA). Officially, the trip was made to "promote better relations between the United States and Saudi Arabia." However, various news sources gleaned that they made the trip to the Middle East so that Kontogiannis could bribe a few influential politicians to gain contracts for his oil business.[20]

These two crooked politicians, Cunningham and Calvert, have been notorious for backroom deals, yet they've managed to placate "family values" voters by projecting that type of persona. That's particularly disturbing because Ken Calvert has been listed three times as one of the most corrupt members of Congress in the annual reports by Citizens for Responsibility and Ethics in Washington (CREW).[21] Nevertheless, his unwavering right-wing voting record has earned him a 92% rating by the Christian Coalition.[22] Predictably, Calvert, along with Cunningham, was very critical of Bill Clinton's extramarital affair. "We can't forgive what occurred between the President and Lewinsky," said Calvert.[23]

This kind of pious affectation apparently helped Calvert avoid an abrupt end to his political career after an incident in 1993 when he was literally caught with his pants down in his car with a prostitute. The police report mentioned that when the officer approached the car the female's head "was laying in the driver's lap" and that Calvert "was placing his penis into his unzipped dress slacks, and was trying to hide it with his untucked dress shirt." Apparently, Calvert's explanation was ironclad. He declared that they were "just talking that's all, nothing else." He even started to drive away after the police discovered him, yet he was never arrested on any charges.[24] Hence, this information wasn't reported across the police blotter. This incident would have never come to the light of day, but one of his political rivals instigated a lawsuit requiring the Corona, CA Police Department to release the details of that report.[25]

Nonetheless, Ken Calvert continues living a charmed life due to multiple re-elections on a morality platform even though his sexual indiscretions and ethical violations have been well-documented. *Fox News* revealed that specific earmark spending had been added to the federal budget by Calvert. Specifically, money for highways and commercial developments were slated for his district. That's not unusual as many other Congressmen do the same thing to help their constituents. It is all part of the legalized corruption on Capitol Hill. In fact, there is a term for this, "pork barrel spending." Be that as it may, Calvert's actions were much more flagrant. His spending projects directly benefited his speculative real estate holdings, entirely for his personal gain![26]

Yes, Ken Calvert, along with many others, embodies the myriad of jokes that compare politicians and prostitutes.[A27] As Ronald Reagan once said, "Politics is supposed to be the second oldest profession. I have come to realize that it bears a very close resemblance to the first."[28] Also, H.L. Mencken once wrote, "A professional politician is a professionally dishonorable man. In order to get anywhere near high office he has to make so many compromises and submit to so many humiliations that he becomes indistinguishable from a streetwalker."[29]

These types of observations are always good for a chuckle, but there is usually a common misunderstanding. Everyone's sense of personal ethics and morality vary, but there is an undisputed understanding that our choices shouldn't negatively affect other people. The corrupt actions of politicians routinely affect other people negatively, whereas prostitution is an act between two

---

[A] There are also many of those comparisons between lobbyists and politicians. A very relevant story emerged in 2015 when the North Carolina Ethics Commission made a controversial decision. They decided that sex between a lobbyist and a government official didn't violate ethics laws. The commission determined that "consensual sexual relationships do not have monetary value," therefore there was no need to report the activity.

consenting adults. In other words, to label some of these politicians as whores would be in fact, a compliment.

Some religious leaders are living a lie to maintain their public image. Some of them have had their sexual scandals, but the televangelists' were probably the most memorable. Jimmy Swaggart's tearful "I have sinned" speech took place months after he criticized Jim Bakker for an affair with his former secretary turned Playboy model, Jessica Hahn. Swaggart didn't directly admit it, but he had been with a prostitute. Notwithstanding, Swaggart's fall from grace didn't lead to him changing his ways. Police pulled him over three years later with a prostitute in his car. Nonetheless, he remained brazen when confronted afterward by his congregation. "The Lord told me it's flat none of your business," declared Swaggart.[30] Making matters worse, he was implicated again in 1998 by CNN's program, "Impact," for separate instances with more prostitutes, in addition to allegations of plundering his ministry's funds.[31]

Gay conversion therapy is now illegal in some states, but it remains a profitable industry even though there have been some well-publicized scandals involving the same religious leaders who have pioneered this practice. The pastor Ted Haggard had been aggressively anti-homosexual with his political activism and served as the president of the National Association of Evangelicals. He was even listed in 2005 by *Time Magazine* as one of the top 25 most influential evangelicals in America. However, his prestige plummeted in the next year when a gay male escort outed him. In fact, that same escort also supplied Haggard with crystal meth during their sexual encounters over a three-year period. After some time passed, Haggard eventually declared that his homosexuality had been "cured" with therapy. He even claimed that it was merely the result of a massage that got out of hand.[32] Who knew that someone would someday use a punchline from *Seinfeld*, "It moved," as a defense? Nevertheless, Ted Haggard has managed to resurrect his career and founded a new church.[33]

In a similar scenario, Rev. George Rekers had a lofty position with one of the leading gay conversion therapy groups, the National Association for Research & Therapy of Homosexuality.

In fact, this status enabled Rekers to receive a $120,000 payment from the Florida Attorney General for his testimony as an "expert" against gay adoption.[34] Therefore, his reputation became a matter of national ridicule after news reports unveiled that he had hired a "travel companion" from the website, RentBoy.com.[B][35] Rekers denied knowing that his young male escort was a prostitute, despite his online profile that touted his "smooth, sweet, tight ass" and "perfectly built 8-inch cock (uncut)." According to Rekers, it wasn't until the midpoint of their trip that he figured out the young man's true profession. However, Rekers insisted that he kept him around because he needed someone to carry his luggage after surgery. But much to his chagrin, Rekers was photographed in the airport pushing his luggage in a cart while his escort stood by.[36]

There have also been several gay sex scandals involving politicians with consistently homophobic voting records. One former California State Representative, Roy Ashburn, was arrested for DUI with another man who accompanied him after leaving a gay bar. Ashburn had actively opposed various homosexual rights issues and even organized a rally against same-sex marriage. Later, when confronted about his lengthy anti-gay voting record, he deflected that criticism by noting that those policies were "the wishes of the people in my district."[37] Certainly, that was a defense mechanism, but those words also cut to the deeper truth that sexually-repressed policies are often purely politics. Ashburn is now openly gay and out of office, but he acknowledges that it would have been next to impossible to be elected on the Republican ticket otherwise.[38] That really emphasizes the need for the Libertarian Party to gain more of a political footing. There is

---

[B] With the threat of ISIS increasing daily, the Department of Homeland Security decided to raid the headquarters of RentBoy.com, which is located just three miles from the New York Stock Exchange. In the process, they confiscated $1.4 million via asset forfeiture. There obviously weren't any allegations of terrorism related to RentBoy.com, nor anything to do with sex trafficking. Rent Boy was part of the low-hanging-fruit trend in which Manhattan prosecutors have ignored the crimes of Wall Street while bearing down on the sex industry within the same zip code. Also, the timing of this raid was quite noteworthy because this occurred just months after Attorney General Eric Holder's deadline had passed for prosecuting any Wall Street executives in relation to the financial crisis of 2007.

no reason that those seeking office should have to align themselves with the Republicans' firmly anti-gay agenda simply because they are economically conservative.

Likewise, the political career of the former Congressman and political adviser to Ronald Reagan, Robert Bauman, ended abruptly after he was caught paying for sex with an underage male prostitute. This happened just before election time when he was a shoe-in for winning his fourth term in the House. Before that arrest, he had been one of the fastest risers within the Republican Party with a distinctive brand as an authoritative moralist. Bauman was known to publicly attack other members of Congress for their less-than-virtuous transgressions and assuaged the religious right wing with his strong anti-gay voting record. In fact, he co-sponsored one such bill, the "Family Protection Act."[39] Bauman's political career ended with his arrest, but he eventually eschewed his socially conservative ways with a career in law and lobbying. He even served as a lobbyist for the Gay National Rights lobby and promoted a variety of libertarian causes.[40]

There are several stories like these involving closeted conservatives living the charade. The poster child of this sort has to be former Rep. Mark Foley (R-FL) who wrote laws with stronger penalties for pedophiles and child pornography. That made it even more disturbing when he was caught sending lewd messages to an underage male Congressional intern in 2006. Foley ultimately never faced any criminal charges.[41]

Many of these scandals are disturbing, but arguably the most cringeworthy of these tales involves a former State Representative from Florida with a strong anti-gay voting record, Bob Allen. He was the co-chairman of John McCain's presidential campaign in Florida before he was arrested for solicitation of prostitution. This man's "tough on crime" reputation had earned him official recognition as the Representative of the Year by Florida's Police Association. He was also the author of a bill against public sex acts, the Lewd or Lascivious Exhibition Act.[42]

According to Allen, the circumstances involved with his arrest were all a "misunderstanding." He only wanted to avoid a thunderstorm when he made his way into the bathroom of a public park. He then offered to pay $20 to perform oral sex on an undercover cop in a bathroom stall. Afterward, Allen insisted that sex wasn't his motive. After all, he "had his name on the damn building." He claimed that his offer was to ward off a potential violent attack because he was afraid of the "stocky black guy and there were a lot of other black guys around in the park." However, recordings show that Bob Allen initiated this conversation. There was never even a hint of a threat, but Bob Allen still insisted that he feared that he "was about to be a statistic."[43] Who knows, maybe he should have been more adamant? *After all, the first technique taught by self-defense instructors is to kneel down and offer a blowjob to any potential attacker*. In the end, a jury didn't believe his racist defense.

Richard Curtis, a Republican Washington State Representative with a homophobic voting record, was also involved in a scandal with a male prostitute. Yes, Curtis had been very hypocritical, but he was the victim of a much more serious crime -- extortion. Initially, most of the media coverage focused on the R-rated aspects of the story as Curtis was allegedly a cross dresser. According to the store's employees, he had hooked up with other gay men that he had met at a particular adult video store (the same place where he met this particular prostitute).[44]

However, this time around Curtis contacted the police after his encounter because he accused the male prostitute of extortion. Indeed, the young man essentially admitted to blackmailing Curtis indirectly by keeping his wallet, but he claimed that it was "for collateral" from insufficient payment for his sexual services. In the end, he was never convicted; Curtis resigned from office and eventually decided to drop the extortion case.[45]

All in all, Americans should be less concerned with their elected officials' sex lives as long as it doesn't affect their work. However, as that last story demonstrates these scandals can leave them open to being compromised. Prostitution scandals have even reached the highest levels of government: the White House. It's widely acknowledged that JFK had many affairs, some of which were with call girls. JFK once reportedly told a friend in private, "You know, I get a migraine headache if I don't get a strange piece of ass every day."[46] In fact, that's why JFK was so visually composed during his famous debate with Nixon, according to

Langdon Marvin (a campaign worker for JFK in 1960). Marvin claims that he arranged a date with a call girl for him just beforehand.[47]

The details of JFK's affairs were censored by reporters while he was in office. Keeping such secrets under wraps seems unimaginable now, but the media was then a much smaller circle. With that said, this sort of blackout didn't happen by accident and some American reporters tried to cover the story. On June 29, 1963, the front page of the *New York Journal American* included an article, "High US Aide Implicated in V-Girl Scandal," which referenced what was later known as the Profumo affair. John Profumo, then Britain's Secretary of War, resigned earlier that month due to his affair with a prostitute who was linked with a suspected Soviet spy. The article by the *New York Journal American* never mentioned JFK by name, only "a man who holds a very high elective office," but suggested that the official had an affair with a prostitute connected to the Profumo affair. This was a tabloid publication, but the reporters were generally accurate in their claims. Regardless, RFK, then serving as the Attorney General, summoned those reporters to his office. They were interrogated and their newspaper was threatened with criminal prosecutions.[48] Needless to say, this encounter served as a warning to everyone else in the industry.

Years had passed before reporters were willing to cover this topic. The Pulitzer Prize-winning journalist, Seymour Hersh, later revealed the deeper implications of JFK's adultery with *The Dark Side of Camelot*. The FBI suspected that one particular call girl, Ellen Rometsch, whom JFK and other D.C. insiders had slept with, was an East German communist spy. In fact, Rometsch was later deported and the Kennedys reportedly paid her to sign a nondisclosure agreement.[49]

A few decades later, on June 29, 1989, *The Washington Times* printed a story with the headline, "Homosexual prostitution inquiry ensnares VIPs with Reagan and Bush: 'Call Boys' took midnight tour of White House.'" This conservative-minded newspaper broke the story about a federal investigation into an underage homosexual prostitution ring. Key officials from the Reagan and Bush administrations were reportedly the suspects in this investigation, including military officers, Congressional aides, along with U.S. and foreign business people entrenched among the political establishment. As a matter of discretion, *The Washington Times* decided to only name people in "sensitive government posts or positions of influence" and included credit card vouchers as evidence.[50]

Charles K. Dutcher, allegedly a client of this escort service, was a former Reagan administration official and Congressional aide to Robert Bauman. As you may recall, Bauman's emerging political career was ruined due to being arrested for soliciting an underage male prostitute. An influential Republican lobbyist, Craig Spence, was also named in the article. He had spent an estimated $20,000 a month with the escort agency and had even arranged for the late-night tours of the White House with his underage male escorts.[51] Spence died months later of a drug overdose in an apparent suicide.[C52]

A separate prostitution scandal began to unravel during the George W. Bush administration when the liberal media watchdog group, Media Matters for America, exposed a reporter named Jeff Gannon. Oddly enough, this story revealed more about the cozy relationship between the press and the government, rather than actual prostitution. In short, Jeff Gannon stuck out like a sore thumb within the White House Press Corps because he refused to feign a pretense of independence. He habitually offered easy, partisan questions to change the direction of White House press conferences. *(Gannon's full story will be addressed later.)*

President Bush called upon Gannon on January 26, 2005 after reporters repeatedly asked about a shady contract deal involving his administration. The U.S. Department of Education paid $240,000 to a conservative media pundit, Armstrong Williams, to promote the No Child Left Behind Law. Before then, it had never been disclosed to the public that he was being paid for his advocacy efforts! In other words, our tax dollars were being used

---

[C] That controversy was included in the "Franklin Cover-up," a scandal with allegations of a massive child pedophile prostitution ring that served business and political leaders from both major political parties.

as part of a propaganda campaign. That decision was clearly unethical, but it was also technically illegal.[D53]

Armstrong Williams' contract was part of a larger $1 million contract from the Department of Education paid to the influential New York-based PR firm, Ketchum Communications. That's the same company that received $11 million from the government to raise awareness about human trafficking. In this instance, Ketchum Communications distributed video news releases, or VNRs, to several news stations that were designed to look like legitimate news reports. The VNRs touted the No Child Left Behind Act and didn't disclose that they were produced on behalf of their client, the U.S. Department of Education. The GAO later determined that this violated federal laws against "covert propaganda."[54] There were also two nationally syndicated reporters, Maggie Gallagher and Mike McManus, who received direct payments from the Department of Health and Human Services to promote George W. Bush's program for encouraging marriage.[55]

Americans, for the most part, are distrustful of the media, but few knew that there were actual reporters on the government's payroll.[E56] With this issue at the forefront, Jeff Gannon came to the President's rescue during his press conference. Gannon served as

---

[D] No Child Left Behind had many of the familiar signs of crony capitalism as some of Bush's closest allies have directly profited from that law, including his brother Neil.

[E] Just three days prior to the report about the Department of Education, the GAO reported on a different example of "covert propaganda." This time it was from the Office of National Drug Control Policy (ONDCP), which had also violated these laws during the Clinton administration. In this particular instance, the ONDCP also produced seemingly real video news releases or VNR's about marijuana, just like the Department of Education. The VNR's were distributed to various news stations and eventually were viewed by 22 million households. The videos didn't disclose that they were produced by the ONDCP and they featured two former legitimate news reporters, Mike Morris and Karen Ryan, who were both working in public relations at that time. Moreover, that wasn't Karen Ryan's only foray involving covert propaganda. She provided VNR's for the Department of Health and Human Services touting the Bush administration's Medicare prescription drug plan while never disclosing that the videos were produced on behalf of the government.

a formidable gatekeeper by redirecting the narrative away from government propaganda with his questioning. However, that question quickly became a matter of national ridicule:

> Thank you. Senate Democratic leaders have painted a very bleak picture of the U.S. economy. Harry Reid was talking about soup lines and Hillary Clinton was talking about the economy being on the verge of collapse. Yet in the same breath, they say that Social Security is rock solid and there's no crisis there. How are you going to work -- you've said you are going to reach out to these people -- how are you going to work with people who seem to have divorced themselves from reality?[57]

Gannon's handy work made its way into pop culture for the first time. He was ridiculed by Jon Stewart on "The Daily Show," along with other pundits. To clarify, the "soup lines" quote from Harry Reid wasn't even an actual quote; Rush Limbaugh had paraphrased "soup lines" from comments made by Reid.[58] As a result, a newfound media microscope focused on Gannon's credibility and it opened Pandora's Box. Gannon had no prior experience in journalism and had been denied a Congressional press pass because he didn't work for a legitimate news organization. His employer, *Talon News*, didn't have any paying subscribers and was owned by a conservative group, GOPUSA. In fact, the headquarters were none other than Gannon's apartment![59] To sum up, *Talon News* served as an obscure mouthpiece for the Republican Party posing as a legitimate news website.[60]

Gannon definitely ruffled the feathers of some Democrats and his opposition was determined to dig up more dirt from his past. To illustrate, Jeff Gannon wasn't even the reporter's real name! It was an alias for James Guckert and that's where the details became much more interesting. It turned out that James Guckert's private life embodied the polar opposite of Republican Party ideals. Guckert had owned, operated, and worked as an escort for his military-themed, gay prostitution websites, MeetLocalMen.com, HotMilitaryStud.com, and MilitaryEscorts.com.[61]

That revelation opened the floodgates for gossip and speculation due to the mysterious circumstances surrounding his comings and goings within the White House. Again, Gannon had been denied a Congressional press pass, but he was able to circumvent the requirements for entering the White House Press Corps because the Secret Service issued day passes to him. He received day passes on more than 200 occasions over a two year period. Furthermore, records show that Gannon visited the White House on several days when there were no press briefings! There were even 14 occasions in which either his entry or exit times were missing.[62] Those circumstances certainly raised questions as to whether prostitution was his "in" for gaining such access to the Bush administration. After all, he clearly had some high-level connections within the White House. And regretfully, the prostitution issue involved in this scandal effectively distracted from the larger issue of media manipulation.

He wasn't directly employed by a government agency, but Gannon clearly was affiliated with the Bush White House. One particular blog post of his was obviously intended to inflame the right-wing base, "Kerry Could Become First Gay President." That particular piece was written a month before the 2004 presidential election and pointed to John Kerry's pro-gay rights voting record.[63] Furthermore, Gannon was apparently working with Karl Rove and played a significant role in spoiling the re-election campaign for then Senate Minority Leader, Tom Daschle (D-SD). Gannon's opposition blogging benefitted Dick Wadham, the campaign manager for Daschle's opponent, who had been a long-time ally of Karl Rove. In fact, *CBS News* mentioned that Gannon was known as the "resident D.C. expert on South Dakota politics" because he received inside scoops for stories that attacked former Senator Daschle's campaign. "This guy (Gannon) became the dumping ground for opposition research," claimed Daschle's aides.[64]

Another political prostitution scandal emerged only two years after the Jeff Gannon controversy concluded. In this case, there was considerably more media coverage because Deborah Jeane Palfrey, dubbed "the D.C. Madam," threatened to "out" many powerful people as part of her defense. She ran an exclusive escort agency that generated over $2 million of revenue and catered to over 10,000 clients within the nation's capital.

Much to Palfrey's surprise, she was arrested not long *after* closing her business, which had operated with little interference for thirteen years. By all means, the sex business was thriving in our nation's capital and there were 83 competing brothels and escort agencies in the area, according to Palfrey.[65] Nonetheless, her business was essentially singled out and became the focus of an investigation by multiple federal agencies that spanned over a six-year period![66] Hence, Palfrey and her attorneys theorized that she was the target of a politically-motivated prosecution. Many have speculated that someone within the Bush administration targeted the D.C. Madam's "black book" for political blackmail purposes, either to target their enemies or protect their allies.[F67]

The federal government came after her with the heavy-handed charges that are intended for mafia cases, the Racketeer Influenced and Corrupt Organizations Act (the RICO Act). If there truly was an underhanded federal conspiracy at hand, then the authorities were out of luck as there was no "black book" to confiscate. Palfrey didn't keep her clients' personal information; instead, she kept 13 years of phone records. Initially, she remained tight-lipped about revealing the identities of her powerful clientele. That is everyone except Dick Morris, *Fox News* contributor and former advisor to Bill Clinton. She publicly mentioned that Morris had been a client because his past involvement with prostitutes was already public knowledge.

She decided to leverage her clients' information and gave a portion of her phone records to Brian Ross of *ABC News* so they could cross reference the phone numbers.[G68] She claimed that this was part of her defense strategy by insisting that these men would certainly testify in her defense. However, she was clearly more intent on exposing the hypocrisy of this case because she knew the government had no interest in prosecuting her clientele.

Within those documents, Brian Ross and *ABC News* were able to identify officials from the White House, Pentagon, NASA, the

---

[F] Palfrey's civil defense attorney, Montgomery Sibley, alleged that Dick Cheney was potentially a client when he was Halliburton's CEO. That information was provided by the investigative journalist Wayne Madsen, a NSA whistleblower with a variety of contacts in the intelligence community.
[G] These were the Sprint phone records for 2002 to 2006.

World Bank, and the IMF. Also, there were CEOs of major corporations, along with military officers, prominent attorneys, powerful lobbyists for both major parties, TV personalities, and a "career Justice Department prosecutor."[H69] *ABC News* was sitting on a bombshell, but this was a peculiar dilemma because not every name was newsworthy. In the end, they decided to censor nearly every client's identity.

The first shoe to drop involved a relatively obscure name within political circles, Harlan Ullman. Ullman is a war-hawk author, military advisor, and a symbol for conservative culture. He is the creator of the "Shock and Awe" doctrine. Palfrey later said that Ullman was such a frequent client that he was allowed to pay by check.[70] Nonetheless, Ullman wasn't a public official and never had any influence on prostitution legislation; therefore this public embarrassment wasn't particularly relevant.

Randall Tobias, on the other hand, was remarkably pertinent in this matter. He was directly responsible for an "anti-prostitution pledge" and had to resign "for personal reasons" on the following day after a story by *ABC News*. Tobias admitted on the air that he had been a client of the D.C. Madam, but he insisted that he didn't have sex with the escorts. Instead, they only gave him "massages," he claimed.[I71]

The fact that Tobias had patronized the D.C. Madam, along with other escort services, was newsworthy because he had been appointed as the Administrator of the U.S. Agency for International Development (USAID). That meant that he was in charge of how our nation's AIDS prevention funding (PEPFAR) would be distributed to different organizations worldwide. During Tobias's tenure, the agency implemented policies rooted in

---

[H] The Justice Department refused to identify the prosecutor. They denied that there was a conflict of interest because the prosecutor had died in 2004.

[I] Bill O'Reilly, a strong critic of legalized prostitution and a "Culture Warrior," summoned his inner Libertarian to defend the right to privacy for Tobias and the rest of Palfrey's clients. He told Brian Ross, "I kind of feel sorry for this guy" and "I'm giving him the benefit of the doubt that he's a lonely guy. He got a couple of women to give him a massage, whatever. I don't really care about that. To me, I don't care. If...there is a quid pro quo then I start to care. But if it's just a guy had nothing to do on Saturday night, I don't care."

conservative ideology, rather than practicality. One of these endeavors included abstinence-only sex education. That was a change from the past as the former Surgeon General of the Clinton administration, Dr. Joycelyn Elders, once noted, "the vows of abstinence break far more often than latex condoms."[72]

There were other symbolic decisions by USAID that fell in line with right-wing principles but contradicted the best available scientific research. In particular, Randall Tobias vigorously defended the agency's requirement for "an anti-prostitution pledge."[73] That meant that no organization could receive funding for AIDS prevention if they "promote or advocate the legalization or practice of prostitution." To put it another way, it's alarmingly apropos that this ridiculous anti-prostitution pledge was an amendment proposed by former Rep. Todd Akin (R-MO) who seems to be living in a utopian conservative fantasy land.[74] Akin's ultra-right-wing ideology has blinded him from accepting obvious scientific facts. For instance, look no further than his response to whether rape victims should have the right to an abortion. He countered nonchalantly, "If it's a legitimate rape, the female body has ways to try to shut that whole thing down."[75]

An anti-prostitution pledge might sound like an insignificant gesture to rally the Republican base, but this has had tangible effects worldwide. The PEPFAR program is by far the most philanthropic effort worldwide by any nation with $15 billion allocated over the first five years. However, the anti-prostitution pledge flies in the face of reason and contradicts this organization's core mission. After all, the most prestigious international health organizations, including the World Health Organization, *support* the decriminalization of prostitution. These health officials know firsthand that criminalizing and further stigmatizing prostitution are major obstacles to AIDS prevention. Human Rights Watch wrote an open letter to former President Bush in opposition to the anti-prostitution pledge. It was signed by 171 leading organizations worldwide, along with 48 notable individuals.[76]

The USAID program has interpreted the terms "promoting or advocating prostitution" in an *extremely* broad manner at times and selectively enforced this rule. As a result, the anti-prostitution pledge has had a chilling effect on outreach work and has thwarted safe sex practices globally. Hence, some NGOs have refused to provide prostitutes with condoms out of fear that it could be considered "promoting prostitution." In fact, the possible defunding from appearing to be "pro prostitution" has scared organizations away from answering even the most basic sex education questions that weren't even related to prostitution. One particular NGO worker, Arpha Nota of Empower Foundation in Thailand, described the anti-prostitution pledge as the "George Bush Discrimination Policy" and has stated the obvious that it restricts the coordination between sex worker groups and non-sex worker groups.[77]

Unfortunately, condom usage rates are typically very low in some developing countries that have very high HIV rates. Therefore, that makes outreach work for sex workers all the more important in those regions of the world. India has the second highest number of AIDS-infected citizens in the world, and one particular Indian NGO, SANGRAM, was solely focused on harm reduction and safe sex practices for the area's sex workers. In fact, SANGRAM had been officially praised by USAID, along with UNAIDS, *before* the anti-prostitution pledge policy was put in place. However, this group was blocked from USAID funding specifically because they refused to follow the conditions of the anti-prostitution pledge.[78]

Several other deserving programs were defunded because of this pledge, but not every nation decided to cower to our authoritarian ways. Above all, Brazil's government made international headlines when it refused to accept $48 million of grant money from the U.S. due to our anti-prostitution pledge. Brazil has had tremendous success with reducing AIDS by not only offering free condoms to sex workers but also by having them participate as leaders in this battle. Sonia Correa, an Aids activist in Brazil who was instrumental in Brazil's HIV-prevention policy, noted that if their government had abided by the anti-prostitution pledge, it would have been "entirely in contradiction with Brazilian guidelines for a program that has been working very well for years."[79] The liberal policy of Brazil's government led to the number of projected AIDS infections being cut in half! That's why their HIV prevention program has been recognized by United

Nations health officials as the best in the world. "We provide information and resources, and don't enter into moral or religious issues," explained Mariangela Simao of the Brazilian national AIDS prevention program.[80]

The anti-prostitution pledge was supposed to become a thing of the past once President Obama took office. He issued an executive order, in one of his first acts as President, to reverse that rule. However, it was only a facade because his administration actually defended the anti-prostitution pledge in federal courts, including the Supreme Court![81] Nevertheless, there is a bright side to this story and the anti-prostitution pledge was eventually overturned because the U.S. Supreme Court ruled in 2013 that it was unconstitutional.[82] Albeit, that was only a partial victory because the Supreme Court's ruling applied to only U.S.-based organizations, not foreign NGOs.

Now, with the full context in mind, it is absolutely disgraceful that Randall Tobias was a firm supporter of the anti-prostitution pledge during his stint as the leader of USAID. In an indirect manner, the D.C. Madam brought this somewhat obscure issue into the light of day. Former Sen. David Vitter (R-LA) was the next big name to drop as one of the D.C. Madam's clients. With this information available to the public, Jeanette Maier, "the Canal Street Madam" from New Orleans who was targeted by the FBI, was all too happy to publicly allege that Vitter, "family values" candidate, had frequented her brothel as well. In fact, plenty of other politicians did so too. "It's the people running our country who visited our house -- mayors who did drugs and Republicans in pantyhose," said Maier.[83] Luckily for Vitter, he wasn't prosecuted in his home state of Louisiana, which has some of the most strict prostitution laws in the U.S.[J84] Nonetheless, Vitter was so flagrant about this activity that he arranged dates with the D.C.

[J] Louisiana still convicts prostitutes for solicitation under a 206-year-old Crime Against Nature law which has a maximum penalty of five years in prison and requires sex offender registry. It's also one of the most backward laws because Louisiana prostitution solicitation statutes only cover vaginal sex. That means by law prostitutes must be charged with a Crime Against Nature if they offer oral sex.

madam's escorts while he was on the floor of Congress, according to his phone records.[85]

It's fitting that David Vitter was the replacement of another "family values" conservative, former Sen. Bob Livingston. Livingston's downfall came about from the pornographer Larry Flynt, owner of Hustler Magazine. Livingston was someone whose head Flynt figuratively wanted on his mantle because Livingston was part of the Republican leadership that demanded Clinton's resignation. Flynt offered a $1 million reward during Clinton's impeachment hearings to anyone who could provide evidence of an affair with a prominent politician. "I just wanted to expose hypocrisy. If these guys are going after the President, they shouldn't have any skeletons in their closet," said Flynt.[86] Well, he certainly was provided with that opportunity when Hustler Magazine's former editor, Allan MacDonell, received a stunning tip from someone at *CBS News*. According to his source, Bob Livingston wasn't merely having an extramarital affair; he was implementing the agendas of various corporate lobbyists in exchange for sexual favors. Livingston certainly seemed to blink first because he resigned only hours after MacDonell publicly made those allegations.[87] Oddly enough, Livingston opened his own powerful lobbying firm after leaving office.

Again, former Sen. David Vitter was Bob Livingston's replacement. Therefore, you may be surprised to learn that the conservative base rallied around Vitter and supported his decision not to resign. Even Bob Livingston said that Vitter should not resign. On the other hand, former Sen. Larry Craig (R-ID) had been arrested for lewd conduct in a public men's restroom one month earlier and he was pressured to resign by his own party. Hmm…why was there such selective moral outrage? As some have aptly pointed out, it was much easier to replace Larry Craig with another Republican Senator in Idaho, but a Democrat would likely have become Vitter's replacement if he had resigned.[88]

The only repercussions that Vitter faced from this scandal were in the form of public embarrassment. In fact, just months after the scandal, Vitter received the "True Blue" award from the Family Research Council (FRC) with a 100% approval rating for "consistently voting in a pro-family manner." Tony Perkins who runs the FRC stated, "He left me convinced that I should give him another chance. He (Vitter) certainly has not changed his positions. If anything, he's gotten stronger and more resolute in his firm conservative stance."[89] For example, Vitter said "protecting the sanctity of marriage" against same-sex marriages was the single most important issue in America.[90]

None of the D.C. Madam's clients were forced to testify nor did any of them face any legal penalties. That may sound unusual, but it is actually the norm with these high-profile madam court cases.[K][91] In the end, the Deborah Jeane Palfrey bore the brunt of the federal government's wrath and was convicted of money laundering, racketeering, and conspiracy. She faced a maximum of 55 years in prison, but two weeks after her conviction, while awaiting sentencing, she was found dead of an apparent suicide by hanging. Naturally, some people have speculated that foul play was involved based upon the suspicious circumstances.[L][92] Others had pointed out that she would have been around 60 years old when she left prison (assuming she was to serve six to eight years) and her entire life savings had been confiscated by the government with asset forfeiture. She also had apparently attempted suicide four days earlier with an overdose of Ambien.[93]

In this instance, only a few prominent Republicans were publicly identified, but these escort services were frequented in a

---

[K] One of the more salacious examples involved the "black book" from Kathy Willets. Her attorney defended her activity by asserting that Willets was a nymphomaniac and that her husband was sometimes impotent. Her husband, a Broward County sheriff, was arrested for acting as her pimp. He routinely watched the sex through a closet and kept notes about each client. One of their clients was Doug Danziger, former Ft. Lauderdale Vice Mayor, who had crusaded against the area's strip clubs and pornography shops. A number of other men on the list formally requested the court to not publicly release their identities.

[L] Palfrey specifically stated that she would never commit suicide and was looking forward to going to trial during an interview on the Alex Jones Radio Show a year earlier. She later added to that assertion by telling the press that, "I guess I'm made of something that Brandy Britton wasn't made of." Brandy Britton escorted part-time for Palfrey while working as a professor at the University of Maryland. However, she hanged herself after her career was ruined from her prostitution arrest.

bipartisan manner. The D.C. Madam case remained out of the public conscious for many years. But that changed during the presidential campaign of 2016 due to an announcement by her former defense attorney, Montgomery Blair Sibley. According to Sibley, one of the remaining candidates at that time (Donald Trump, John Kasich, Ted Cruz, Bernie Sanders, or Hillary Clinton) had patronized the D.C. Madam.[94]

Sibley held on to roughly 5,000 unreleased phone records relating to 815 of the D.C. Madam's former clients. According to Sibley, he wanted to keep that information as a form of negotiating power, but the judge issued a restraining order in 2007 barring anyone from releasing those records.[95] Nonetheless, Sibley appealed that decision all the way to the U.S. Supreme Court. In May of 2016, the U.S. Supreme Court upheld the restraining order because Sibley didn't have the legal right to that information. He obtained those records as a defense attorney for Deborah Jeane Palfrey, but she fired him before her trial concluded. Therefore, he had to hand over all files by law.[96] We'll never know if there was any truth to Sibley's accusations, but his announcement came at a time when rumors surrounding the sex life of ultra-conservative Ted Cruz were mentioned in the news by way of the tabloids. For what it's worth, the *National Enquirer* launched an anonymously-sourced story titled, "A HOOKER, A TEACHER & COWORKERS: 5 romps that will destroy Ted Cruz!"

In fairness to the Republican Party, this chapter has focused primarily on conservative leaders because the hypocrisy is more glaring. However, some of the most notable political prostitution scandals have involved renowned Democrats. Many people reveled in the fall from grace of former Rep. Wayne Hays (D-OH), one of the most influential Congressmen at the time. Hays, "the Archie Bunker of Capitol Hill," had a hard-nosed reputation for abusing his power. He resigned in 1976 after it surfaced that his mistress had been employed as his secretary for two years at the taxpayer's expense. Her only real responsibilities were sexual. His mistress, Elizabeth Ray, told reporters, "I can't type. I can't file. I can't even answer the phone."[97]

A media frenzy unfolded two years earlier involving the former Chairman of the House Ways and Means Committee,

Wilbur Mills. Police apprehended Mills driving drunk with a stripper from Argentina who went by the stage name "Fannie Foxe." During the traffic stop, the police discovered injuries from an apparent fight between the two. Wilbur had a bloody nose and scratches on his face; Fannie Foxe had two black eyes.[98] This incident surprisingly didn't ruin Mills' political career and he managed to be re-elected one more time. The final nail in the coffin was struck just weeks after the election when he visited Fannie Foxe at a strip club in Boston. He even drunkenly stepped on stage and held an impromptu press conference for some members of the media in the audience. To sum up, the negative press spread quickly and the Democratic leadership pressured him never to seek re-election again.[99]

Historically speaking, the liberal base has been more forgiving when a Democrat has been involved in a prostitution scandal.[M][100] For instance, former Congressman Joe Waggonner was re-elected after a prostitution arrest in 1976. Granted, the circumstances surrounding Waggonner's case were unique because he was immediately released from jail. Believe it or not, his release was based on an obscure law which granted immunity to all Congressmen from any misdemeanor charges. On a positive note, this well-publicized arrest prompted that law to be changed.[101]

Former Congressman Fred Richmond was re-elected two times after being arrested for soliciting sex with a 16-year-old male prostitute in 1978. Remarkably, his lawyers managed to get the charges dropped because he agreed to receive psychiatric treatment.[102] His get-out-of-jail-free card eventually expired and his legal woes intensified two years later when federal investigators found that Richmond was guilty of corruption involving military contracts. Also, he forced his staffers to buy him marijuana and cocaine. Nonetheless, the judicial system still granted Congressman Richmond tremendous leniency. In fact, an

---

[M] Jerry Springer is well known for his wild TV show, but his former career was in politics. He was a city councilman in Cincinnati, before he was forced to resign. He had been implicated in a brothel raid because he paid a prostitute with a personal check. Apparently, Springer was somewhat self-deprecating and humbled by the experience which helped him to be re-elected in 1975 as a city councilman. He later became Cincinnati's mayor in 1979.

unidentified man was found dead in his apartment from a drug overdose before his sentencing. Yet, he only served nine months in prison after pleading guilty to tax evasion, possession of marijuana, and improper payments to a federal employee.[103]

A prostitution scandal didn't ruin former Congressman Barney Frank's career either. He was already out of the closet when in 1989 he admitted that he had an intimate relationship with a male prostitute, Stephen Gobie. He also hired Gobie as his personal assistant and allowed him to move into his apartment. According to Frank, he was unaware that Gobie continued to operate his escort service while living with him. Afterward, Frank testified that he ended the relationship once his landlord notified him about what was happening during the daytime. Frank said, "I assumed it was something he personally was doing, not that he was arranging it for other people." In the end, the House Committee on Ethics concluded that he committed several violations but couldn't prove that he was aware of the extent of Gobie's escort business.[N104]

There are several more examples of these types of scandals, but only one of these politicians had publicly supported the decriminalization of prostitution *before* the scandal occurred; it was Barney Frank. Barney Frank was a Massachusetts State Representative in 1975 when he introduced legislation that would have officially recognized the "Combat Zone" district of Boston as an adult entertainment district. The Combat Zane was a small section of Boston comprised of mostly adult theaters and strip clubs. Barney Frank's bill would have recognized the area as a de facto red-light district with decriminalized prostitution. Barney Frank's bill was never passed even though it was at the behest of the Boston Police Commissioner at that time.[105]

Unlike the other politicians who've been criticized in this chapter, Barney Frank shouldn't be labeled as a hypocrite. With that said, Dick Morris, of all people, attacked Barney Frank for his relationship with an escort during an appearance on the Sean

---

[N] He "acted improperly" by using his influence to see that Gobie's 33 parking tickets (cited while using Frank's car) were thrown out. Also, considering Frank's role as Gobie's employer, "the congressman interceded with probation authorities on behalf of Mr. Gobie."

Hannity Show in 2009. He mocked Frank for running "a gay prostitution ring out of his house office."[106] Yes, that's the same Dick Morris who was fired from Bill Clinton's campaign due to a prostitution scandal.[O][107]

Barney Frank and Ron Paul have been the only high-profile politicians on Capitol Hill brave enough to support decriminalizing prostitution. Those are bold stances as there isn't much political momentum for decriminalizing prostitution. However, these viewpoints weren't coincidental because neither man was beholden to their respective parties. In spirit, Ron Paul is a Libertarian and Barney Frank is a Progressive. Bear in mind, the Progressives were instrumental in implementing prostitution laws in the early 20th century, but they are now generally associated with very liberal social policies.

The last major poll of this kind was conducted in 2008 with New York respondents after the Eliot Spitzer scandal. By a margin of 62% to 30%, they opposed legalized prostitution.[108] However, opinions are changing and YouGov.com conducted a similar poll seven years later after Amnesty International issued their report supporting decriminalized prostitution. YouGuv.com found that 44% of Americans supported legalized prostitution with 46% opposed.[P][109]

All things considered, decriminalized prostitution seems to be now supported at a rate that is similar to legalized marijuana in the mid-2000s.[110] Remember, the American public drastically reevaluated the marijuana issue because the stigma had dwindled due to a few states voting for legalization. That kind of momentum shift can happen very quickly, but it takes a lot of advocacy effort. All that is needed is for one city, county, or maybe even a state to

---

[O] "Hard Copy" interviewed Sherry Rowlands, the woman who exposed Morris. She said that Morris actually allowed her to listen silently to a phone call he had with Bill Clinton.

[P] A simple google search provides polls from a variety of websites and usually the results show very strong support for legalizing prostitution. Obviously, online polls don't fully represent the diverse demographics of Americans and have more methodological flaws than professional services. However, they differ in one very important aspect; they offer more anonymity. Therefore, there may be a slight "stigma bias" in which some Americans truly support decriminalized prostitution, but only as long as they can do so anonymously.

make the change and it will send a signal of credibility to voters nationwide. Luckily, twenty-four states have the ballot initiatives in which citizens can propose law changes via petitions.[111] In fact, that is how recreational marijuana was legalized in eight states and the District of Columbia. The takeaway is that you can't depend on your elected officials to bring about this change.

Some activists, such as Robyn Few (founder of the Sex Worker Outreach Program), have accepted the challenge. She obtained more than 2,000 signatures in a petition drive in Berkeley, CA in 2004 for a ballot measure to decriminalize prostitution. Robyn Few, who dubbed herself the "patriotic prostitute," came about her nickname as a dig at the FBI due to her arrest in 2002 for conspiracy to promote prostitution as a result of a PATRIOT ACT investigation.[112] The nickname also alludes to the fact that this issue affects society as a whole and involves several other factors such as public safety and health, privacy, fiscal responsibility, etc. Nevertheless, even in a liberal city like Berkeley, most voters were reluctant to become the first city in decades to formally overturn their prostitution laws. In the end, Measure Q was voted down at a rate of 63.5%.[113] However, Robyn Few acknowledged before the vote, "The point is to start a groundswell and a dialogue. This thing didn't start in Berkeley and it won't end in Berkeley."[114]

She also pioneered a similar measure that received over 12,000 signatures in San Francisco in 2008. And this time around there was more official support for this initiative by people in prominent positions, including the Democratic County Central Committee, the city's Health Department Director of STD control and prevention, a former District Attorney, among others.[115] The measure would have saved the city millions of dollars annually in law enforcement costs, but Proposition K was also voted down, albeit this time around at a less decisive rate of 59%.[116]

These kinds of persistent grassroots efforts will likely be necessary to pass a decriminalization bill. You shouldn't hold your breath waiting for your local government officials to draft that type of proposal, but Hawaii was an exception. In 2007 legislation was written (SB 706 and its companion bill HB 982) that would have decriminalized indoor prostitution and established specific zones for prostitution. The bill even had 13 sponsors in the Hawaiian

House of Representatives and one in the Senate. It was supported by the ACLU, along with some women's rights groups, but the bill didn't make it past the House. Despite the results, one of the bill's sponsors, Rep. Bob Herkes pointed out that simply writing legislation was a step in the right direction. He said, "It's one of those bills you do it for public dialogue instead of trying to get it passed."[117]

The New Hampshire state legislature wrote a proposal to decriminalize prostitution in 2016 as well. And hold onto your hat, it came about in the aftermath of a local political figure being arrested for prostitution.[118] *Who could have seen that one coming?* Nonetheless, this was a bipartisan effort and the authors of the bill were inspired by Amnesty International's recommendations.[119] Likewise, a Washington D.C. Council member proposed a similar bill just months earlier specifically due to Amnesty International's report.[120]

It takes some thick skin to be a trailblazer with this issue, but there are mature Americans who are ready for this to happen. In fact, Hawaii's decriminalization bill was even well received by some local religious leaders. "In general, talking about sex is scary for people," said the Rev. Pam Vessels of the United Church of Christ in Kalaupapa on Moloka'i. "We need to talk about it, not get excited about it and throw rocks at each other. Do we really care if consenting adults are engaging in sexual acts for money?"[121] You know, maybe those wise words will catch on someday. After all, our elected leaders can't consistently abide by these laws.

To wrap up, the issue of prostitution is alarmingly similar to drugs and gambling. It would be great to live in a world where no one is addicted to drugs or gambling, and no one feels the need to sell sex to survive. However, that is an unrealistic ideal. Sure, these vices are harmful to society in a variety of ways, but banning them has caused considerably worse collateral damage. Simply put, the prohibition is worse than the vice. To say it another way, the cure is worse than the disease. Enforcing these laws has been a very wasteful expense for the taxpayers and those efforts have failed to noticeably impact the supply and demand.

There are several unintended consequences from these vice laws. For every impractical law that a government imposes, society loses respect for the rule of law. History has proven that the government can't legislate morality. These are not winnable battles; thus legalization, decriminalization, regulation, education, and harm reduction are the keys to combating these matters most effectively.

The law enforcement side of our government is no longer capable of addressing these issues in an impartial manner. There are too many conflicts of interest and financial incentives that benefit the prison industrial complex. "Every great cause begins as a movement, becomes a business, and eventually degenerates into a racket." This popular paraphrasing of a quote by the author Eric Hoffer captures the reality of the wars on drugs, gambling, and prostitution.

The Declaration of Independence guaranteed the right to "life, liberty, and the pursuit of happiness." That means tolerating the people who have made life choices that you disagree with, including drugs, gambling, and prostitution. The problem is that the symbolic nature of these three vices provides a platform for ambitious politicians to brand themselves as "moral crusaders." By the same token, the stigma associated with the legalization of drugs, gambling, and prostitution is difficult to overcome.

Few Americans believe that we should return to the days of the prohibition of alcohol. With that in mind, if you think that alcohol should remain legal no one would suggest that you hope to see our country morph into a nation of pathetic drunks. That's a ridiculous thought, but that is a common misperception with the legalization of drugs, gambling, and prostitution. Advocates for legalization have been labeled as "un-American," "junkie enablers," "supporters of predatory gambling," and/or "purveyors of human trafficking."

The other connotation is that drugs, gambling, and prostitution are frivolous issues. And that couldn't be further from the truth. These three crimes have flooded our prisons with non-violent offenders who didn't need to be incarcerated. Due to the sheer volume of criminal cases, judges have been forced to unofficially issue lengthier prison sentences as a deterrent for those who take their cases to trial. Clearly, that has led an untold number of people to plead guilty to crimes that they didn't commit. We can't stand by and allow that to happen anymore.

If marijuana and skill-based gambling, such as sports betting and online poker, were legalized it would create hundreds of thousands of jobs and produce billions of dollars of tax revenues. Not to mention, if the drug war had ended 40 years ago, it would have wiped a trillion dollars off of our national debt. Ending the drug war would not only reduce the violence in our streets, but it would also drastically reduce the death toll throughout the world. Likewise, an untold amount of violence has been caused by keeping gambling and prostitution in the shadow of the black market. There would unquestionably be fewer overdose deaths, more addicts receiving rehabilitation services, and a reduction in the spread of deadly diseases if drug addiction and prostitution were addressed as public health issues and treated with proven harm reduction methods. And those are just a few of the benefits of legalization.

As a reminder, in the introduction of volume one of this book series, it was mentioned that an auditorium of liberal-minded voters laughed at the idea of legalizing drugs, gambling, and prostitution during President Obama's earliest days. Has there been much progress since then? Absolutely. Recreational marijuana is now legal in eight states and the District of Columbia. The stigma associated with harm reduction for harder drugs is also rapidly declining. Furthermore, various world leaders have suggested ending the drug war. In addition, online poker is now legal in three states; daily fantasy sports is legal in eight states. Congress may even vote on a bill to legalize sports gambling in the next year. Lastly, New Hampshire nearly decriminalized prostitution. And there have been several other examples of progress, but we have a long way to go. Thankfully, the activists who were responsible for these changes weren't swayed by the president's skepticism. For this momentum to continue, we are all going to have to contribute. So please get involved and don't be afraid to let your voice be heard.

NAMES AND ORGANIZATIONS

Almodovar, Norma Jean – Former LAPD officer turned sex worker and activist. She is the author of *Cop to Call Girl*.

Calvert, Ken – Republican Congressman from California was once caught by the police with a prostitute in his car. He is also known for his unethical earmark spending.

Conforte, Joe – Nevada brothel owner who manipulated the political process to legalize prostitution in his county.

(COYOTE) (Call Off Your Old Tired Ethics) – One of the pioneering sex worker activist organizations, which was founded by Margo St. James.

"D.C. Madam" (Debra Jeane Palfrey) - Some of the most powerful men from government and business patronized her escort service. This scandal resulted in a media firestorm.

(ESPLERP) (Erotic Service Providers Legal Education, and Research Project) – This group has a pending lawsuit against the state of California that challenges the constitutionality of prostitution laws.

Gannon, Jeff (real name James Guckert) - Reporter for Talon News that was a proxy for the Republican Party. He also owned and operated a few gay escort services.

Goldman, Emma – Anarchist activist who opposed all conservative restrictions on women's fundamental rights.

International Day to End Violence Against Sex Workers (December 17th) A serial killer, Gary Ridgeway, was sentenced on this date. This day now serves a memorial for all sex workers who have been murdered.

Leigh, Carol – Sex worker rights activist who coined the term "sex worker."

McCahon, Sam – Former federal prosecutor who is a leading whistleblower concerned with human trafficking violations committed by subcontractors of the U.S. military.

St. James, Margo – Founder of COYOTE whose lawsuit prompted the state of Rhode Island to reform its prostitution laws.

Project RENEW (Revitalizing and Engaging Neighborhoods by Empowering Women) – A diversion program in Pawtucket, RI to help sex workers find the necessary services to escape the sex industry.

ROKS – Swedish organization that provides women's shelters. Some Swedish political leaders are linked with this organization and its brand of radical feminism.

Sex Workers Project at the Urban Justice Center – This non-profit organization supports sex worker rights and provides academic studies on topics related to the sex industry.

(SWOP) Sex Workers Outreach Project – Sex worker rights organization with chapters throughout the world. SWOP has been one of the leading lobbyist groups pushing for ballot initiatives to decriminalize prostitution.

Tobias, Randall – Client of the D.C. Madam who was the Administrator of the U.S. Agency for International Development (USAID) and a supporter of the "Anti-Prostitution Pledge."

Woodhull, Victoria – This "free love" activist was the first female Presidential nominee. She and her sister, Tennessee Claflin, were the first women to publish their own newspaper and open a brokerage on Wall Street.

References and Notes

Chapter 1

[1] Gerda Lerner. *The Creation of Patriarchy*. New York: Oxford University Press, 1986. Print. P 131
[2] Mary Dian Molton and Lucy Ann Sikes. *Four Eternal Women*. Carmel, CA: Fisher King Press, 2011. Print. P 83
[3] Eric Berkowitz. *Sex and Punishment: Four Thousand Years of Judging Desire*. Berkeley, CA: Counterpoint, 2012. Print. P 38
[4] Larry Siegel. *Criminology*. Belmont, CA: Cengage Learning, 2009. Print. P 483
[5] Nils Johan Ringdal. *Love For Sale: A World History of Prostitution*. New York: Grove Press, 2004. Print. P 54-57
[6] Ibid.
[7] Vern Bullough and Bonnie Bullough. *Women and Prostitution: A Social History*. New York: Prometheus Books, 1987. Print. P 39
[8] Reay Tannahill. *Sex in History*. New York: Scarborough House, 1991. Print. P 101
[9] Vern Bullough and Bonnie Bullough. P 50
[10] Vern Bullough and Bonnie Bullough. P 48
[11] Eric Berkowitz. P 102
[12] Nils Johan Ringdal. P 86
[13] Eric Berkowitz. P 107
[14] Vern Bullough and Bonnie Bullough. P 55
[15] *What Life Was Like Was Like When Rome Ruled the World: The Roman Empire 100 BC – AD 200*. Alexandria, VA: Time-Life Books, 1997. Print.
[16] Henry Mayhew. *London Labour and the London Poor: Volume IV*. New York: Cosimo, 2009. Print. P 193
[17] "Historical Timeline: History of Prostitution from 2400 BC to the Present." *ProCon.org*.
[18] Havelock Ellis. *Studies in the Psychology of Sex*. New York: Random House, 1942. Print. P 240
[19] Nils Johan Ringdal. P 137-139
[20] Kathryn Nordberg. *History of Women in the West: III. Renaissance and Enlightenment Paradoxes*. Ed. Natalie Zemon Davis and Arlette Farge. Cambridge and London: The Belknap Press of the Harvard University Press, 1993. Print. P 458
[21] Nils Johan Ringdal. P 153
[22] Reay Tannahill. P 278
[23] Melissa Hope Ditmore. *Encyclopedia of Sex Work and Prostitution Vol. II*. Westport, CT: Greenwood Publishing Group, 2006. Print. P 389

[24] Nils Johan Ringdal. P 174
[25] Melissa Hope Ditmore. *Encyclopedia of Sex Work and Prostitution Vol. II.* P 390, 394
[26] John D'Emilio and Estelle B. Freedman. *Intimate Matters: A History of Sexuality in America.* New York: Harper & Row Publishers, 1988. Print. P 50
[27] Larry Flynt and David Eisenbach. *One Nation Under Sex: How Private Lives of Presidents, First Ladies and their Lovers Changed the Course of American History.* New York: Palgrave Macmillan, 2011. Print. P 5
[28] Larry Flynt and David Eisenbach. P 5
[29] Barbara Meil Hobson. *Uneasy Virtue: The Politics of Prostitution and the American Reform Tradition.* New York: Basic Books Inc, 1987. Print. P 17-24
[30] Jack Tager. *Boston Riots: Three Centuries of Social Violence.* Boston: Northeastern University Press, 2001. Print. P 163
[31] Timothy J. Gilfoyle. *City of Eros: New York City, Prostitution, and the Commercialization of Sex, 1790 – 1920.* New York and London: W.W. Norton & Company, 1992. Print. P 77-78
[32] Nils Johan Ringdal. P 277
[33] Michael Rutter. P 28
[34] "America's Secret Slang." *History Channel.* Season one Episode Four
[35] Marion S. Goldman. *Gold Diggers & Silver Miners: Prostitution and Social Life on the Comstock Lode.* Ann Arbor, MI: University of Michigan Press, 1981. Print. P 16
[36] Michael Rutter. P 80
[37] Herbert Asbury. *The Barbary Coast: An Informal History of the San Francisco Underworld.* New York: Garden City Publishing, 1933. Print. P 32
[38] Anne M. Butler. *Daughters of Joy, Sisters of Misery: Prostitutes in the American West, 1865-90.* Urbana: University of Illinois Press, 1985. Print. P 135-145
[39] Michael Rutter. *Upstairs Girls: Prostitution in the American West.* Helena, MT: Farcountry Press, 2005. Print. P 40
[40] Michael Rutter. P 38-40
[41] John D'Emilio and Estelle B. Freedman. P 134
[42] Edwin G. Burrows and Mike Wallace. *Gotham: A History of New York City to 1898.* Oxford: Oxford University Press, 1999. Print. P 484
[43] Ibid.
[44] Anne M. Butler. P 122
[45] William Moss Wilson. "The Nashville Experiment." *New York Times.*
[46] Timothy J. Gilgoyle. P 112
[47] Jan MacKell. *Brothels, Bordellos, & Bad Girls: Prostitution in Colorado, 1860 – 1930.* University of New Mexico Press, 2004. Print. P 34
[48] Michael Rutter. P 14
[49] Karen Abbott. *Sin in the Second City: Madams, Ministers, Playboys, and the Battle for America's Soul.* New York: Random House, 2007. Print. P 6, 68

[50] Jan MacKell. P 7-10
[51] Mara L. Keire. *For Business & Pleasure: Red-Light Districts and the Regulation of Vice in the United States, 1890 – 1933*. Baltimore: Johns Hopkins University Press, 2010. Print. P 31
[52] Jan MacKell. P 1
[53] Anne Seagraves. *Soiled Doves: Prostitution in the Early West*. Hayden, ID: Wesanne Publications, 1994. Print. P 59
[54] Lecture by Sherita Thompson at Gettysburg College on June 25, 2011. CSPAN.
[55] Timothy J. Gilfoyle. P 124
[56] Ruth Rosen. *Lost Sisterhood: Prostitution in America, 1900-1918*. Baltimore: Johns Hopkins University Press, 1982. Print. P 48
[57] Barbara Meil Hobson. P 99
[58] Christine Stansell. *City of Women: Sex and Class in New York City, 1789-1860*. New York: Knopf, 1986. Print. P 156
[59] John D'Emilio and Estelle B. Freedman. P 214
[60] Michael Rutter. P 5
[61] Nils Johan Ringdal. P 264-273
Vern Bullough and Bonnie Bullough. P 125
[62] Anne Seagraves. P 28
[63] Allen Eugene Wagner. *Good Order and Safety: A History of the St. Louis Metropolitan Police Department, 1861-1906*. Columbia, MO: University of Missouri Press, 2008. Print. P 117
[64] Allen Eugene Wagner. P 108
[65] Allen Eugene Wagner. P 117
[66] Vern Bullough and Bonnie Bullough. P 224
[67] Timothy J. Gilfoyle. P 141
[68] Sharon E. Wood. *The Freedom of the Streets: Work, Citizenship, and Sexuality in a Gilded Age City*. Chapel Hill: U of North Carolina, 2005. Print. P 184
[69] Joel Best. "Keeping the Peace in St. Paul: Crime, Vice, and Police Work, 1869-74." *Minnesota History*. Vol. 47, No. 6 (summer 1981): p. 240-248.
[70] Ruth Rosen. P 16-17
[71] Richard Zacks. *Island of Vice: Theodore Roosevelt's Doomed Quest to Clean up Sin-Loving New York*. New York: Doubleday, 2012. Print. P 8
[72] Karen Abbott. P 273
[73] Ruth Rosen. P 14
Michael McGerr. *A Fierce Discontent: The Rise and Fall of the Progressive Movement in America, 1870-1920*. New York: Free Press, 2003. Print. P 89
[74] Mike Dash. *Satan's Circus: Murder, Vice, Police Corruption, and New York's Trial of the Century*. New York: Crown Publishing, 2007. Print.
[75] Richard Zacks. P 88
[76] Timothy J. Gilgoyle. P 203

[77] Mark Thomas Connelly. *The Response to Prostitution in the Progressive Era.* Chapel Hill: University of North Carolina Press, 1980. Print. P 1, 26
[78] Mara L. Keire. P 9-10
[79] Gary Krist. *Empire of Sin: A Story of Sex, Jazz, Murder, and the Battle for Modern New Orleans.* New York: Crown Publishers, 2014. Print. P 71-72
[80] Melissa Hope Ditmore. *Encyclopedia of Sex Work and Prostitution Vol. I.* Westport, CT: Greenwood Publishing Group, 2006. Print. P 329
[81] Herbert Asbury. *The French Quarter: An Informal History of the New Orleans Underworld.* New York: Old Town Books, 1936. Print. P 436
Gilbert King. "The Portrait of Sensitivity: A Photographer in Storyville, New Orleans' Forgotten Burlesque Quarter." *Smithsonian Magazine.*
[82] Gary Krist. P 182, 236, 237
[83] Melissa Hope Ditmore. *Prostitution and Sex Work: Historical Guides to Controversial Issues in America.* P 52
[84] Melissa Hope Ditmore. *Encyclopedia of Sex Work and Prostitution Vol. II.* P 462
[85] Vern Bullough and Bonnie Bullough. P 283
[86] Mara L. Keire. P 97
[87] Ruth Rosen. P 116
[88] Anne Seagraves. P 136
[89] Jan MacKell. P 194
[90] Herbert Asbury. *The Barbary Coast: An Informal History of the San Francisco Underworld.* P 172
[91] Herbert Asbury. *The Barbary Coast: An Informal History of the San Francisco Underworld.* P 168
Michael Rutter. P 41-46
[92] Karen Abbott. P 123
[93] Brian Donovan. *White Slave Crusades: Race, Gender, and Anti-Vice Activism, 1887-1917.* Urbana: University of Illinois Press, 2006. Print. P 90
[94] Brian Donovan. P1-2
[95] Ruth Rosen. P 115
[96] Mark Thomas Connelly. P 118
[97] Brian Donovan. P 63
[98] David J. Langum. P 34
[99] James R. Petersen. *The Century of Sex: Playboy's History of the Sexual Revolution, 1900-1999.* New York: Grove, 1999. Print. P 55
[100] Gail Collins. *America's Women: Four Hundred Years of Dolls, Drudges, Helpmates, and Heroines.* New York: William Morrow, 2003. Print. P 322
[101] Timothy J. Gilfoyle. P 302
[102] Karen Abbott. P 221
[103] Brian Donovan. P 91-92
[104] Ibid.
[105] Brian Donovan. P 94-107

[106] David J. Langum. P 33-34
[107] Mark Thomas Connelly. P 130
[108] Brian Donovan. P 75
[109] Brian Donovan. P 32
[110] Karen Abbott. P 122, 129, 145
Joanne McNeil. "The 'White Slavery' Panic." *Reason*.
Timothy J. Gilfoyle. P 265-266
[111] Laura Hapke. *Girls Who Went Wrong: Prostitutes in American Fiction, 1885-1917*. Bowling Green State University Popular Press, 1989. Print. P 124
[112] David J. Langum. P 35
[113] Karen Abbott. P 222
[114] James A. Morone. *Hellfire Nation: The Politics of Sin in American History*. New Haven & London: Yale University Press, 2003. Print. P 269
[115] Mark Thomas Connelly. P 55-58
[116] Karen Abbott. P 223
[117] Matthew R. Linderoth. *Prohibition on the North Jersey Shore: Gangsters on Vacation*. Charleston, SC: The History Press, 2010. Print. P 20
[118] Jessica R. Pliley. *Policing Sexuality: The Mann Act and the Making of the FBI*. Cambridge and London: Harvard University Press, 2014. Print. P 95
[119] Mark Thomas Connelly. P 75, 65
[120] James A. Morone. P 267
[121] Ibid.
[122] David J. Langum. P 75, 148, 65
[123] David J. Langum. P 49
[124] *Unforgivable Blackness. The Rise and Fall of Jack Johnson*. Dir. Ken Burns. PBS Home Video. 2005. DVD.
[125] David J. Langum. P 180
[126] Karen Abbott. P 181
[127] *Unforgivable Blackness: The Rise and Fall of Jack Johnson*.
Rhodri Jeffreys-Jones. *The FBI: A History*. Caravan Books, 2007. Print.
[128] Associated Press. "Congress Approves Jack Johnson Pardon."
[129] David J. Langum. P 185
[130] Melissa Hope Ditmore. *Prostitution and Sex Work: Historical Guides to Controversial Issues in America*. P 82
[131] Theodore Roosevelt letter to Charles B. Davenport. January 3, 1913.
[132] David J. Pivar. *Purity and Hygiene: Women, Prostitution, and the "American Plan," 1900-1930*. Westport, CT: Greenwood Press, 2002. Print. P 111-129
[133] Edwin Black. *War Against the Weak: Eugenics and America's Campaign to Create a Master Race*. New York: Four Walls Eight Windows, 2003. Print. P 258, 418
[134] Michael Nevins. *Abraham Flexner: A Flawed American Icon*. Bloomingdale, IN: iUniverse, 2010. Print. P 20

[135] Melissa Hope Ditmore. *Encyclopedia of Sex Work and Prostitution Vol. I.* P 146
[136] Edwin Black. P 68
[137] Ruth Rosen. P 21
[138] Elizabeth Cohen and Jon Bonifield. "California's dark legacy of forced sterilizations." *CNN.*
[139] James A. Morone. P 276
[140] David J. Pivar. P 154
[141] Susan Currell and Christina Cogdell. *Popular Eugenics: National Efficiency and American Mass Culture in the 1930s.* Athens, OH: University of Ohio Press, 2006. Print. P 37
[142] Edwin Black. P 123
[143] Edwin Black. P 78
[144] Mara L. Keire. P 107
Barbara Meil Hobson. P 149
[145] Gary Krist. P 300
[146] Barbara Meil Hobson. P 166
[147] Barbara Meil Hobson. P 165
[148] Barbara Meil Hobson. P 180
[149] Mark Thomas Connelly. P 138
[150] Mara L. Keire. P 106
[151] Barbara Meil Hobson. P 166-176
[152] Ruth Rosen. P 35
[153] Mara L. Keire. P 109
[154] Melissa Hope Ditmore. *Prostitution and Sex Work: Historical Guides to Controversial Issues in America.* P 71
[155] Melissa Hope Ditmore. *Prostitution and Sex Work: Historical Guides to Controversial Issues in America.* P 78
[156] Mara L. Keire. P 97
[157] Timothy J. Gilfoyle. P 310
[158] Alfred McCoy. *The Politics of Heroin in Southeast Asia.* New York: Harper & Row, 1972. Print. P 19
[159] Frederick Lewis Allen. *The 1920s.* Ed. John F. Wukowits. San Diego: Greenhaven Press, 2000. Print. P 151
[160] Timothy J. Gilfoyle. P 312
Thomas Maier. *Masters of Sex: The Life and Times of William Masters and Virginia Johnson, the Couple Who Taught America How to Love.* New York: Basic Books, 2009. Print. P 82
[161] Matthew Bandyk. "The SuperFreakonomics of Prostitution: Levitt and Dubner in Trouble Again." *U.S. News & World Report.*
[162] Martin A. Monto. "Focusing on the Clients of Street Prostitutes: A Creative Approach to Reducing Violence against Women – Final Report."

[163] Jane Mersky Leder. *Thanks for the Memories: Love, Sex, and World War II.* Westport, CT: Praeger Publishers, 2006. Print. P 34
[164] "Brothels that Built America." *American Heroes Channel.*
[165] Beth Bailey and David Farber. "Prostitutes on Strike: The Women of Hotel Street during World War II."
[166] Ibid.
[167] Jane Mersky Leder. P 36
[168] Ted Chernin. "My Experiences in the Honolulu Chinatown Red-Light District."
[169] Robert J. MacCoun and Peter Reuter. *Drug War Heresies: Learning from Other Vices, Times, and Places.* Cambridge, U.K.: Cambridge University Press, 2001. Print. P 152
[170] Barbara Meil Hobson. P 217
[171] Melissa Hope Ditmore. *Prostitution and Sex Work: Historical Guides to Controversial Issues in America.* P 111.
Carol Leigh. *Whores and Other Feminists.* Ed. Jill Nagle. New York: Routledge, 1997. Print. P. 223-231.
[172] Nils Johan Ringdal. P 377
Valerie Jenness. P 56
[173] Lynn Arditi. "How R.I. opened the door to prostitution." *Providence Journal.*
[174] Melanie Shapiro. "Sex Trafficking and Decriminalized Prostitution in Rhode Island."
[175] Scott Cunningham and Manisha Shah. "Decriminalizing Prostitution: Surprising Implications for Sexual Violence and Public Health."
[176] Melissa Hope Ditmore. *Prostitution and Sex Work: Historical Guides to Controversial Issues in America.* P 32
[177] Lynn Arditi. "How R.I. opened the door to prostitution."
[178] Ian Donnis. "Prostitution Now Outlawed In R.I., But Is That Good?" *NPR.*
[179] Scott Cunningham and Manisha Shah. "Decriminalizing Prostitution: Surprising Implications for Sexual Violence and Public Health."
[180] Valerie Vande Panne. "Will California Legalize Prostitution Next? Inside the Crowd-Sourced Fundraising." *The Daily Beast.*
[181] "You Have a Right to Buy and Sell Sex. Will the Courts Protect It By Legalizing Prostitution?" *Reason TV.*
[182] Jesse Folk. "Two Cincinnati lawyers file suit to legalize prostitution in California." *WCPO 9 Cincinnati.*
[183] "You Have a Right to Buy and Sell Sex. Will the Courts Protect It By Legalizing Prostitution?" *Reason TV.*

[1] Russell Clark and Elaine Hatfield. "Gender Differences In Receptivity To Sexual Offers." *Journal of Psychology & Human Sexuality*: Vol. 2 (1) P. 39-55. 1989.

[2] < http://www.havocscope.com/number-of-prostitutes/>

[3] Illinois Academy of Criminology presentation on Wings Court. Women in Need of Gender Specific Services.

[4] J. Pearl. "Highest Paying Customers - America's Cities and the Costs of Prostitution Control." *Hastings Law Journal* Volume: 38 Issue: 4 Dated: (April 1987) Pages:769-800

[5] Lucas Sullivan, Jacqui Boyle, and Kelsey Cano. "Prostitution policing efforts are costly for taxpayers." *Springfield News-Sun.*

[6] Laurie Becklund. "Prostitution Arrests Cost $2,000 Each, Study Finds." *Los Angeles Times.*

[7] "San Francisco Task Force on Prostitution Final Report 1996." *Bayswan.org.*

[8] Noah Pransky. "Tampa Police turning profits off vehicle seizures." *Channel 10 News Tampa.*

[9] Elizabeth Nolan Brown. "Sex Work and Civil Asset Forfeiture Increasingly Go Hand in Hand." *Reason.*

[10] Michael Shively, Ph.D., Kristina Kliorys, Kristin Wheeler, and Dana Hunt, Ph.D. "An Overview of Vehicle Seizures for Sex Buyers in the United States." *The National Institute of Justice.*

[11] George Hunter and Doug Guthrie. "Wayne Co. profits from police property seizures." *Detroit News.*

[12] Ibid.

[13] Mike Riggs. "Michigan Cops Used Asset Forfeiture Funds to Buy Drugs, Prostitutes, and a Tanning Salon." *Reason.*

[14] Joseph O'Sullivan. "Let police seize sex-buyers' cars, cash?" *Seattle Times.*

[15] Robert J. MacCoun and Peter Reuter. *Drug War Heresies: Learning from Other Vices, Times, and Places.* Cambridge, U.K.: Cambridge University Press, 2001. Print. P 149

[16] "Letter to the Editor: Prostitution Laws Serve to Protect Weak from Exploitation; Hypocrisy's High Cost." *New York Times.*

[17] Jeff Leen, Gail Epstein, and Lisa Getter. "Dade Cops Like To Play 'Collars For Dollars.'" *Miami Herald.*

[18] "Strip club busted on prostitution charges." *FOX 23 News Tulsa, Oklahoma.*

[19] Amaris Elliott-Engel. "Pay for Play: Cops Can't Pay Snitch's Tab for Sex With Hookers." *New York Law Journal.*

[20] Matt Pulle. "Sex Stings Reined In." *Nashville Scene.*

[21] Norma Jean Almodovar. "The Abuse and Consequences of Arbitrary Enforcement of Prostitution Laws." PoliceProstitutionAndPolitics.com.

[22] Mark Memmott. "In Hawaii, Sex With a Prostitute May Be Legal For Undercover Sports." *NPR.*

[23] Jennifer Sinco Kelleher. "Women arrested in Honolulu prostitution sting face unusual charge of sex assault." *Associated Press*.
[24] Duaa Eldeib. "In DePaul study of Chicago pimps, most were abused as children." *Chicago Tribune*.
[25] Steven D. Levitt and Stephen J. Dubner. *Super Freakonomics: Global Cooling, Patriotic Prostitutes, and Why Suicide Bombers Should Buy Life Insurance*. New York: William Morrow, 2009. Print. P 45
[26] Norma Jean Almodovar. "The Abuse and Consequences of Arbitrary Enforcement of Prostitution Laws."
[27] Irving Dejohn. "Portland's professional cuddler Samantha Hess expanding business and adding employees." *New York Post*.
[28] Ian Forest. "Professional cuddler: 'I literally could cuddle 24 hours a day.'" *FOX 12 Oregon*.
[29] Ted Balaker. "Cuddle Crackdown! Police Think Snugglers Are Actually Hookers: Don't cops have better things to do?" *Reason*.
[30] Jody Babydol Gibson. *Secrets of a Hollywood Super Madam*. Los Angeles, CA: Corona and Music, 2007. Print. P 255
[31] <https://www.seekingarrangement.com/about-us>
"Part 1: How Student Debt Can Lead to Survival Sex." *Polaris Project*.
[32] Michael S. Scott. "Street Prostitution." *U.S. Department of Justice Office of Community Oriented Policing Services*.
[33] Norma Jean Almodovar. *Cop To A Call Girl*. New York: Avon Books, 1993. Print. P 57
[34] Norma Jean Almodovar. *Whores and Other Feminists*. Ed. Jill Nagle. New York: Routledge, 1997. Print. P 211
[35] Uniform Crime Reporting by the FBI. "Crime in the United States 2013."
[36] "Move Along: Policing Sex Work in Washington D.C." *Alliance for a Safe & Diverse DC*.
[37] San Francisco Task Force on Prostitution Final Report 1996.
[38] Dr. Joycelyn Elders Opening Keynote Address at the 2010 Annual Conference of the Desiree Alliance, Las Vegas, NV, July 26, 2010.
[39] "US: Louisiana Fuels HIV Epidemic." *Human Rights Watch*.
[40] Megan McLemore. "Distributing, Then Confiscating, Condoms." *New York Times*.
[41] Rebecca Corral. "Condoms No Longer Allowed As Evidence In San Francisco Prostitution Cases." *CBS San Francisco*.
"Unused condoms no longer evidence of prostitution in NYC." *Associated Press*.
[42] Juhu Thukral, Melissa Ditmore, and Berny Horowitz. "Revolving Door: An Analysis of Street-Based Prostitution in New York City." *Sex Workers Project at the Urban Justice Center*.
[43] Adam Reiss. "Health clinic helps addicts shoot up." *CNN*.

44 Martha Felini, Deepika Talari, Elyse Ryan, and Raquel Qualls-Hampton. "Prostitution Diversion Initiative – New Life Program - Annual Report: 2011-2012."
45 Ana Ley. "The impact of specialty courts: 'I've seen girls from prostitution to college.'" *Las Vegas Sun*.
46 David Klepper. "Program helps R.I. prostitutes get off the street." *Associated Press*.
47 "Project Renew: Transforming Women & A Neighborhood." *YouTube*.
48 "Rethinking Arrest: Street Prostitution & Public Policy in Rhode Island: Open Doors Policy Report 2009." *Open Doors*.
49 Martha Felini, Amy Abraham, Gloria Mendoza, Louis Felini, Renee' Breazeale. ""Prostitution Diversion Initiative – New Life Program - Annual Report: October 2008 – September 2009."
50 Martha Felini, Deepika Talari, Elyse Ryan, and Raquel Qualls-Hampton. "Prostitution Diversion Initiative – New Life Program - Annual Report: 2011-2012."
51 Ian Urbina. "For Runaways, Sex Buys Survival." *New York Times*.
52 Carol Christian. "Houston police arrest 8 men, 1 woman on prostitution charges." *Houston Chronicle*.
53 "Former Prostitute Works To Keep Women Off The Streets." *NPR's Here & Now*.
54 "Houston's abusive prostitution diversion program & Kathryn Griffin." *YouTube of SexWorkerNation*.
55 O'Reilly Factor July 23, 2008 with guest Carol Leigh.
56 "PART Victories." *Chicago Coalition for the Homeless*.
57 Illinois Academy of Criminology presentation on Wings Court. Women in Need of Gender Specific Services
58 Martha Felini, Amy Abraham, Gloria Mendoza, Louis Felini, Renee' Breazeale. "Prostitution Diversion Initiative – New Life Program - Annual Report: October 2008 – September 2009."
59 "Rethinking Arrest: Street Prostitution & Public Policy in Rhode Island: Open Doors Policy Report 2009." *Open Doors*.
60 David Segal. "Rhode Island Moves Closer To Banning Prostitution." *Huffington Post*.
61 U.S. House of Representatives Judiciary Subcommittee on Crime, Terrorism, and Homeland Security. Hearing on Domestic Minor Sex Trafficking. September 15, 2010.
62 Ibid.
63 Titania Kumeh. "'It's Not Selling Your Body, It's More Like Controlled-Access Rental.'" *Mother Jones*.
64 Zach Weissmueller and Will Neff. "Legalize Prostitution to Fight Sex Trafficking? Sex Workers Say 'Yes.'" *Reason*.
65 Rebecca Leung. "Part 2: Uneasy Street." *CBS News*.

[66] Rebecca Leung. "The Canal Street Brothel." *CBS News.*
[67] Ibid.
[68] Ibid.
[69] "FBI probe of brothel criticized amid 9/11." *Washington Times.*
[70] Matt O'Connor. "'Gold Coast Madam' sentenced to prison." *Chicago Tribune.*
[71] David Jackson. "Gold Coast Madam still pointing finger." *Chicago Tribune.*
[72] Robert Nolin. "Cooperation Wins Lighter Sentences In Call Girl Ring." *Sun Sentinel.*
[73] Matt O'Connor. "'Gold Coast Madam' sentenced to prison." *Chicago Tribune.*
[74] Connie Fletcher. *What Cops Know: Cops Talk about What They Do, How They Do It, and What It Does to Them*. New York: Villard Books, 1991. Print. P 23
[75] Catherine Murphy. "Sex Workers' Rights are Human Rights." *Amnesty International.*
[76] Mark Prothero and Carlton Smith. *Defending Gary: Unraveling the Mind of the Green River Killer*. San Francisco: Jossey-Bass, 2006. Print. P. 496
[77] Elaine Porterfield. "Green River Killer pleads guilty to 49th murder." *Reuters.*
[78] Annie Sprinkle. "Help Stop Violence Against Sex Workers." *Alternet.*
[79] John J. Potterat, Devon D. Brewer, Stephen Q. Muth, Richard B. Rothenberg, Donald E. Woodhouse, John B. Muth, Heather K. Stites, and Stuart Brody. "Morality in Long-term Open Cohort of Prostitute Women." *American Journal of Epidemiology.* Vol. 159, Issue 8, 778-85
[80] Brad Hamilton. "Sick cell call is strongest clue in search for Long Island serial killer." *New York Post.*
[81] "Police announce crackdown in Chillicothe after 4 women found dead, 2 missing." *FOX 8 Cleveland.*
[82] Priscilla Alexander. *Whores and Other Feminists*. Ed. Jill Nagle. New York: Routledge, 1997. Print. P 97
[83] Elizabeth Sisco. *Critical Condition: Women on the Edge of Violence*. Ed. Amy Scholder. San Francisco: City Lights Books, 1993. Print. P. 43
[84] Elizabeth Sisco. P. 45
Richard Serrano. "New Review of S.D. Prostitute Killing Ordered." *Los Angeles Times.*
Mark Platte. "No Police Link Made in Slaying of Prostitutes." *Los Angeles Times.*
[85] Norm Stamper. *Breaking Rank: A Top Cop's Exposé of the Dark Side of American Policing*. New York: Nation Books, 2005. Print. P 46-51
[86] House Oversight and Government Reform Committee hearing on allegations of sexual misconduct in the Drug Enforcement Administration (DEA). April 14, 2015.

[87] Mark Arax. "Judge Says Law Doesn't Protect Prostitutes, Drops Rape Count." *Los Angeles Times.*
[88] Lee Moran. "Texas prostitute's jilted killer acquitted, was trying to 'retrieve stolen property' says jury." *New York Daily News.*
[89] "Judge Criticized for Considering Gang Rape on Prostitute 'Theft of Services.'" *Associated Press.*
[90] Ibid.
[91] Priscilla Alexander. *Whores and Other Feminists.* Ed. Jill Nagle. New York: Routledge, 1997. Print. P 85
[92] Lenore Kuo. *Prostitution Policy: Revolutionizing Practice through a Gendered Perspective.* New York: New York University Press, 2002. Print. P 85
[93] Juhu Thukral, Melissa Ditmore, and Alexandra Murphy. "Behind Closed Doors: An Analysis of Indoor Sex Work in New York City." *Sex Workers Project at the Urban Justice Center.*
[94] Ibid.
[95] Nils Johan Ringdal. *Love For Sale: A World History of Prostitution.* New York: Grove Press, 2004. Print. P 342
[96] Ronald Weitzer. *Legalizing Prostitution: From Illicit Vice to Lawful Business.* New York: New York University Press, 2012. Print. P 28
[97] Ibid.
[98] Juhu Thukral, Melissa Ditmore, and Alexandra Murphy. "Behind Closed Doors: An Analysis of Indoor Sex Work in New York City." *Sex Workers Project at the Urban Justice Center.*
[99]

Uniform Crime Reporting Statistics - UCR Data Online
http://www.ucrdatatool.gov/

Estimated forcible rape rate per 100,000 population

	2011 Forcible Rape Rate	2012 Forcible Rape Rate
United States	27	26.9
Alabama	28.5	26.9
Alaska	60.2	79.7
Arizona	38.6	34.7
Arkansas	41.9	42.3
California	20.3	20.6
Colorado	44.7	40.7
Connecticut	19.2	25.6
Delaware	33.8	26.5
Florida	27.6	27.2
Georgia	21.1	21.4
Hawaii	25.6	20.5

Idaho	28	30
Illinois	23.6	27.7
Indiana	27	25.5
Iowa	28.3	28.3
Kansas	39.1	36.5
Kentucky	34.3	29
Louisiana	27.6	25.2
Maine	29.7	28
Maryland	20.5	21
Massachusetts	25	24.7
Michigan	44	46.4
Minnesota	39.5	30.5
Mississippi	29	27.5
Missouri	24.4	25.1
Montana	36.7	37.7
Nebraska	37.9	38.3
Nevada	33.6	33.7
New Hampshire	44.1	34
New Jersey	11.4	11.7
New Mexico	41.2	45.9
New York	14.1	14.6
North Carolina	20.3	20.3
North Dakota	38.8	38.9
Ohio	31.9	31.7
Oklahoma	37.3	41.6
Oregon	32	29.2
Pennsylvania	26.2	26.1
Rhode Island	30.4	27.4
South Carolina	35.9	35.5
South Dakota	61.1	70.2
Tennessee	32.7	31.5
Texas	29.2	29.6
Utah	32	33
Vermont	23.3	19.3
Virginia	19.6	17.7
Washington	34	31.8
West Virginia	20.1	22.7
Wisconsin	20.8	21.3
Wyoming	25.7	26.7

Uniform Crime Reporting Statistics - UCR Data Online
http://www.ucrdatatool.gov/

Estimated forcible rape rate per 100,000 population in Rhode Island vs. national average

Year	Rhode Island	National Average
1980	17.1	36.8
1981	17.9	36
1982	19.4	34
1983	16.8	33.8
1984	21.3	35.7
1985	26.1	36.8
1986	21.4	38.1
1987	24.4	37.6
1988	30.5	37.8
1989	26.7	38.3
1990	24.7	41.1
1991	30.9	42.3
1992	30.9	42.8
1993	28.6	41.1
1994	27.4	39.3
1995	27	37.1
1996	29	36.3
1997	36.8	35.9
1998	35.5	34.5
1999	39.5	32.8
2000	39.3	32
2001	39.3	31.8
2002	37	33.1
2003	46.9	32.3
2004	29.6	32.4
2005	30.1	31.8
2006	27.1	31.6
2007	24.4	30.6
2008	26.8	29.8
2009	28.1	29.1

[100] Martin A. Monto. "Focusing on the Clients of Prostitutes: A Creative Approach to Reducing Violence against Women – Summary Report."
[101] Ronald Weitzer. *Sex for Sale: Prostitution, Pornography, and the Sex Industry*. New York: Routledge, 2000. Print. P 244
[102] Chris Atchison and Carol Thorbes. "Study paints compassionate picture of johns." Simon Frasier University Public Affairs and Media Relations Release January 14, 2010.

Chris Atchison. "Report of the Preliminary Findings for John's Voice: A Study of Adult Canadian Sex Buyers." *John's Voice Project*.
[103] Mary Papenfuss. "FBI seizure of 'My Red Book' website spurs San Francisco bid to decriminalize prostitution." *Reuters*.
[104] Joan Kennedy Taylor. *Whores and Other Feminists*. Ed. Jill Nagle. New York: Routledge, 1997. Print. P 257
[105] Tom Chivers. "Does porn cause sexual violence? Probably not. But we're allowed to want to protect children from it anyway." *Telegraph*.

Chapter 3

[1] Joe Conforte and David W. Toll. *Breaks, Brains & Balls: The Story of Nevada's Fabulous Mustang Ranch*. Virginia City, NV: Gold Hill Publishing, 2011. Print.
[2] Alexa Albert. *Brothel: Mustang Ranch and its Women*. New York: Random House, 2001. Print. P 34
[3] Lenore Kuo. *Prostitution Policy: Revolutionizing Practice through a Gendered Perspective*. New York: New York University Press, 2002. Print. P 80
"Legalized Prostitution in Nevada." *C-Span*.
[4] Daria Snadowski. "The Best Little Whorehouse is Not in Texas: How Nevada's Prostitution Laws Serve Public Policy, and How Those Laws May Be Improved." *Nevada Law Journal*.
[5] Pete Earley. *Super Casino: Inside the "New" Las Vegas*. New York: Bantam Books, 2000. Print. P 52-53
Robert D. McCracken. *Las Vegas: The Great American Playground*. Reno, NV: University of Nevada Press, 1997. Print. P 23
Jeff Burbank. *Las Vegas Babylon: The True Tales of Glitter, Glamour, and Greed*. Plymouth: Rowman and Littlefield Publishing Group, 2008. Print. P 35
[6] Alexa Albert. P 37
[7] "Legalized Prostitution in Nevada." *C-Span*.
Dave Downing. "Beverly Harrell – a Fearless beauty of class and intellect." *Death Valley Gateway Gazette*.
[8] American Greed. "The Mustang Ranch: Money, Women and Murder." Season 3, Episode 7. *CNBC*.
[9] Joe Conforte and David W. Toll. *Breaks, Brains & Balls: The Story of Nevada's Fabulous Mustang Ranch*.
[10] Alexa Albert. P 41
[11] Paul Dean. "Joe Conforte's Legal Tangles." *Los Angeles Times*.
[12] Ibid.
[13] Jane Ann Morrison. "Raggio's legend caught fire with his battle against pimp." *Las Vegas Review-Journal*.
[14] Paul Dean. "Joe Conforte's Legal Tangles."
[15] Howard W. Herz. "The 'Gray Bar Hotel & Casino' The Nevada State Prison Casino." *Casino Chip and Token News*. Summer of 2006 edition.

American Greed. "The Mustang Ranch: Money, Women and Murder." Season 3, Episode 7. *CNBC*.
John L. Smith. *Of Rats and Men: Oscar Goodman's Life from Mob Mouthpiece to Mayor of Las Vegas*. Las Vegas: Huntington Press, 2003. Print. P 160, 161
"Nevada's Most Infamous Brothel, Mustang Ranch, Back In Business." *Associated Press*.
[16] Alexa Albert. P 41
[17] Joe Conforte and David W. Toll.
[18] Ovid Demaris. *Boardwalk Jungle: How Greed Corruption and the Mafia Turned Atlantic City into the Boardwalk Jungle*. New York: Bantam Books, 1986. Print. P 291
Chris Serioty. "Palms to pay $1 million fine to settle drug, prostitution complaint." *Las Vegas Review-Journal*.
[19] Alexa Albert. P 41
Melissa Hope Ditmore. *Encyclopedia of Sex Work and Prostitution Vol. I*. Westport, CT: Greenwood Publishing Group, 2006. Print. P 253
[20] Steve Oney. "The Little House in the Desert." *New York Times*.
[21] "The Best Little Whorehouse in Texas." *ABC News 13 Houston, TX*.
[22] Steve Oney. "The Little House in the Desert."
[23] Melissa Hope Ditmore. P 253
[24] Alison Vekshin. "Brothels in Nevada Suffer as Web Disrupts Oldest Trade." *Bloomberg*.
[25] "US Federal and State Prostitution Laws and Related Punishments." *ProCon.org*.
[26] Alexa Albert. P 163-165
[27] David CM-Azares. "Law Officers Know Pilot As Publicity-seeker." *Sun Sentinel*.
[28] Kirsten Scharnberg. "Nevada's brothels get touch look." *Chicago Tribune*.
[29] "Pimps force underage girls to work in Nevada brothels, Oregon police say." *Las Vegas Sun*.
[30] Kirsten Scharnberg.
[31] Patt Morrison. "Prostitution — it isn't 'Pretty Woman'" *Los Angeles Times*.
[32] Melissa Farley. "Indoor Versus Outdoor Prostitution in Rhode Island." *Prostitution Research & Education*.
[33] Ronald Weitzer. "Flawed Theory and Method in Studies of Prostitution." George Washington University.
[34] Maggie McNeil. "A Load of Farley." *The Honest Courtesan*.
[35] "Response to Melissa Farley." *Sex Workers Without Borders*.
[36] Melissa Farley. "Trafficking for Prostitution: Making the Connections." American Psychological Association. 115th Annual Convention August 17, 2007. San Francisco.
[37] Melissa Farley and Vanessa Kelly. "Prostitution: A Critical Review of the Medical and Social Sciences Literature." *Women & Criminal Justice*.

[38] Abigail Goldman. "UNLV academics look into Nevada's brothel industry." *Las Vegas Sun.*
[39] Barbara Brents. "Nevada's Legal Brothels Make Workers Feel Safer." *New York Times.*
[40] Kathryn Hausbeck, Barbara Brents, and Crystal Jackson. "Sex Industry and Sex Workers in Nevada." UNLV Center for Democratic Culture.
Doug McMurdo. "Brothels fire back at Harry Reid." *Las Vegas Review-Journal.*
[41] Lora Shaner. *Madam: Inside A Nevada Brothel.* Las Vegas: Huntington Press, 2003. Print. P 45
[42] Leonard Greene. "Meet the brothel workers who found Lamar Odom collapsed." *New York Daily News.*
[43] Kathryn Hausbeck and Barbara Brents. *Sex For Sale: Prostitution, Pornography, and the Sex Industry*. Ed. Ronald Weitzer. New York: Routledge, 2010. Print. P 267
[44] Annie Lowrey. "Stimulus Spending." *Slate.*
[45] Bob Baker. "Study of Brothel Prostitutes Finds Little Venereal Disease: Health: Nevada houses fund research by ex-UCLA professor. Infection has fallen to near zero since condoms were required." *Los Angeles Times.*
[46] Alexa Albert. P 163
[47] Doug McMurdo. "Brothels fire back at Harry Reid."
[48] Barbara Brents and Kathryn Hausbeck. "State-Sanctioned Sex: Negotiating Formal and Informal Regulatory Practices in Nevada Brothels." *Sociological Perspectives.* Vol. 44 Number 3 P 307-332.
[49] Barbara Brents and Kathryn Hausbeck. "Violence and Legalized Brothel Prostitution in Nevada: Examining Safety, Risk, and Prostitution Policy." *Journal Of Interpersonal Violence*, Vol. 20 No. 3, March 2005 P 270-295
[50] Alexa Albert. P 27
[51] Hotline for Migrant Workers. "The Legalization of Prostitution: Myths and Reality: A Comparative Study of Four Countries."
[52] Cy Ryan. "ACLU appeals federal court decision upholding Nevada's brothel ad ban." *Las Vegas Sun.*
Doug McMurdo. "U.S. Supreme Court won't stop Nevada from banning brothel ads." *Las Vegas Review-Journal.*
[53] Kathryn Hausbeck and Barbara Brents. *Sex For Sale: Prostitution, Pornography, and the Sex Industry*. Ed. Ronald Weitzer. P 275
[54] Henry Brean and Steve Tetreault. "Brothels fear Reid will seek their demise." *Las Vegas Review-Journal.*
[55] Annie Lowrey. "Stimulus Spending."
Hunter Schwartz. "Harry Reid calls Nevada lawmakers 'cowards' for not banning prostitution." *Washington Post.*
[56] Brian Duggan. "Reid's comments catch business leaders off guard." *Tahoe Daily Tribune.*

Sandra Chereb. "Harry Reid: Time To Ban Brothels In Nevada." *Associated Press*.
[57] Ray Hagar. "Brothel owner helped seal Nevada's Tesla deal." *Reno Gazette-Journal*.
[58] Dave Toplikar. "Goodman: Despite what Harry Reid says, prostitution isn't hurting Nevada's economy." *Las Vegas Sun*.
[59] "10 fastest-growing cities." *CNN Money*.
[60] Alexa Albert. P 48-49
[61] Lenore Kuo. P 81

Chapter 4

[1] "Swiss Prostitutes Trained To Use Defibrillators In Brothels." *Huffington Post*.
[2] Paul Sims. "Councils for disabled to visit prostitutes and lap-dancing clubs from £520m taxpayer fund." *Daily Mail*.
[3] "Australian and Danish Governments Providing Prostitutes for the Disabled." *LifeSiteNews.com*.
[4] Melissa Hope Ditmore. *Encyclopedia of Sex Work and Prostitution Vol. I*. Westport, CT: Greenwood Publishing Group, 2006. Print. P 26
[5] Melissa Hope Ditmore. *Encyclopedia of Sex Work and Prostitution Vol. II*. Westport, CT: Greenwood Publishing Group, 2006. Print. P 480
[6] Nick Squires. "Switzerland opens drive in 'sex boxes' to make prostitution safer." *The Telegraph*.
[7] Patrick Jackson. "How the Dutch protect their prostitutes." *BBC News*.
[8] Paul Bisschop, Kastoryano, and Bas Van Der Klaauw. "Street Prostitution Zones and Crime."
[9] Nomi Levenkron and Ella Keren. "The Legalization of Prostitution: Myth and Reality: A Comparative Study of Four Countries." *Hotline For Migrant Workers*.
[10] "Dutch Policy on Prostitution: Questions and Answers 2012." *Dutch Ministry of Foreign Affairs*.
[11] A.L. Daalder. "Prostitution in the Netherlands since Lifting the General Ban on Brothels." *La Strada International*.
Charlotte Bailey. "Prostitutes in Holland to be awarded 'street miles.'" *The Telegraph*.
[12] Greggor Christian Mattson. *Governing Loose Women Rationalizing European Prostitution, 1998-2004*. UMI Dissertation Publishing. 2008. Print. P 10
[13] Nisha Lilia Diu. "Welcome to Paradise." *The Telegraph*.
[14] "Unprotected: How Legalizing Prostitution Has Failed." *Der Spiegel*.

[15] "Germany National Report on HIV and Sex Work." TAMPEP European Network for HIV/STI Prevention and Health Promotion among Migrant Sex Workers.
[16] Stephanie Ott. "Switzerland: Zurich launches 'sex drive-ins.'" *CNN*.
[17] Nicholas Kulish. "In Germany, Sex Workers Feed A Meter." *New York Times*.
[18] "German 'Sex Meters' Taxing Street Prostitutes Hailed As Successful By Bonn Officials (VIDEO)." *Huffington Post*.
[19] Melissa Hope Ditmore. *Encyclopedia of Sex Work and Prostitution Vol. I*. P 140
[20] "Full disclosure: The Dutch central bank fires an inspector who failed to report her part-time job." *The Economst*.
[21] Philip Oltermann. "Germany rethinks its liberal ways on sex workers." *The Guardian*.
[22] "German prostitutes in rights plea." *BBC News*.
[23] Nisha Lilia Diu. "Welcome to Paradise."
[24] Laura Barnett, Lyne Casavant, and Julia Nicol. "Prostitution: A Review of Legislation in Selected Countries." *Legal and Legislative Affairs Division Parliamentary Information and Research Service*.
[25] Michelle Goldberg. "Should Buying Sex Be Illegal?" *The Nation*.
[26] Abigail Abrams. "Dutch Brothel Owners Must Speak Sex Workers' Language, EU Court Rules." *International Business Times*.
[27] "Trafficking in Human Beings: First Report of the Dutch National Rapporteur (2002)." *National Rapporteur on Trafficking in Human Beings and Sexual Violence against Children: The Hague*.
"Trafficking in Human Beings: Ten Years of Independent Monitoring. (2010)" *National Rapporteur on Trafficking in Human Beings and Sexual Violence against Children: The Hague*.
[28] "Unprotected: How Legalizing Prostitution Has Failed." *Der Spiegel*.
[29] U.S. Department of State Trafficking in Persons Reports 2010.
[30] U.S. Department of State Trafficking in Persons Reports 2012.
[31] U.S. Department of State Trafficking in Persons Reports 2010.
[32] Seo-Young Cho. "Human Trafficking: Germany Only Average When It Comes To Protecting Victims." *DIW Economic Bulletin*.
[33] U.S. Department of State Trafficking in Persons Reports 2015.
[34] Ibid.
[35] Nomi Levenkron and Ella Keren.
[36] Barbara Sullivan. *The Politics of Prostitution: Women's Movements, Democratic States and the Globalisation of Sex Commerce*. Cambridge, UK: Cambridge University Press, 2004. Print. P 22
[37] Suzanne Carbone. "Daily Planet listing centered on a new bottom line." *The Age*.
"Liberals divided on proposed brothel laws." *Perth Now*.
[38] "NSW prostitution laws 'ambiguous, contradictory.'" *ABC.net*.

[39] Danny Rose. "Legal or not, sex industry powers on." *Sydney Morning Herald.*
[40] Michael Edwards. "Study backs decriminalization of prostitution." *ABC.net.*
[41] John Godwin. "Sex Work and the Law in Asia and the Pacific Laws: HIV and human rights in the context of sex work." United Nations Development Programme.
[42] "Australia HIV and AIDS Statistics." *Avert.org.*
[43] HIV estimates from Wikipedia via three tables from the World Health Organization in conjunction with UNICEF

35 "Advanced Economies	Prostitution Status	HIV Rate
Australia	Legal	0.2%
Austria	Legal	0.4%
Belgium	Legal	0.3%
Canada	Decriminalized	0.3%
Cyprus	Legal	<0.1%
Czech Republic	Legal	<0.1%
Denmark	Legal	0.2%
Estonia	Legal	**1.3%**
Finland	Swedish Model	0.1%
France	Swedish Model	0.4%
Germany	Legal	0.1%
Greece	Legal	0.2%
Hong Kong	Decriminalized	0.1%
Iceland	Swedish Model	0.3%
Ireland	Decriminalized	0.3%
Israel	Decriminalized	0.2%
Italy	Legal	0.4%
Japan	Decriminalized	<0.1%
Luxembourg	Legal	0.3%
Malta	Illegal	0.1%
Netherlands	Legal	0.2%
New Zealand	Legal	0.1%
Norway	Swedish Model	0.1%
Portugal	Decriminalized	**0.7%**
Singapore	Legal	0.1%
Slovakia	Decriminalized	<0.1%
Slovenia	Decriminalized	0.1%
South Korea	Illegal	0.1%

Spain	Decriminalized	0.4%
Sweden	Swedish Model	0.2%
Switzerland	Legal	0.4%
Taiwan	Illegal for seller not buyer	0.1%
United Kingdom	Decriminalized	0.3%
United States	Illegal	**0.6%**

[44] "Policy consultation on decriminalisation of sex work." *Amnesty International*.
[45] Susan Brink. "Legalizing Prostitution Would Protect Sex Workers From HIV." *NPR*.
[46] Catherine Healy, Calum Bennachie, and Anna Reed. *Taking the Crime Out of Sex Work: New Zealand Sex Workers' Fight for Decriminalisation*. Ed. Gillian Abel, Lisa Fitzgerald, Catherine Healy, and Aline Taylor. Bristol, UK: The Policy Press, 2010. Print. P 47, 52, 53, 107
[47] Ibid.
"Report of the Prostitution Law Review Committee on the operation of the Prostitution Reform Act of 2003." *New Zealand Ministry of Justice*.
[48] Gillian Abel, Lisa Fitzgerald, and Cheryl Brunton. "The Impact of the Prostitution Reform Act on the Health and Safety Practices of Sex Workers: Report to the Prostitution Law Review Committee." University of Otago.
[49] "Prostitution reform has little effect." *New Zealand Herald*.
[50] "Prostitution law reform in New Zealand." *New Zealand Parliament*.
[51] Bob Fredericks. "Hooker wins sexual harassment case against brothel owner." *New York Post*.
[52] John Godwin. "Sex Work and the Law in Asia and the Pacific Laws: HIV and human rights in the context of sex work." United Nations Development Programme.
[53] Talia Shadwell. "Man charged with failing to use condom with prostitute." *Stuff.co.nz*
[54] Nicole Westmarland. *International Approaches to Prostitution: Law and Policy in Europe and Asia*. Ed. Geetanjali Gangoli and Nicole Westmarland. Bristol, UK: The Policy Press, 2006. Print. P 21-30.
[55] Andrew Levy. "Vice law chaos after mother-of-two, 49, acquitted of running brothel from her village home." *Daily Mail*.
[56] Ronald Weitzer. *Legalizing Prostitution: From Illicit Vice to Lawful Business*. New York: New York University Press, 2012. Print. P 26.
[57] Juhu Thukral, Melissa Ditmore, and Alexandra Murphy. "Behind Closed Doors: An Analysis of Indoor Sex Work in New York City." *Sex Workers Project at the Urban Justice Center*.
[58] Alan Travis. "For men who pay for sex with trafficked women, ignorance is no longer a defence." *The Guardian*.

59 "Dominique Strauss-Kahn acquitted of 'aggravated pimping.'" *BBC News.*
60 Ian Sparks. "Looking like a prostitute is now LEGAL in France after bizarre law banning 'passive' soliciting is overturned." *Daily Mail.*
61 Jane Fae Ozimek. "Canada prostitution laws pulverised: politicians apoplectic." *The Register.*
62 Kirk Makin. "Judge decriminalizes prostitution in Ontario, but Ottawa mulls appeal." *The Globe and Mail.*
James Keller. "Vancouver police passed the buck on Pickton case." *The Canadian Press.*
63 Josh Wingrove. "Tory prostitution bill gets Senate approval." *The Globe and Mail.*
64 Tonda MacCharles. "Laws targeting 'johns' only increase dangers to prostitutes, report warns." *The Star.*
65 Erin Corrigan and Martin Donohoe. "Regulatory Approaches to Prostitution: Comparing Sweden, Denmark, and Nevada, USA."
66 Ibid.
67 Ibid.
68 Gwladys Fouche. "View from the streets: New Nordic sex laws are making prostitutes feel less safe." *The Independent.*
69 "We want to save you. And if you don't appreciate it, we will punish you!" *Sex Workers' Rights Advocacy Network (SWAN).*
70 Angela Waters. "Sweden prostitution reduction model's success a myth, skeptics warn." *Washington Times.*
71 Michelle Goldberg. "Swedish prostitution law is spreading worldwide – here's how to improve it." *The Guardian.*
72 "The Human Cost of 'Crushing' the Market: Criminalization of Sex Work in Norway." *Amnesty International.*
73 "We want to save you. And if you don't appreciate it, we will punish you!" *Sex Workers' Rights Advocacy Network (SWAN).*
74 "Sex workers cry foul over activist's death." *TheLocal.se*
Michelle Goldberg. "The Netherlands Vs. Sweden: Should Buying Sex Be Illegal?" *Pulitzer Center.*
75 Greggor Christian Mattson. P 12
76 Susanne Dodillet and Petra Östergren. "The Swedish Sex Purchase Act: Claimed Success and Documented Effects." Conference paper presented at the International Workshop: Decriminalizing Prostitution and Beyond: Practical Experiences and Challenges. The Hague, March 3 and 4, 2011.
77 "Dr Jay Levy, Researcher and Consultant, Discusses the Outcomes of the Criminalisation of the Purchase of Sex in Sweden." *RuthJacobs.co.uk.*
78 Angela Waters. "Sweden prostitution reduction model's success a myth, skeptics warn."
79 Susanne Dodillet and Petra Östergren.
80 Cajsa Wikstrom. "Sweden feminists roar into political arena." *Al Jazeera.*

[81] Karl Ritter. "Swedish Politicians Can Cheat on Spouses, but Not on Taxes." *Los Angeles Times*.
[82] "Has Swedish feminism gone too far?" *Euronews*.
[83] Gunilla Ekberg. "The Swedish Law That Prohibits the Purchase of a Sexual Service: Best Practices for Prevention of Prostitution and Trafficking in Human Beings." *Violence Against Women*.
[84] *Könskriget "The Gender War."* Dir. Evin Rubar. Nordisk Films, 2005. Sweriges Television.
[85] Ibid.
[86] U.S. Department of State Trafficking in Persons Reports 2011.
[87] Susanne Dodillet and Petra Östergren.
[88] Ibid.
[89] Ibid.

Chapter 5

[90] Moira Hoiges. "From the Inside Out: Reforming State and Local Prostitution Enforcement to Combat Sex Trafficking in the United States and Abroad." *Minnesota Law Review*.
[91] Duren Banks and Tracey Kyckelhahn. "Characteristics of Suspected Human Trafficking Incidents, 2008-2010." *U.S. Department of Justice Office of Justice Programs Bureau of Justice Statistics*.
[92] Melissa Ditmore. "The Use of Raids to Fight Trafficking in Persons." *Sex Workers Project*.
[93] Heather J. Clawson, Nicole Dutch, and Megan Cummings. "Law Enforcement Response to Human Trafficking and the Implications for Victims: Current Practices and Lessons Learned." *U.S. Department of Justice*.
[94] Courtneyshouse.org.
[95] Tina Frundt testimony before the House Committee on the Judiciary Subcommittee on Crime, Terrorism, and Homeland Security. "Domestic Minor Sex Trafficking." September 15, 2010.
[96] Alexandra Lutnick's testimony during 10/20/2015 California Assembly Committee on Public Safety and Human Trafficking.
[97] Marisa Gerber. "Crackdown on pimps fuels a rise in human trafficking charges in L.A. County." *Los Angeles Times*.
[98] Hannah Albarazi. "Oakland Police Underage Sex Scandal Prompts Protest At Headquarters." *CBS San Francisco*.
[99] David Debolt. "Oakland police in 13th year of federal oversight." *Mercury News*.
[100] Darwin BondGraham and Ali Winston. "The Real Reason Why Oakland's Police Chief Was Fired." *East Bay Express*.
[101] David Debolt. "Oakland police scandal spreads: Woman claims sex with dozens of officers." *Mercury News*.

[102] Conchita Sarnoff. "Billionaire Pedophile Goes Free." *The Daily Beast.*
[103] Ibid.
[104] James Hill and James Mosk. "Victims: Feds Hid 'Sweetheart' Deal for Sex Offender With Deep Political Ties." *ABC News.*
[105] Michele Dargan. "New documents reveal Palm Beach billionaire sex offender Jeffrey Epstein's 'sweetheart deal' with prosecutors." *Palm Beach Daily News.*
[106] Conchita Sarnoff. "Billionaire Pedophile Goes Free."
[107] Neal Conan. "Amb. CdeBaca Combats Sex Trafficking in the U.S." *NPR.*
[108] Melissa Ditmore. "The Use of Raids to Fight Trafficking in Persons."
[109] Alison Parker and Meghan Rhoad. "US: Victims of Trafficking Held in ICE Detention." *Human Rights Watch.*
[110] David Henry Sterry and R.J. Martin Jr. *Hos, Hookers, Call Girls, and Rent Boys: Professionals Writing on Life, Love, Money, and Sex.* Brooklyn: Soft Skull Press, 2009. Print. P 332.
[111] "Human Trafficking: Better Data, Strategy, and Reporting Needed to Enhance U.S. Antitrafficking Efforts Abroad." *U.S. Government Accountability Office.*
[112] Jerry Markon. "Human Trafficking Evokes Outrage, Little Evidence." *Washington Post.*
[113] Jessica Dickinson Goodman. "Severe Shelter Beds Shortage for Survivors of Human Trafficking." *Polaris Project.*
[114] Heather J. Clawson, Nicole M. Dutch, Amy Salomon, and Lisa Goldblatt Grace. "Study of HHS Programs Serving Human Trafficking Victims." *U.S. Department of Health and Human Services.*
[115] Alison Knezevich. "For human trafficking victims, state offers 'a new beginning'."
[116] U.S. Department of State Trafficking in Persons Reports 2011.
[117] April Rieger. "Missing the Mark: Why the Trafficking Victims Protection Act Fails to Protect Sex Trafficking Victims in the United States." *Harvard Journal of Law and Gender.*
[118] U.S. Department of State Trafficking in Persons Reports 2012.
[119] Heather J. Clawson, Nicole Dutch, and Megan Cummings. "Law Enforcement Response to Human Trafficking and the Implications for Victims: Current Practices and Lessons Learned."
[120] Ibid.
[121] Melissa Ditmore. "The Use of Raids to Fight Trafficking in Persons."
[122] Jerry Markon. "Human Trafficking Evokes Outrage, Little Evidence."
[123] "DOJ Exaggerated Aid To Human Trafficking Victims: IG Report." *The Crime Report.*
Robyn Shepherd. "ACLU Lens: Using Religion as an Excuse for Discrimination." *ACLU.*

[124] Patricia Montemurri. "How bar of soap can save human trafficking victim." *Detroit Free Press.*
[125] Tom Ragan. "Nevada movement draws the line on human trafficking." *Las Vegas Review-Journal.*
[126] Anne Elizabeth Moore. "Special Report: Money and Lies in Anti-Human Trafficking NGOs." *Truthout.*
[127] Jerry Markon. "Human Trafficking Evokes Outrage, Little Evidence."
[128] "ILO Global Estimate of Forced Labour." *International Labor Office.*
[129] U.S. Department of State Trafficking in Persons Reports 2011.
[130] U.S. Department of State Trafficking in Persons Reports 2015.
[131] Sara E. Gilmer. *Toward a Human Rights Framework for Human Trafficking: Examining the U.S. Government Approach to Trafficking in Persons.* Washington D.C.: American University, 2007. Print. P 36
[132] E. Benjamin Skinner. *A Crime So Monstrous: Face-To-Face With Modern-Day Slavery.* New York: Simon and Schuster, 2008. Print. P 53
[133] Andrea Maria Bartone. *Human Trafficking on the International and Domestic Agendas: Examining the Role of Transnational Advocacy Networks between Thailand and United States.* College Park, MD: University of Maryland, 2008. Print. P 172
[134] Jerry Markon. "Human Trafficking Evokes Outrage, Little Evidence."
[135] Jerry Markon. "Anti-Human Trafficking Bill Would Send FBI Agents on Trail of Pimps." *Washington Post.*
[136] Letter to John Conyers from U.S. Department of Justice Office of the Assistant Attorney General. November 7, 2007.
Alison Siskin and Clare Ribando Seelke. "Select Differences Between S. 3061 and H.R. 3887." *Congressional Research Service.*
[137] Kerry Howley. "Congress as Sex Slave Factory." *Reason.*
[138] "Trafficking: New Slave Trade or Moral Panic?" *Battle of Ideas.*
[139] Dan Baum. *Smoke and Mirrors: The War on Drugs and the Politics of Failure.* Boston: Little, Brown and Company, 1996. Print. P 226
[140] Debbie Nathan. "ABC's Primetime Fakery." *CounterPunch.org.*
[141] Ariane Lange. "Sex Workers Say A&E Show Lied To Them About Providing Resources And Protecting Their Privacy." *BuzzFeed.*
 Tara Burns. "How Self-Described 'Whore Nation' Killed the TV Show '8 Minutes.'" *Alternet.*
[142] Maggie McNeil. "Lies, damned lies, and sex work statistics." *Washington Post.*
[143] Pete Kotz. "Super Bowl prostitution: 100,000 hookers didn't show, but America's latest political scam did." *Dallas Observer.*
[144] Pete Kotz. "The Super Bowl Prostitute Myth: 100,000 Hookers Won't Be Showing Up in Dallas." *Dallas Observer.*
[145] Ibid.

[146] Susy Solis. "Arlington Makes Dozens of Super Bowl Prostitution Arrests." *NBC Dallas Fort Worth.*
[147] Pete Kotz. "Super Bowl prostitution: 100,000 hookers didn't show, but America's latest political scam did."
Matt Peterson. "Efforts of sex trafficking task force led to 133 arrests in run-up to Super Bowl XLV." *Dallas Morning News.*
[148] Jessica L. Huseman. "Top FBI agent in Dallas praises Super Bowl security effort, sees no evidence of expected spike in child sex trafficking." *Dallas Morning News.*
[149] "Results of the anti-human trafficking campaign during Super Bowl of 2012." Indiana Attorney General.
[150] "Situational Awareness: Possible Sex Trafficking During Super Bowl XLVIII." *Human Smuggling and Trafficking Center.*
[151] Dr. Annalee Lepp lecture, "Sex Trafficking and the Olympics," at the FIRST Public Forum, June 16, 2009, Vancouver.
[152] Carl Bialik. "The Elusive Link Between Sex Trafficking and Sporting Events." *Wall Street Journal.*
[153] Julie Ham. "What's the Cost of a Rumour? A guide to sorting out the myths and the facts about sporting events and trafficking." *Global Alliance Against Traffic in Women.*
[154] Marlow Stern. "The World Cup of Prostitution: How the Soccer Tourney Is Affecting Brazil's Sex Workers." *Daily Beast.*
[155] U.S. Department of State Trafficking in Persons Reports 2014.
[156] "Have sex trafficking levels been exaggerated?" *BBC Newsnight.*
[157] Nick Davies. "Inquiry fails to find single trafficker who forced anybody into prostitution." *The Guardian.*
[158] Rebecca Beitsch. "More States Separate Prostitution, Sex Trafficking." *Pew Charitable Trusts.*
[159] Lynn Bartels. "Colorado prostitution bill solicits no comments from senators." *Denver Post.*
[160] Rob Port. "North Dakota State's Attorney: Human Trafficking Laws Have Complicated Prostitution Issue." *SayAnythingBlog.com.*
[161] Jordan Flaherty. "Is the State of Alaska Fighting Sex Trafficking or Targeting Women?" *Truthout.*
[162] Noah Berlatsky. "Alaska's Prostitution Law Isn't Working." *The Atlantic.*
[163] Tara Burns. "People in Alaska's Sex Trade: Their Lived Experience and Policy Recommendations."
[164] Panel Discussion about Proposition 35 (the CASE Act) on human trafficking in California. Program for Human Rights Panel Discussion-October 23, 2012. Stanford University.
[165] Perla Flores, Lynette Parker, and John Vanek. "Perla Flores, Lynette Parker and John Vanek: Prop 35: More harm than good for victims of human trafficking." *San Jose-Mercury News.*

[166] Panel Discussion about Proposition 35 (the CASE Act) on human trafficking in California. Program for Human Rights Panel Discussion-October 23, 2012. Stanford University.
[167] "The Stream - Should buying and selling sex be a crime?" *Al Jazeera.*
[168] Aziza Ahmed. "Think Again: Prostitution." *Foreign Policy Magazine.*
[169] Sopheng Cheang. "Cambodian prostitutes protest police crackdown." *USA Today.*
[170] Noy Thrupkaew. "The Crusade Against Sex Trafficking." *The Nation.*
[171] Elaine Pearson. "Violence Against Cambodia's Sex Workers." *Human Rights Watch.*
[172] Noy Thrupkaew. "Beyond Rescue." *The Nation.*
[173] Ibid.
[174] Aziza Ahmed. "Think Again: Prostitution."
[175] John Godwin. "Sex Work and the Law in Asia and the Pacific Laws: HIV and human rights in the context of sex work." United Nations Development Programme.
[176] Anne Elizabeth Moore. "Here's why it matters when a human rights crusader builds her advocacy on lies." *Salon.*
Anne Elizabeth Moore and Ten Soksreinith. "Author Looks at Forced Labor in Cambodia's Sex and Garment Industries." *VOA Cambodia.*
[177] Poypiti Amatatham and Thomas Fuller. "Cambodia's Scam Orphanages." *New York Times.*
[178] "Truth or Lies: Somaly Mam." *Al Jazeera.*
[179] Simon Marks. "Somaly Mam: The Holy Saint (and Sinner) of Sex Trafficking." *Newsweek.*
[180] Ibid.
[181] Ibid.
[182] "Truth or Lies: Somaly Mam." *Al Jazeera.*
[183] Elizabeth Nolan Brown. "Another High-Profile Sex Trafficking Tale May Be Falling Apart." *Reason.*
[184] "Breaking Out – Timeline." *Facebook.com*
< https://www.facebook.com/BreakingOut/posts/708922209196425>
[185] Carmen Fishwick, Kate Hodal, Chris Kelly, and Steve Trent. "Slave labour producing prawns for supermarkets in US, UK: your questions answered." *The Guardian.*
[186] "Five things you need to know about coltan." *International Consortium of Investigative Journalists.*
[187] Traver Riggins. "Human trafficking allegations test diplomatic immunity." *Center for Public Integrity.*
Chuck Neubauer. "Diplomats immuned to charges of human trafficking." *Washington Times.*
[188] Senate Foreign Relations Committee. April 13, 2016.
[189] Cam Simpson. "U.S. stalls on human trafficking." *Chicago Tribune.*

Brett D. Schaefer. "United Nations Peacekeeping: The U.S. Must Press for Reform." *Heritage Foundation*.
[190] Senate Foreign Relations Committee. April 13, 2016.
[191] "UN whistleblower in CAR sex abuse case resigns." *Associated Press*.
[192] House Armed Service Committee. "Fiscal Year 2006 Defense Budget." March 10, 2005.
[193] James M. Carter. "War Profiteering From Vietnam to Iraq." *Counter Punch*.
[194] Scot J. Paltrow. "Special Report: The Pentagon's doctored ledgers conceal epic waste." *Reuters*.
[195] Lauren Lyster. "Want to Cut Government Waste? Find the $8.5 Trillion the Pentagon Can't Account For." *Daily Ticker*.
[196] Kelley Beaucar Vlahos. "'Windfalls of war': Companies with spotty records making billions off Afghanistan." *FOX News*.
[197] House Armed Service Committee. "Fiscal Year 2006 Defense Budget." March 10, 2005.
[198] Alastair Good. "Kathyrn Bolkovac: interview with the original 'Whistleblower'." *The Telegraph*.
[199] Kathryn Bolkovac and Cari Lynn. *The Whistleblower: Sex Trafficking, Military Contractors, and One Woman's Fight for Justice.* New York: Palgrave Publishing, 2011. Print. P 151
[200] Todd Robberson. "Employees not convinced whistle-blowers are safe."
[201] Jason Linkins. "WikiLeaks Reveals That Military Contractors Have Not Lost Their Taste For Child Prostitutes." *Huffington Post*.
Jason Linkins. "U.S. Military Contractor 'Used Armored Cars To Transport Prostitutes.'" *Huffington Post*.
[202] Joseph Goldstein. "U.S. Soldiers Told to Ignore Sexual Abuse of Boys by Afghan Allies." *New York Times*.
[203] David Mark. "Green Beret who beat Afghan official over alleged child assault to stay in Army." *CNN*.
"The Dancing Boys of Afghanistan." *PBS Frontline*.
[204] James Risen. "Before Shooting in Iraq, a Warning on Blackwater." *New York Times*.
[205] Justin Rood. "Blackwater Chief Accused of Murder, Gun-Running." *ABC News*.
Carol D. Leonnig and Nick Schwellenbach. "Former Blackwater employees accuse security contractor of defrauding government." *Washington Post* with *Center for Public Integrity*.
[206] Jeremy Scahill. "Blackwater's New Sugar Daddy: The Obama Administration." *The Nation*.
"Pentagon outsources War on Drugs to Blackwater." *RT*.
[207] Steven M. Watt. "Your Tax Dollars at Work? U.S. Military Contractors and Human Trafficking in War Zones." *ACLU*.
[208] "America's War Workers." *Al Jazeera Fault Lines*.

209 "Labour Trafficking in the Middle East." Lecture by Sindhu Kavinamannil and Sam McCahon before the Observer Research Foundation.
210 Steven M. Watt. "Court Rejects Military Contractor's Attempt to Avoid Trial for Human Trafficking." *ACLU.*
211 Nick Schwellenbach. "War contracting commission cites Center article on trafficking." *Center for Public Integrity.*
212 Damien McElroy. "US 'used forced labour to build Iraq embassy.'" *The Telegraph.*
213 Carlos H. Conde. "Company accused of abducting Filipinos to build U.S. Embassy in Iraq." *New York Times.*
214 David Phinney and Pratap Chatterjee. "U.S. Embassy in Baghdad built by trafficked workers in squalid working conditions." *Corp Watch.*
David Isenberg and Nick Schwellenbach. "Documents Reveal Details of Alleged Labor Trafficking by KBR Subcontractor." *Project on Government Oversight.*
David Isenberg. "What the U.S. Government Knew About Najlaa." *Huffington Post.*
215 Jessica Schulberg. "The American Government Is Funding Human Trafficking." *New Republic.*
216 Ibid.
217 Executive Order - Strengthening Protections Against Trafficking In Persons In Federal Contracts. September 25, 2012.
218 Sam Black. "After 12 years of war, labor abuses rampant on US bases in Afghanistan." *Al Jazeera.*
219 *Iraq for Sale: The War Profiteers.* Dir. Robert Greenwald. Brave New Films, 2006.
220 Sam Black. "After 12 years of war, labor abuses rampant on US bases in Afghanistan."
221 Traver Riggins. "Human trafficking allegations test diplomatic immunity." *Center for Public Integrity.*
222 Ian Urbina. "U.S. Flouts Its Own Advice in Procuring Overseas Clothing." *New York Times.*

Chapter 6

1 Maggie McNeil. "In Their Own Words." *The Honest Courtesan.*
2 Maggie O'Neill. *Prostitution and Feminism: Towards a Politics of Feeling.* Cambridge, UK: Blackwell Publishers, 2001. Print. P 19
3 Sheila Jeffreys. *The Idea of Prostitution.* Melbourne, AU: Spinifex Press, 1997. Print. P 226
4 Maggie McNeil. "In Their Own Words." *The Honest Courtesan.*
5 Catharine A. MacKinnon. *Toward a Feminist Theory of the State.* Cambridge, MA: Harvard University Press, 1989. Print. P 174

[6] Andrea Dworkin. *Intercourse*. New York: Basic Books, 1987. Print. P 174
[7] Myra MacPherson. *Scarlett Sisters: Sex, Suffrage, and Scandal in the Gilded Age*. New York: Hatchet Book Group, 2014. Print.
[8] Myra MacPherson. P 60
[9] Vivian Gornick. "Emma Goldman Occupies Wall Street." *The Nation*.
[10] Oliver Stone's Untold History of the United States / Series Directed, Co-written and Narrated by Oliver Stone. DVD.
[11] "Timeline: Anarchism and Emma Goldman." *PBS American Experience*.
[12] Emma Goldman. "The Traffic in Women." *Mother Earth*.
[13] David J. Langum. *Crossing Over the Line: Legislating Morality and the Mann Act*. Chicago: University of Chicago Press, 1994. Print. P 158
[14] Ibid.
[15] Timothy J. Gilfoyle. *City of Eros: New York City, Prostitution, and the Commercialization of Sex, 1790 – 1920*. New York and London: W.W. Norton & Company, 1992. Print. P 288
[16] "Trafficking: New Slave Trade or Moral Panic?" *Battle of Ideas*.
[17] Liv Jessen. "Prostitution seen as Violence Against Women - a supportive or oppressive view?" *Bayswan.org*.
[18] Stacy Reed. *Whores and Other Feminists*. Ed. Jill Nagle. New York: Routledge, 1997. Print. P. 184
[19] Sheila Jeffreys. P 164
[20] Melissa Ditmore. *Prostitution and Sex Work: Historical Guides to Controversial Issues in America*. Santa Clara, CA: Greenwood Publishing Group, 2011. Print. P 144
[21] National Organization For Women website
[22] "Women need rehabilitation not penalties." Letter by Josephine Martell, Rhode Island NOW Legislative Chair, June 29, 2009.
[23] Ronald Weitzer. *Legalizing Prostitution: From Illicit Vice to Lawful Business*. New York: New York University Press, 2012. Print. P 8
[24] Testimony by Bella Robinson on January 28, 2016 before the New Hampshire State committee on House Bill 1614.
[25] Sheila Jeffreys. *The Idea of Prostitution*. P 90
[26] Cosi Fabian. *Whores and Other Feminists*. Ed. Jill Nagle. P. 51
[27] Sheila Jeffreys. *The Idea of Prostitution*. P 81
[28] Robin Reisig. "Sisterhood & prostitution." *Village Voice*. December 16, 1971, Vol. XVI, No. 50.
[29] Gail Sheehy. *Hustling: Prostitution in Our Wide-Open Society*. New York: Delacorte Press, 1973. Print. P 197
[30] Robin Reisig. "Sisterhood & prostitution." *Village Voice*.
[31] Jill Nagle. *Whores and Other Feminists*. Ed. Jill Nagle. P. 3
[32] Teri Goodson. *Whores and Other Feminists*. Ed. Jill Nagle. P. 249
[33] Thomas Streissguth. *The Roaring Twenties: An Eyewitness History*. New York: Infobase Publishing, 2001. Print. P 43

34 Thaddeus Russell. *A Renegade History of the United States.* New York: Free Press, 2010. Print. P 101
35 Catherine Gourley. *Flappers and the New American Woman: Perceptions of Women from 1918 through the 1920s.* Minneapolis: Twenty-First Century Books, 2008. Print. P 59
36 Michael A. Lerner. *Dry Manhattan: Prohibition in New York City.* Cambridge, MA: Harvard University Press, 2008. Print. P 181
37 Glenna Matthews. *The Rise of Public Woman: Woman's Power and Woman's Place in the United States, 1630-1970.* New York: Oxford University Press, 1992. Print. P 4
38 Richard Zacks. *Island of Vice: Theodore Roosevelt's Doomed Quest to Clean up Sin-Loving New York.* New York: Doubleday, 2012. Print. P 189
39 Richard Zacks. P 194
40 Gail Collins. *America's Women: Four Hundred Years of Dolls, Drudges, Helpmates, and Heroines.* New York: William Morrow, 2003. Print. P 331
41 Karen Halttunen. *Confidence Men and Painted Women: A Study of Middle-Class Culture in America, 1830-1870.* New Haven: Yale University Press, 1982. Print. P. XV
42 Thaddeus Russell. *A Renegade History of the United States.* P 112-114
43 Kathy Peiss. *Cheap Amusements: Working Women and Leisure in Turn-of-the-Century New York.* Philadelphia: Temple University, 1986. Print. P 101
44 Kathy Peiss. P 102
45 Kathy Peiss. P 98
46 Catherine Gourley. *Flappers and the New American Woman: Perceptions of Women from 1918 through the 1920s.* P 59
47 Mara Laura Keire. *For Business and Pleasure: Red-Light Districts and the Regulation of Vice in the United States, 1890-1933.* Baltimore: Johns Hopkins University Press, 2010. Print. P 51
48 Thaddeus Russell. *A Renegade History of the United States.* P 121
49 Gary Krist. *Empire of Sin: A Story of Sex, Jazz, Murder, and the Battle for Modern New Orleans.* New York: Crown Publishers, 2014. Print. P 114

Chapter 7

1 Norm Stamper. *Breaking Rank: A Top Cop's Exposé of the Dark Side of American Policing.* New York: Nation Books, 2005. Print. P 43
2 David Nakamura and Carol D. Leonnig. "Investigator of Secret Service prostitution scandal also linked to prostitution." *Washington Post.*
3 Mike Edison. *Dirty! Dirty! Dirty!: Of Playboys Pigs, and Penthouse Paupers: An American Tale of Sex and Wonder.* Berkeley: Counterpoint, 2011. Print.
4 Robert Brenner. "Sins of Commission: The 40th Anniversary of the Illustrated Presidential Report of the Commission on Obscenity and Pornography." *Huffington Post.*

[5] Mike Edison. *Dirty! Dirty! Dirty!: Of Playboys Pigs, and Penthouse Paupers: An American Tale of Sex and Wonder.*

[6] Richard Nixon's Statement About the Report of the Commission on Obscenity and Pornography on October 24, 1970.

[7] Mike Edison. *Dirty! Dirty! Dirty!: Of Playboys Pigs, and Penthouse Paupers: An American Tale of Sex and Wonder.*

[8] Elizabeth Purdy. *Encyclopedia of White-Collar & Corporate Crime, Volume 2.* Ed. Lawrence M. Salinger. Thousand Oaks, CA: Sage Publications, 2005. Print. P 476

[9] "Charles Keating, the Financier Behind the Savings and Loan Scandal, Dies at 90." *The Real News.*

[10] Philip Shenon. "Did Charles Keating Go to Jail for Nothing?" *POLITICO.*

[11] Eric M. Jackson. *The Paypal Wars: Battles with EBay, the Media, the Mafia, and the Rest of Planet Earth.* Los Angeles: World Ahead Publishing, 2006. Print. P 224, 237

Nina Bernstein. "Foes of Sex Trade Are Stung by the Fall of an Ally." *New York Times.*

[12] "As Spitzer Prostitution Scandal Dominates Headlines, a Look at the Plight of Sex Workers: March 12, 2008." *Democracy Now!*

George Marlin. *"Eliot Spitzer: Confessed criminal." New York Post.*

[13] William K. Rashbaum. "Revelations About Governor Began in Routine Tax Inquiry." *New York Times.*

Brian Ross. "It Wasn't the Sex; Suspicious $$ Transfers Led to Spitzer." *ABC News.*

[14] United States of America V Mark Brener, a/k/a "Michael," Cecil Suwal, a/k/a "Katie," a/k/a "Kate,"
Temeka Rachelle Lewis, a/k/a "Rachelle," and Tanya Hollander, a/k/a "Tania Hollander,"

[15] Benjamin Weiser. "No Prison for Booker at the Escort Service Tied to Spitzer." *New York Times.*

[16] Jake Tapper, Edward Meagher, and Sherisse Pham. "Tough questions for Eliot Spitzer on hypocrisy of never being charged with breaking the law he signed." *CNN.*

[17] Bob Lamendola. "J.H. Burke, Congressman 12 Years, Dies." *Sun Sentinel.* Martin Langeveld and Dirk Langeveld. "J. Herbert Burke: only there for the articles." *The Downfall Dictionary.*

[18] George E. Condon Jr. and Marcus Stern. "Imprisoned Cunningham outlines depths of corruption to FBI." *UT San Diego.*

[19] Kitty Kelley. "Ace in the Hole: Duke Cunningham's Wife Tells All." *New Republic.*

[20] Joe Cantlupe. "Ex-congressman's friend emerges as mystery man." *UT San Diego.*

[21] Lawrence Delevingne. "The Most Corrupt Members Of Congress." *Business Insider.*
[22] www.ontheissues.com
Lawrence Delevingne. "The Most Corrupt Members of Congress." *Business Insider.*
[23] Joe Conason. *Big Lies: The Right-Wing Propaganda Machine and How It Distorts the Truth.* New York: Thomas Dunne Books, 2003. Print. P 125
[24] Satyam Khanna. "Calvert Caught In The Act With Prostitute, Lied, Attempted To Run From Police." *Think Progress.*
[25] Stanley G. Hilton and Anne-Renee Testa. *Glass Houses: Shocking Profiles of Congressional Sex Scandals and Other Unofficial Misconduct.* New York: St. Martin's Press, 1998. Print.
[26] "FOX News Documentary Shows Congressmen Sent Millions in Earmarks to Their Own Families." *FOX News.*
[27] Olivia Nuzzi. "North Carolina Lobbyists Can Officially Screw Politicians Legally." *Daily Beast.*
[28] Kerry Picket. "Reagan at 100 - The humor and wit of Ronald Reagan." *Washington Times.*
[29] *LIFE* magazine, Vol. 21, No. 6, (5 August 1946), P 48
[30] Edwin L. Battistella. *Sorry About That: The Language of Public Apology.* New York: Oxford University Press, 2014. Print. P 78-79
[31] Michael James Guliano. *Thrice-Born: The Rhetorical Comeback of Jimmy Swaggart.* Macon, GA: Mercer University Press, 1999. Print. P 116
[32] Stephanie Simon. "Humbled Haggard Climbs Back in Pulpit." *Wall Street Journal.*
[33] Josh Scheer. "Mike Jones on Ted Haggard and Hypocrisy." *Truthdig.com.*
[34] John Schwartz. "Scandal Stirs Legal Questions in Anti-Gay Cases." *New York Times.*
[35] Kevin Dugan. "Eric Holder launches 90-day crusade against bank leaders." *New York Post.*
Jonathan Dienst. "Feds Take Down Rentboy.com, 'World's Largest Male Escort Site,' in Manhattan; 7 Arrested." *NBC Channel 4 New York.*
[36] Penn Bullock and Brandon K. Thorpe. "Christian right leader George Rekers takes vacation with 'rent boy.'" *New Miami Times.*
[37] Patrick Mcgreevy. "State Sen. Roy Ashburn says he's homosexual." *Los Angeles Times.*
[38] Ben Adler. "Five Years Later, Ashburn Reflects On His Journey." *Capital Public Radio.*
[39] Robert E. Bauman. "A Former Congressman, Once a Staunch Foe of Gay Rights, Confronts His Own Homosexuality." *People Magazine.* September 19, 1983. Vol. 20 No. 12.
[40] Lou Chibbaro Jr. "Gay ex-congressman shuns politics in Florida." *Washington Blade.*

[41] Charles Babington and Jonathan Weisman. "Rep. Foley Quits In Page Scandal." *Washington Post*.
< http://www.ontheissues.org/fl/Mark_Foley.htm>
[42] "McCain state co-chairman arrested for soliciting sex." *CNN*.
[43] Phil Landeros. "State rep. blames fear in sex arrest." *Channel 10 News Tampa*.
Kerry Lauerman. "LGBT's worst foe: The Closet Monster." *Salon*.
[44] Dan Savage. "Straight Acting." *The Stranger*.
[45] Nicholas K. Geranios. "Ex-legislator's extortion case dropped." *Seattle Times*.
[46] Jerome A. Kroth. *Conspiracy in Camelot: The Complete History of the Assassination of John Fitzgerald Kennedy*. New York: Algora Publishing, 2003. Print. P. 264
[47] Larry Flynt and David Eisenberg. *One Nation Under Sex: How the Private Lives of Presidents, First Ladies and Their Lovers Changed the Course of American History*. New York: Palgrave Macmillan, 2011. Print. P 173, 174
[48] Larry Flynt and David Eisenberg. P 183, 184
[49] Seymour Hersh. *The Dark Side of Camelot*. Boston: Little, Brown, 1997. Print.
[50] Paul M. Rodriguez and George Archibald. "Homosexual prostitution inquiry ensnares VIPs with Reagan and Bush: 'Call Boys' took midnight tour of White House.'" *Washington Times*.
[51] Ibid.
[52] John DeCamp. *The Franklin Cover-up: Child Abuse, Satanism, and Murder in Nebraska*. Lincoln, NE: AWT, 1992. Print.
[53] Rachel Maddow Show on July 8, 2014. MSNBC.
Alan Scher and Sam Burchard. "# 12 Bush Profiteers Collect Billions From No Child Left Behind." *Project Censored*.
[54] Christopher Lee. "Law Cautions Against Outside PR Spending -- Sort Of." *Washington Post*.
[55] Dan Collins. "3rd Columnist On Bush Payroll." *CBS News*.
[56] Steve Fox, Paul Armentano, and Mason Twert. *Marijuana is Safer: So Why are We Driving People to Drink?* White River Junction, VT: Chelsea Green Publishing Company, 2009. Print. P 88,89
Robert C. Aldridge. *America in Peril*. Pasadena, CA: Hope Publishing House, 2008. Print. P 204-206
[57] Jamie Barge and Jamison Foser. "Talon News 'Reporter' lobs Bush another softball; is Talon a news organization or an arm of the Republican Party?" *Media Matters*.
[58] Andrew Seifter. "Limbaugh bragged that his show inspired Talon News 'reporter's' erroneous question to Bush." *Media Matters*.
[59] David Margolick and Richard Gooding. "Wrong Man, Wrong Place." *Vanity Fair*.

[60] Jeremy Cluchey. "Talon News 'reporter' lifts from GOP documents verbatim for 'news reports.'"
[61] Elizabeth Gerteiny. *The President of War and the Cowards, Villains, and Fools Behind Him: An Unfolding Record of the George W. Bush Administration, 2001-2009 In Verse*. Bloomington, IN: XLibris Corp, 2009. Print. P 32
[62] John Byrne. "Secret Service records raise new questions about discredited conservative reporter." *Raw Story*.
[63] Frank Rich. "The White House Stages Its 'Daily Show.'" *New York Times*.
[64] Joel Roberts. "Rove-Gannon Connection?" *CBS News*.
[65] Vicky Ward. "No Way to Treat a Lady." *Vanity Fair*.
[66] Montgomery Sibley. *Why Just Her: The Judicial Lynching of the D.C. Madam, Deborah Jeane Palfrey*. Full Court Press Inc., 2009. Print. P 565
[67] Montgomery Sibley. P 260
[68] Montgomery Sibley. P 238
[69] Montgomery Sibley. P 234-237
[70] Montgomery Sibley. P 188
[71] Montgomery Sibley. P 216, 225
Brian Ross and Justin Rood. "Senior Official Linked to Escort Service Resigns." *ABC News*.
[72] Dr. Joycelyn Elders Opening Keynote Address at the 2010 Annual Conference of the Desiree Alliance, Las Vegas, NV, July 26, 2010.
[73] "Interviews - Randall Tobias – The Age of AIDS." *PBS Frontline*.
[74] House Bill H.R. 4754...H.Amdt.653 — 108th Congress (2003-2004)
[75] John Eligon and Michael Schwirtz. "Senate Candidate Provokes Ire With 'Legitimate Rape' Comment." *New York Times*.
[76] "U.S.: Restrictive Policies Undermine Anti-AIDS Efforts: Letter to President Bush Opposing Mandatory 'Anti-Prostitution Pledge,' which Threatens Lives of Sex Workers and Trafficking Victims." *Human Rights Watch*.
[77] "Taking the Pledge." Prod. Sex Worker Project. Interviews and edited by Erin Siegal.
[78] Rachel Thomas. "Spotlight on Meena Seshu, SANGRAM: Sex Worker Rights in Rural India." *Open Society Foundations*.
[79] Sarah Boseley and Suzanne Goldenberg. "Brazil spurns US terms for Aids help." *The Guardian*.
[80] Monte Reel. "Where Prostitutes Also Fight AIDS." *Washington Post*.
[81] Chi Mgbaka. "Overturn US anti-prostitution pledge to support sex workers and combat HIV." *The Guardian*.
[82] Mark Sherman. "Supreme Court Strikes Down Anti-Prostitution Pledge As Condition For AIDS Funding." *Huffington Post*.
[83] David Jackson. "Gold Coast Madam still pointing finger." *Chicago Tribune*.
[84] Trymain Lee. "Sex Crimes In New Orleans, Separate And Unequal." *Huffington Post*.
[85] Joel Roberts. ""D.C. Madam" Called Vitter During Votes." *CBS News*.

[86] Howard Kurtz. "Larry Flynt, Investigative Pornographer." *Washington Post*.
[87] "HUSTLER, GENERATION KILL & LA Punk with Evan Wright & Allan MacDonell: Harper Simon's Talk Show." *The LipTV*.
[88] John Nichols. "Larry Craig, Expendable Senator." *The Nation*.
Glenn Greenwald. "Forcing Larry Craig's resignation while embracing David Vitter." *Salon*.
[89] "Vitter Scores! Controversial Louisiana Lawmaker Earns Perfect Rating From FRC." *Americans United For Separation of Church and State*.
[90] Glenn Greenwald. "Sen. David Vitter, a leading Christian social conservative." *Salon*.
[91] Mary T. Schmich. "Husband-wife Prostitution Case Turns Into Bizarre Cliffhanger." *Chicago Tribune*.
[92] Montgomery Sibley. P 236
<http://www.infowars.com/media/230707palfrey.mp3>
Darragh Johnson. "Trial Nearing, Alleged Call Girl Found Dead." *Washington Post*.
[93] Montgomery Sibley. P 580
[94] Steven Nelson. "D.C. Madam's Attorney Says Call Log Bombshell Could Upend 2016 Race." *U.S. News & World Report*.
[95] Ibid.
[96] Spencer. S. Hsu. "U.S. Supreme Court rejects 'D.C. Madam' attorney bid to release customer records." *Washington Post*.
[97] "Wayne Hays, a Scourge of Congress, Dies: Longtime Lawmaker's Career Ruined by Affair With Staff Clerk." *United Press International*.
[98] Stephen Green and Margot Hornblower. "Mills Admits Being Present During Tidal Basin Scuffle." *Washington Post*.
[99] Edward D. Berkowitz. *Something Happened: A Political and Cultural Overview of the Seventies*. New York: Columbia University Press, 2006. Print.
[100] "Politicians And Prostitutes." *Real Clear Politics*.
[101] Ibid.
[102] "A Timeline of Politicians and Prostitutes." *U.S. News & World Report*.
[103] George Childs Kohn. *The New Encyclopedia of American Scandal*. New York: Infobase Publishing, 2000, 1989. Print. P 332
[104] "In the Matter of Representative Barney Frank: Report of the Committee on Standards of Official Conduct U.S. House of Representatives."
[105] Stuart E. Weisberg. *Barney Frank: The Story of America's Only Left-handed, Gay, Jewish Congressman*. Amherst, MA: University of Massachusetts Press, 2009. Print. P 125
[106] "On Hannity, Dick Morris Repeats False Claim That Rep. Frank Ran 'Gay Prostitution Ring Out Of His House Office.'" *Media Matters*.
[107] Howard Kurtz. "The Hooker, Line And Sinker." *Washington Post*.
[108] Sewell Chan. "Poll Says Yes to Paterson, No to Legalized Prostitution." *New York Times*.

[109] Peter Moore. "Country split on legalizing prostitution." *YouGov.com*
"Dirty Money: The Business of High-End Prostitution." *CNBC.*
"Poll: Should prostitution be legalized?" *NJ.com.*
Juliette Frette. "Poll: Should prostitution be legalized?" *Examiner.com.*
"Poll: Should prostitution be legal?" *Naples Daily News.*
Nick Sloan "POLL: Should prostitution be legal?" *Kansas City Kansan.*
< http://www.misterpoll.com/polls/321786/results>
[110] Lydia Saad. "U.S. Support for Legalizing Marijuana Reaches New High." *Gallup.*
[111] "State-by-State List of Initiative and Referendum Provisions." *Initiative & Referendum Institute at the University of Southern California.*
[112] < http://www.swopusa.org/about-us/founder-robyn-few/>
[113] "Measure Q: Prostitution Enforcement City of Berkeley." *Smartvoter.org.*
[114] Carolyn Marshall. "Bid to Decriminalize Prostitution in Berkeley." *New York Times.*
[115] John M. Glionna. "Proposition to protect sex work splits S.F." *Los Angeles Times.*
[116] Evelyn Nieves. "With Proposition K, San Francisco Considers Decriminalizing Prostitution." *Associated Press.*
"Proposition K: Changing the Enforcement of Laws Related to Prostitution and Sex Workers City of San Francisco." *Smartvoter.org.*
[117] Mark Niesse. "Bill to legalize prostitution looks for more support." *Associated Press.*
[118] Caitlin Beauregard. "State rep from Manchester proposes bill to decriminalize prostitution in NH." *NH1 News Network.*
[119] Elizabeth Nolan Brown. "Prostitution Decrim Debated by New Hampshire Lawmakers." *Reason.*
[120] Perry Stein. "D.C. reduced punishment for pot. Could prostitution come next?" *Washington Post.*
[121] Mark Niesse. "Bill to legalize prostitution looks for more support." *Associated Press.*

www.ingramcontent.com/pod-product-compliance
Lightning Source LLC
Chambersburg PA
CBHW020252030426
42336CB00010B/731